T0321174

Human Dimensions of Cybersecurity

Human Dimensions of Cybersecurity

Terry Bossomaier, Steven D'Alessandro,
and Roger Bradbury

CRC Press is an imprint of the
Taylor & Francis Group, an **informa** business
AN AUERBACH BOOK

CRC Press
Taylor & Francis Group
6000 Broken Sound Parkway NW, Suite 300
Boca Raton, FL 33487-2742

International Standard Book Number-13: 978-1-138-59040-3 (Hardback)

Library of Congress Cataloging-in-Publication Data

Names: Bossomaier, Terry R. J. (Terry Richard John), author. |
D'Alessandro, Steven, author. | Bradbury, R. H. (Roger H.), author.
Title: Human dimensions of cybersecurity / by Terry Bossomaier, Steven
D'Alessandro, Roger Bradbury.
Description: Boca Raton : CRC Press, [2020] | Includes bibliographical
references and index. | Summary: "The book identifies the technological
features that give rise to security issues. It describes the structure
of the Internet and how it is compromised by malware, and examines some
of the more common security issues. It then looks at aspects of human
persuasion and consumer choice, and how these affect cyber security. It
argues that social networks and the related norms play a key role as
does government policy, as each impact on individual behavior of
computer use. The book identifies the most important human and social
factors that affect cybersecurity. It illustrates each factor using case
studies, and examines possible solutions from both technical and human
acceptability viewpoints"– Provided by publisher.
Identifiers: LCCN 2019038924 (print) | LCCN 2019038925 (ebook) |
ISBN 9781138590403 (hardback) | ISBN 9780429490989 (ebook)
Subjects: LCSH: Computer security–Case studies. | Computer
security–Social aspects. | Computer networks–Security measures. |
Data protection. | Computer security–Government policy.
Classification: LCC QA76.9.A25 B6395 2020 (print) | LCC QA76.9.A25
(ebook) | DDC 005.8–dc23
LC record available at https://lccn.loc.gov/2019038924
LC ebook record available at https://lccn.loc.gov/2019038925

Visit the Taylor & Francis Web site at
http://www.taylorandfrancis.com

and the CRC Press Web site at
http://www.crcpress.com

Contents

Foreword

Professor Paul Cornish
Visiting Professor, LSE IDEAS, London School of Economics
Editor, The Oxford Handbook to Cyber Security (Oxford University Press, forthcoming 2020)
Associate Director, Global Cyber Security Capacity Centre, University of Oxford (2013–18)

Cybersecurity has several dimensions and characteristics. The first, the most obvious and the most important of these, is that cybersecurity is concerned with an environment that is not natural, but man-made. In other words, this environment, which we know as cyberspace, is an artifact, defined in the *Concise Oxford Dictionary* as "a product of human art and workmanship." For all its technological sophistication, which many of us can scarcely comprehend, cyberspace is essentially human. Cyberspace was invented, developed, and is validated by human beings: by men and women who devised ways to encode and decode and encrypt and decrypt vast amounts of information at extraordinary speed; by people who could design and build a global digital communication infrastructure; by experts who can maintain cyberspace as a system of networks and processes and who constantly find ways to improve and develop that system; and by the ever-increasing proportion of humanity who use cyberspace in many aspects of our daily life. And we should not forget that there are also more than enough people devoting substantial time and resources to subvert this system for various malign reasons. Another distinctive feature of cybersecurity is that it is a discussion that never stands still; it evolves very rapidly, while our ideas about the proper governance, management, security, and safety of cyberspace often seem to move at a glacially slow pace at best. But whenever the technology seems just too bewildering, the pace of change just too uncomfortable, and our security just a little too precarious, it is vital that we remember the importance of our own, human agency (both constructive and destructive). Unlike the natural environments of land, sea, air, and outer space, cyberspace is our own work in progress; humans are in charge and, for the time being at least, we make the decisions.

Cybersecurity is concerned with the avoidance, management, and mitigation of risk—the risk of harm and damage that might occur as the result of everything, from individual carelessness to organized criminality, to industrial and national security espionage and, at the extreme end of the scale, to disabling attacks against a country's critical national infrastructure. But as any university lecture on international and national security would point out, the pursuit of security from financial loss, physical damage, etc., should not be seen as an end in itself. Security must also be for something; more than simply the avoidance of risk, security is also the maximization of benefit. This important point is often explained by analogy: we lock our front door to protect our house, ourselves, and our property from thieves and predators. But we don't do this because we see ourselves as an arm of law enforcement: we do so in order that we can enjoy what we have, live as we choose and grow as we need. Security—including cybersecurity—is protective, but it is also liberating and enabling. This applies at every level—individually, nationally, and globally. The central purpose of cybersecurity could not therefore be clearer or more positive—and, again, it could hardly be more human.

Finally, it is because cyberspace is technologically sophisticated, because it reaches into everything that we do, and because it affects individual freedom, quality of life, and fulfilment that we need a rounded, inclusive approach to our understanding and management of it. Just as Georges Clemenceau once quipped that "war is too important to be left to military men," so we might say, rather dismissively perhaps, that cyberspace is too important to be left to computer scientists. But what Clemenceau probably meant was that generals were a necessary yet not sufficient component of any reasonable and useful discussion of war and all that it entails. Something similar can be said of cybersecurity. It would be just as absurd for nonscientific users of cyberspace (i.e., most of humanity) to ignore the science of cyberspace (perhaps on the grounds that it's too difficult to understand or moves too fast) as it would be for computer scientists, mathematicians, and physicists to insist that the social sciences (such as politics, sociology, economics, psychology, and development studies) have nothing useful to say about cyberspace and generate questions that are little more than derivative.

Having observed the Australian cybersecurity environment at close hand, I rate the quality of the policy/academic debate as second to none. In Human Dimensions of Cybersecurity, Terry Bossomaier, Steven D'Alessandro, and Roger Bradbury have produced a book that both exemplifies the depth and sophistication of the Australian debate and shows how it is indeed possible to achieve what we all need: a multidisciplinary, rigorously researched and argued, and above all accessible account of cybersecurity—what it is, why it matters, and how to do it.

Preface

The idea for this book began several years ago with the workshops run by Roger at the Australian National University, which focused on issues beyond the merely technical aspects of cybersecurity. It took shape as Terry and Steve began to formulate the importance of complex systems to the social sciences and hence their influence on understanding the hazards of cybersecurity. The social science perspectives that enabled us to see many hazards in cybersecurity were brought about by the hostile actions of both outsiders and insiders and by the carelessness and lack of knowledge of the affected parties. Over a morning coffee, we would discuss our shared concerns that the information and connected age was also a time of possible great concern and danger.

The need for a multidisciplinary approach was paramount as cybersecurity has become a fundamental issue of risk management for us as individuals, at work, and with government and nation states. In short, cybersecurity is too much of an important issue to just be an IT issue. Terry very much led the conversation about the need to bring the perspectives and skills of computer science and IT to give users a basic understanding of what is under the hood and how this can be protected. Steve looked towards a framework to encourage safer behaviors (in Marketing, this is often called social marketing). To do so, we both saw the need for a book that would explain in enough rigor the issues of cybersecurity, but most importantly, in simple language, what a man or woman on the street could do about this. We see that the real need may be in the area of assisting people who are starting a business, often at home, as this is a step up in IT requirements for people who are not experts, but need to use this technology as part of their business operations. The risk here is that these people may lack information and resources to combat increasingly clever cybercriminal networks.

What are some simple things that can be done for them to avoid risk? We call these simple rules to avoid nasty situations *cybernuggets*, and they are sprinkled throughout the book. These cybernuggets can be read as themselves as simple dos and don'ts of cybersecurity, but the context we have provided behind them is detailed yet, we hope, accessible to a broad part of the population. All being said, no book can be a complete guide, and as we found in writing this text, the environment of cybersecurity is constantly changing. This is shown by new technologies with their weaknesses being exploited by others. Then there is the new development of social engineering that has led to new ways of convincing people to part unwillingly with their most important assets, their identity, and their personal information. Complicating matters, both technical and social engineering approaches are used in cyberattacks these days, and there are ample guides on the Dark Web. This would all seem rather depressing. A useful analogy and the one we hope you take home from this book is that, just like your home or car, no security is foolproof. Determined people can and do break into houses and steal cars. What we all do to manage risk is have locks, alarms, and follow basic protocols, such as locking up after we leave and having unique keys, which we are cautious about sharing with people. In essence, these technical and behavioral approaches make your house, car, or business a hard target for criminals, and insurance companies recognize this by reducing your risk premiums.

So it is in cybersecurity as well. We as individuals, businesses, employees, governments, and nations can make it difficult for criminals and hostile states, so that their attention and actions are elsewhere. The threats, though, are always evolving, and, like an arms race, many security organizations, nations and we as individuals must share their expertise and intelligence on the threats and how to deal with them. We urge you as the reader of this book to keep up to date with the nature of threats in this area, but to not be afraid, but concerned and vigilant. After all, any business, government, or nation state that has a good cybersecurity culture has a long-term competitive advantage as a safe partner with which to do business.

An investment in cybersecurity can be seen as analogous to insurance for goods, chattels, and life itself. With cybersecurity, there is the added dimension of securing personal and private information from unwanted eyes.

Happy panning for cybernuggets.

This book was typeset in LaTeX, built, of course, on TeX: thus, thanks to Leslie Lamport and Donald Knuth. *Emacs*, despite its long heritage, continues in daily use and was a cornerstone of the production of the book. Thus, thanks also to Richard Stallman.

Glossary

ADMD ADministrative Management Domain. 155, 156

AES Advanced Encryption Standard. 123, 124, 125

AH Authorization Header. 144

APT Advanced Persistent Threat. 83, 90

ARP Address Resolution Protocol. 86

ARPANET Advanced Research Projects Agency Network — forerunner to the internet. 3

ASD Australian Signals Directorate. 6, 108

assortativity network property where nodes with some particular property tend to be connected. Similar to homophily. 47

BadRabbit A suspected variant of Petya, BadRabbit, is a ransomware, malicious software that infects a computer and restricts user access to the infected machine until a ransom is paid to unlock it. BadRabbit spreads via fake Adobe Flash updates, tricking users into clicking the malware by falsely alerting the user that their Flash player requires an update. 18

baiting Baiting is in many ways similar to phishing attacks. However, what distinguishes them from other types of social engineering is the promise of an item or good that hackers use to entice victims. Baiters may offer users free music or movie downloads, if they surrender their login credentials to a certain site. Infected USBs have been successfully used in baiting attacks, as most users being curious just plug them into their computers. 87, 88

BEC Business Email Compromise. 6, 9, 22

biometrics an identification/authorization using some aspect of the human body, such as fingerprints or iris scans. 62, 115, 135, 136

blockchain A blockchain is a *distributed ledger* using cryptography to secure a chain of blocks of information, with each new block including a hash of the existing chain. 115, 156

bot an autonomous software agent. 11

botnet A botnet is a collection of internet-connected devices, which may include PCs, servers, mobile devices, and internet of things devices that are infected and controlled by a common type of malware. Users are often unaware of a botnet infecting their system. 11, 13, 88, 149, 173

CA Certificate Authority. 151

chatbot A software agent for mediating a conversation, usually by text on a website. 26

clickjacking a security attack grabbing keystrokes. 72, 149

coin mining Coin mining cyberattacks are aimed at stealing computer power for mining operations for cryptocurrencies. Coin mining is a computationally intensive process that computers comprising a cryptocurrency network complete to verify the transaction record, called the blockchain, and receive digital coins in return. 79, 80, 88, 149

concept creep changes in the definition of a concept rather than its frequency of occurrence. 43

daemon a background software process, providing various services, such as management of a printer. 74

DAO Decentralized Autonomous Organisation. 158

dark web A highly encrypted hidden part of the Web, accessed through the ToR browser and the GRAMS search engine. 18, 20, 41, 72, 147, 149

DDoS Distributed Denial of Service. 7, 9, 10, 12, 13, 30, 83, 84, 85, 86, 149, 173

deep web The vast part of the internet that is hidden from view, either in databases or concealed networks, such as the Dark Web. 147

DEK Data Encrypting Key. 125

Diffie–Hellman The eponymous Diffie–Hellman key exchange is used for exchanging a private key over a public channel. xxvi, 32, 120, 122, 123, 125, 126, 133, 143

DKIM Domain Keys Identified Mail. 155, 156, 157

DMARC Domain-Based Message Authentication, Reporting and Conformance. 43, 155

DNS Domain Name Server. 10, 86, 140, 141, 142, 155, 156, 157

DoS Denial of Service. 10, 12

ECC Elliptic Curve Cryptography. 117, 122, 133

end-to-end encryption Encryption at the initial sending device (such as a phone) and decryption at the receiving device, with no intermediate decryption and reencryption. 56

ESP Encapsulating Security Payload. 144

ethernet A protocol for sending messages (frames) along cable and optical fiber, used widely throughout the internet. 137, 139, 140

EV SSl Extended Validation SSL. 150

firewall Software that controls access to an external network. 144

FSMA Financial Services Modernization Act. 98

FTC Federal Trade Commission. 98

GDPR General Data Protection Regulation. 57, 159, 171

GFW Great Firewall of China. 29, 30

GPU Graphics Processing Unit. 132

GRAMS A search engine for the Dark Web. 147

Hacktivist Computer hacker whose goals are primarily political. 9, 13, 80, 81

hash Hash functions are trapdoor functions, where it is easy to go one way but not the other. They are widely used in cryptography and computer science generally. 157

hexadecimal numbers to base 16. 139, 140

HIPAA Health Insurance Portability and Accountability Act. 98

homophily A social network property where nodes (people) are connected to people with similar likes and preferences. 34, 47

HTTP HyperText Transfer Protocol. 9, 30, 124, 137, 139, 144, 150

HTTPS HyperText Transfer Protocol Secure. 10, 30, 31, 36, 37, 125, 133, 137, 144, 145, 150, 165, 171

ICANN Internet Corporation for Assigned Names and Numbers. 142

ICT Information and Communication Technology. 65

IETF Internet Engineering Task Force. 154

IKE Internet Key Exchange. 143

IoT Internet of Things. 11, 85, 145, 146

IP Internet Protocol. 137, 138, 139, 143, 156

IPSec secure internet packet. 133, 143

ISMS Information Security Management Systems. 98, 99

KEK Key-Encrypting Key. 125

keylogger malware which logs keystrokes on a personal computer, laptop, or mobile device. 62, 149

LAN Local Area Network. 139, 144

MAC Medium Access Control. 86

malware Malware is shorthand for malicious software. It is a software developed by cyberattackers with the intention of gaining access or causing damage to a computer or network, often while the victim remains oblivious to the fact there's been a compromise. xxv, 10, 12, 14, 18, 20, 21, 22, 26, 61, 62, 68, 78, 79, 81, 82, 83, 84, 86, 87, 88, 89, 139, 144, 149

master file table A feature of the Windows NTFS file system, which keeps a record of every file on the system. 21

MD5 A 128 bit message digest. 126

MIME Multipurpose Internet Mail Extensions. 152

MITM Man in the Middle Attack. 36, 86, 125, 150, 161

MTA Mail Transfer Agent. 156

MTAH Motivation To Avoid Harm. 20, 25, 33, 67, 75

NHS National Health Service, UK. 18

NIST National Institute of Standards and Technology. 94, 103, 105, 106, 107, 108, 111, 112, 124, 126

NotPetya The NotPetya virus superficially resembles Petya, but seemingly purely destructive and self-propagating. 18, 21, 22

NSA National Security Agency. 18, 20, 33, 38, 39

Petya Petya is a family of encrypting ransomware, which targets Microsoft Windows-based systems, demanding a ransom to unlock the disk it has encrypted. 8, 18, 20, 21, 22, 66

PEU Perceived Ease of Use. 71, 72, 76

phishing Phishing is the attempt to obtain sensitive information such as usernames, passwords, and credit card details (and money), often for malicious reasons, by disguising as a trustworthy entity in an electronic communication. 43, 62, 83, 87, 153, 166, 167

PKI Public Key Infrastructure. 151

PoP Point of Presence. 139

port number The number of a port (channel) used for input and output from a machine to its local network. 144

PPKC Public-Private Key Cryptography. 117

PT Penetration Testing. 101, 102

PU Perceived Usefulness. 33, 71, 72, 76

quid pro quo Quid pro quo attacks promise a benefit in exchange for information. This benefit usually assumes the form of a service, whereas baiting frequently takes the form of a good. One of the most common types of quid pro quo attacks involve fraudsters who impersonate IT service people and who spam call as many direct numbers that belong to a company as they can find. These attackers offer IT assistance to each and every one of their victims. The fraudsters will promise a quick fix in exchange for the employee disabling their antivirus program and for installing malware on their computers that assumes the guise of software updates. 87

rainbow table a technique for cracking passwords using precomputed hash tables. 132

ransomware Ransomware is a form of malicious software (or malware), which encrypts the contents of a computer disk. Once it's taken over the computer, threatens the user with harm, usually by denying access to the disk. The attacker demands a ransom from the victim, promising to restore access to the data upon payment. xxv, 21, 22, 62, 66, 70, 75, 77, 79, 83, 149, 166

RC4 A stream cypher invented by Ron Rivest, now modified for greater security. 116, 124

RFC Request for Comment: used by IETF for standards documents. 143, 144, 154

RR Resource Record. 140, 156

RSA RSA algorithm developed by Rivest, Shamir, and Adleman. 117, 120, 122

S3 Simple Storage System. An Amazon cloud computing service. 28, 150

salt a way of increasing encryption security by concatenating a random string before encryption. 132

SHA Secure Hash Algorithm, digest function, beginning with SHA = 1 at 160 bits and now up to SHA-3. 126, 151

SMTP Simple Mail Transfer Protocol. 139

spam mass unsolicited email, often with malintent. 13, 43, 62, 83, 88

SPF Sender Policy Framework. 43, 155, 156, 157

spoofing sending an email with a bogus from address. 153, 154

SSID Service Set Identifier. 140

supply chain attack Theft of data along its route, often referring to scraping of confidentially data from commercial websites. 26

tailgating or piggybacking, another social engineering attack, involving someone lacking the proper authentication following an employee into a restricted area or a software equivalent. 87

TAM Technology Acceptance Model. 61, 70, 71

TCP Transport Control Protocol. ix, 139, 141, 143, 144

TCP/IP Transport Control Protocol/Internet Protocol. 137

thread A software fragment operating independently of surrounding software but sharing some of its resources. 149

TI Threat Intelligence. 101, 102

TLD Top-Level Domain. 141, 142

TLS Transport Layer Security. 9, 36, 133, 135

ToR The Onion Router. 147, 149

TRA Theory of Reasoned Action. 61, 65, 73

transport mode Secure internet in which the TCP/IP is encrypted within the original IP header. 143

Trojan horse A Trojan or Trojan horse is a type of malware that is often disguised as legitimate software. Trojans can be employed by cyberthieves and hackers trying to gain access to users' systems. Users are typically tricked by some form of social engineering into loading and executing Trojans on their systems. 13, 87, 163

tunnelling mode Secure internet in which the whole IP packet is encrypted and placed within a new IP packet. 143

UDP User Datagram Protocol. ix, 139, 141

VPN Virtual Private Network. xxvi, 29, 57, 59, 74, 142, 143, 145, 146, 147, 172

WAN Wide Area Network. 139

Wannacry Wannacry is a worm that spreads by exploiting vulnerabilities in the Windows operating system. Once installed, it encrypts files and demands a payment to decrypt them. 7, 8, 18, 19, 20, 21, 22, 33, 75

WEP Wired Equivalent Privacy. 140

whaling cyberattacks against high-profile individuals. 23, 140

WIDS Wireless Intrusion Detection System. 140

WIPS Wireless Intrusion Protection System. 140

worm A worm is a stand-alone malware computer program that replicates itself in order to spread to other computers. Often, it uses a computer network to spread itself, relying on security failures on the target computer to access it. 11

WPA WiFi Protected Access. 140

XOR bitwise exclusive OR (true if two bits are different, false if they are the same. 116, 124

zero day attack A zero-day attack exploits a previously unknown security vulnerability. A zero-day attack is also sometimes defined as an attack that takes advantage of a security vulnerability on the same day that the vulnerability becomes generally known. 142, 163

List of Cyber Nuggets

Authors

Professor Terry Bossomaier set up the Centre for Research in Complex Systems, **CRiCS,** at Charles Sturt University to integrate numerous areas of research, from neuroscience to parallel computing and information theory. He is the co-author of numerous academic papers and five research-oriented books.

Dr Steven D'Alessandro is a professor in the School of Management and Marketing at Charles Sturt University. Steve has published 113 refereed papers in leading international journals (including *The European Journal of Marketing, Journal of Business Research, International Marketing Review, Psychology and Marketing, Marketing Letters, Journal of Services Marketing, Journal of Macromarketing, International Journal of Consumer Studies, Food Quality and Preference, Journal of Retailing and Consumer Services, Accounting and Finance*, and *Journal of Environmental Management and Applied Economics*), books, and conferences. Steve has also worked as a market research consultant for bluechip companies such as Pacific Dunlop, ANZ, Challenge Bank, BHP, Telstra, and Ford. He has published some market-leading textbooks on Market Research, Consumer Behaviour and Services Marketing. Steve was chief investigator of the Cooperative Research Centre Cybersecurity of $140 million Australian dollars in 2017. He is currently coeditor of the *Journal of Consumer Behaviour*. Steve would again like to dedicate this book to his wife, Michelle D'Alessandro, the real cyber expert in his family.

Professor Roger Bradbury began his career as an ecologist, where he developed a long-term interest in complex systems. He left academia to work in government, in the Office of National Assessment with high-level security clearance, amongst other departments. Following retirement from government, he took up a professorship at the National Security College at the Australian National University.

Chapter 1

Introduction

The year this book was written, 2018, cyberscams of one sort or another appeared almost every week. They were often big ones, such as the Marriott/Starwood loyalty program, where millions of people were impacted. Governments were not immune, either, while state-based cyberwarfare rose on the world agenda.

In many of these cyberattacks, technological weakness was only a part, sometimes a small part, of the overall vulnerability; the bigger factor was human. To assume this vulnerability was the result of ignorance or laziness misses the bigger picture. Cybersecurity is very complex. Most people, who are not computer professionals, have little idea what is important and what to believe. To help this large majority is the primary goal of this book.

Thus, the psychological and social aspects of computer security are vitally important, and this is where marketing, a discipline that fuses these domains of knowledge, drawing in many principles from economics, business, and the technological world, comes in.

1.1 That Could Have Been Me

As Odie left the house for work, his wife, Penelope, said to him, "Odysseus, have good day and don't spend any money." The day had not started well. The mail had contained a letter from the bank, saying they were reviewing all housing loans, which might have negative equity implications. His was one. An argument with his anally-retentive employer caused him to miss morning coffee, where there was free cake. Driving into town for lunch, one of the many gigantic potholes destroyed a tyre, which squandered $300 and an hour of his afternoon.

Midafternoon, desperate for a coffee, he found Aga, who was rostered to get new coffee beans, had forgotten to do so, meaning no proper coffee.

Doing a final check of his email before going home, he got an email offering him a housing loan refinancing at a much better rate than he was currently on. It had the bank's logo, was well written, knew his address, and, presumably, the tenuous nature of his existing loan. Tired and frustrated, he clicked on the link at the bottom, which brought up an excellent facsimile of his bank's internet logon page. He entered his username and password.

But he didn't get to his account page. Instead, a sniggering, horned figure popped up. Dreading the worst, he contacted his bank, to discover that $10,000, his mortgage payment for the month, had just been withdrawn. Annoyed, but not alarmed, he assumed the bank would cover the loss. Unfortunately, in Section 6.66 on page 43 of the new terms and conditions, titled *Now you are really stuffed*, was a statement that the bank would no longer be responsible for Trojan Horse attacks.

Odysseus was indeed stuffed. He should have read Cyber Nugget 1. When one is tired and stressed, it is easy to make mistakes. With cyberattacks, there is usually no time to swear profusely and undo the error. One click and it is all over immediately.

Cyber Nugget 1: *Avoid critical computer tasks, such as finance, when tired or stressed.*

Of course if he'd read the terms and conditions, all 67 pages, he would have been aware of the increased risk of financial loss from cyberfraud. However, our lives would be entirely consumed by reading the terms and conditions if we were to read every variant that came along. However, if he'd googled new terms and conditions from Cutthroat Bank, he would have immediately hit Penelope's finance blog, where she highlighted Section 6.66. Thus,

Cyber Nugget 2: *Web forums may highlight important features of new terms and conditions.*

Odysseus fell for an old trick, the Trojan Horse use by his ancient namesake in the oldest work of Western literature. The software technology to implement it is steam-age. Building the fake web page is a trivial endeavor. Spoofing the email address (Section 7.13.1) is not much harder. The failing here was Odysseus, exhibiting a human failing. It is the human dimension of cybersecurity which is the theme of this book.

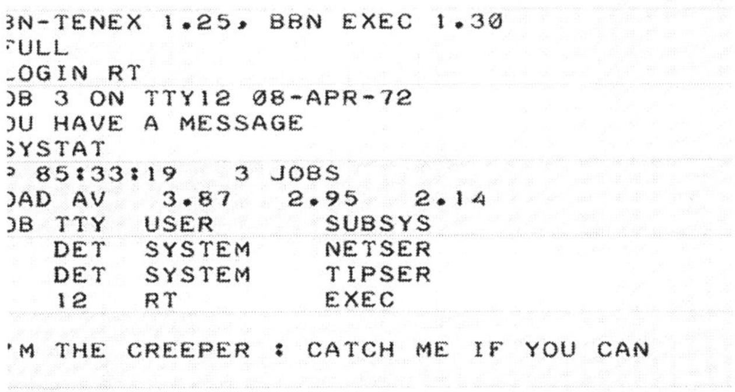

```
3N-TENEX 1.25, BBN EXEC 1.30
FULL
LOGIN RT
)B 3 ON TTY12 08-APR-72
)U HAVE A MESSAGE
SYSTAT
P 85:33:19    3 JOBS
)AD AV    3.87    2.95    2.14
)B TTY   USER        SUBSYS
   DET   SYSTEM      NETSER
   DET   SYSTEM      TIPSER
   12    RT          EXEC

'M THE CREEPER : CATCH ME IF YOU CAN
```

Figure 1.1: CREEPER. The first computer virus.

1.2 A Brief History of Cybersecurity

The history of cybersecurity began with a research project in the early 1970s. Bob Thomas working at Bolt, Beranek and Newman, Inc. realized that it was possible for a computer program to move across a network, leaving a small trail wherever it went. He named the program *CREEPER*, and designed it to travel between telex terminals on the early ARPANET, printing the message *THE CREEPER: CATCH ME IF YOU CAN* (everything was uppercase in those days) (Figure 1.1). A colleague Ray Tomlinson saw this idea and made the program self-replicating, the first computer worm. Then, he wrote another program, *REAPER* , the first antivirus software, which would chase CREEPER and delete it (Big-data made simple, 2018[1]).

The next major recorded cybersecurity incident was between 1976 and 2006, and was an insider attack (these are discussed in detail in Chapter 2). Greg Chung of Boeing stole over 30 years some US $2 billion dollars of aerospace documents and gave them to China. Some 225,000 items of trade secret information were found in his home. This cyberattack was not just a threat to Boeing, but included stealing secrets of national importance about aerospace and space technology, and shows how early on companies were targeted by hostile states[1].

The Russians also used cyberattacks as part of espionage. In 1986, the German computer hacker Marcus Hess hacked an internet gateway in Berkeley, and used that connection to piggyback on the ARPANET. He hacked 400 military computers, including mainframes at the Pentagon, with the intent of selling their secrets to the KGB. He was only caught when an astronomer named Clifford

[1] Eight breakthrough events in the history of cybersecurity - Infographic. https://bigdata-madesimple.com/8-breakthrough-events-in-the-history-of-cybersecurity-infographic/ *Accessed:* 7 Jan 2019.

Stoll detected the intrusion and deployed a honeypot technique (SentinelOne, 2018[2]). At this point in the history of cybersecurity, computer viruses began to become less of an academic prank and more of a serious threat. Late in 1988, a man named Robert Morris wanted to gauge the size of the internet. To do this, he wrote a program designed to propagate across networks, infiltrate Unix terminals using a known bug, and then copy itself. This last instruction proved to be a blunder. The Morris worm replicated so destructively that the early internet slowed to a crawl, causing extensive damage. Robert Morris became the first person charged under the Computer Fraud and Abuse Act. This act also led to the formation of the Computer Emergency Response Team (the precursor to US-CERT), which functions as a nonprofit research center for systemic issues that might affect the internet as a whole.

After the Morris worm, viruses started getting lethal and deadlier, affecting more and more systems. It seems as though the worm foretold the era of massive internet outages in which we now live. You also began to see the rise of antivirus as a commodity, and 1987 saw the release of the first dedicated antivirus company.

The Morris worm also brought with it one last irony. The worm took advantage of the sendmail function in Unix, which was related to the email function originally created by Ray Tomlinson. In other words, the world's first famous virus took advantage of the first worm author's most famous creation.

In 1994, the first major financial cybercrime was reported. A Russian hacker group led by Vladimir Levin, a renowned hacker, perpetrated the attack. Vladimir accessed the accounts of several large corporate customers of Citibank via their dial-up wire transfer service (Financial Institutions Citibank Cash Manager) and transferred funds to accounts set up by accomplices in Finland, the United States, The Netherlands, Germany, and Israel. US $10 million was fraudulently transferred out of the bank and into a bank account in Switzerland. Vladimir was allegedly using his office computer at AO Saturn, a computer firm in St. Petersburg, Russia, to break into Citibank computers. He was finally arrested at Heathrow airport on his way to Switzerland. After the compromise of their system, Citibank updated their systems to use Dynamic Encryption Card, a physical authentication token. Later, it was claimed by Russian hackers that Levin lacked the technical knowhow to hack into Citibank's computers, and simply bought the information to do so for $100.

As we will discuss in Chapter 5, from an early stage, major cybercriminals have not had to be technical experts, but can purchase that expertise at little cost, if they are connected to the right hackavist networks[1]. Later in 2012, we have the largest data breach in history to date. This was when Yahoo reported that hackers had stolen some 3 billion records, including names, addresses, passwords, and security questions. Yahoo failed to report this breach and was fined some

[2] The history of cybersecurity: Everything you wanted to know. www.sentinelone.com/blog/history-of-cyber-security/ *Accessed:* 7 Jan 2019.

$35 million dollars by the Security and Equity Exchange in the United States. The breaches brought down the share price by some $350 million dollars. The Yahoo breach was a major catalyst for government legislation in privacy and the reporting of data breaches in the EU, the United Kingdom, and Australia[1]. Since this time, as covered in the case studies in the next chapter, we have seen a more dynamic set of cyberevents including ransomware attacks, threats to privacy, as shown by the Cambridge Analytica (Section 2.8) scandal and inside threats from Snowden, to many disgruntled or careless employees. All these events in the history of cybersecurity, a term coined in 1989, involve human dimensions as well as advances in technological knowhow. It is very much the purpose of this book to explain how to avoid a repetition of such events by understanding how humans interact with technology and that any system of security is only as good as its weakest link.

1.2.1 The German Celebrity Hack

Just as this book is being finalized on in early 2019, Deutsche Welle television news announced another large-scale hack of politician and celebrity data. Mobile phone and private phone numbers were amongst the items stolen, and even the then German Chancellor, Angela Merkel, was a victim. Some of the aspects of this attack in these initial announcements are central to the theme of this book.

First, the attack had been going on since early December and the hacked items being released on Twitter. The tweeting accounts have now been closed, but one tweet on Dec. 8, 2018 referred to German actor Til Schweiger. Thus, the data had been compromised a month before it became a news story. Nobody had noticed.

Second, how was the data stolen? As yet, speculation varies between Russian hackers and politically aligned German groups. Such large datasets tend, by their very nature, to have many authorized users, and thus many attack points.

Third, there are vast quantities of legacy software and data out there, in organizations, government, and even private individuals. Still in use it relies on old formats, operating systems, or hardware, but is too valuable to risk downtime while attempts are made to bring it up to date. It is both costly and risky to move this data to a more secure framework. The difficulty is summed up by these anguished comments from somebody involved in maintaining a database [86].

> Every few months we get a new software release. Putting it into production requires a lot of work...is painful and the major source of stress around here.

There is a trade-off in risk between being hacked versus loss of data, as the legacy software is updated or rewritten. The balance seems to be shifting towards the former.

These three aspects get to the heart of this book: human factors are of paramount importance in the protection of data everywhere.

Other human factors range from rogue individuals (Section 2.10) to bad authentication (Section 7.5.2). Authentication is steadily improving. The latest IoS (the operating system for iPhones and for iPads) comes with two-factor authentication (Section 7.5.4). Fingerprint and other biometrics are now appearing, such as Apple's FaceID on the iPhone X.

1.2.2 The Australian Parliamentary Hack

Hot on the heels of the German attack, the Australian government announced in February 2019 that it also had been the victim of an attacker. A foreign nation state was thought to be responsible, and it was not immediately clear what had been stolen or what damage had been done.

The attack shows the importance of securing internal networks and encrypting sensitive data. It is also suggested that user behavior in networks be monitored to provide baselines of normal behavior so that intruders on the networks can be more easily identified. Cyberattacks are not just about stealing data or gaining intelligence. As David Braue points out,[3] these attacks can be used to steal identities/approvals of approved users. The actions of asking users to change passwords is seen as an important step in mitigating this risk. It has also been argued that restricting administrative privileges based on user duties is a vital security policy, and forms part of the Australian Signals Directorate (Australian Signals Directorate (ASD)) Essential Eight guidelines, which are mandated for government bodies including Parliament House. Ironically, strong encryption of key data with no backdoors (something not favored by security agencies) is seen as a key internal safeguard. What is not known is how the attack occurred. However, one could reasonably assume that this may have followed a Business Email Compromise (BEC) (Section 2.3), which was a means by which a state actor gained access to the US Democrat email servers in 2016 (Section 2.3).

1.3 The Big Picture

As we shall see in the case studies in Chapter 2 and later in our discussion of risk in Chapter 5, there are numerous ways security may be breached. Overall there seem to be just a few major drivers:

- Social norms, discussed in Chapter 3, are not strongly in favor of cybersecurity, akin to indifference to parking tickets.

[3] www.cso.com.au/article/657638/parliament-house-attack-tough-lesson-credential-security/ *Accessed:* 19 Feb 2019.

- Access: large government or corporate IT systems tend to have many users, increasing the chance that some privileged user will have a dumb password or will allow an unauthorized person to use her account.
- Casualization: where people are hired ad hoc on short, maybe zero-hour contracts, their commitment to the organization may be inadequate.
- Legacy systems with known vulnerabilities are a risk, but the overhead and risk of transition failures or even meltdown, impedes upgrading. The Wannacry attack on the UK National Health Service is discussed in Section 2.2.1.
- Operating system upgrades, which break software or force a disadvantageous licensing arrangement.
- The cashless society is convenient, but, as network outages demonstrate, can be very frustrating for small businesses, such as coffee shops, bakeries, which can lose a part, or a whole day's trade.
- Government services are often now totally online, or risk people opting out for cybersecurity or privacy reasons (Section 2.4).

A common element through all of these is that cybersecurity does not belong just to the IT group. Managers who opt for increasing casualization may not feel that cybersecurity is their problem.

When a large corporation is breached, there will be embarrassment, maybe fines, maybe compensation, but then all will continue as if nothing happened. However, the cost to individuals and small companies can be immense. Identity theft, ransomware, and downtime of a website or corporate database can be devastating. This book is not so much a roadmap for such users, since the roads to safe cyberpractices are at best indistinct and shifting all the time. It is more akin to a compass bearing on rough seas, with no immediate indication of calm weather.

1.4 Overview

We begin in Chapter 2 with a general discussion of a number of case studies, such as

- The Distributed Denial of Service (DDoS) attack on DYN, which impacted numerous large organizations, including Amazon, Twitter, and Netflix (Section 2.1).
- Wannacry ransomware, which seriously disrupted numerous organizations, including the National Health Service in the UK (Section 2.2.1).

- The Petya variant of Wannacry, which was particularly interesting, because it relied on the same vulnerabilities as Wannacry. In other words, many people had ignored the warning signal of Wannacry (Section 2.2.2).

The next three chapters provide a conceptual framework: Chapter 3 introduces social networks, social norms, and their resilience, and Chapter 4 provides a wider marketing perspective and looks at theories of consumer choice and contextualizes poor security behavior.

Chapter 7 is a technical primer, describing in qualitative terms, accessible to the general reader, the cyberelements needed to understand the traps and tricks of the rest of the book. We conclude this chapter with a cyberchecklist for nontechnical people, anyone from parents wanting to protect their children to owners of small businesses. There are many excellent frameworks for cybersecurity policy for technical experts and policy advisors in large organizations or government. What we offer here is a few pointers complementing the cybernuggets.

Many computer scientists of our acquaintance are avid coffee consumers. Most of the book is non-technical, but where we need to venture a little deeper into the computing world, we flag the section with one or more espresso symbols, where two cups indicates the need for a double shot of coffee and three cups a triple. Readers can skip such sections at a first reading, or even ignore them altogether.

The book concludes with an idiosyncratic look at the future in Chapter 8. With the theoretical framework and case studies in place, the book goes on to consider cyberrisk and how to reduce it in Chapter 5 and government policy and statecraft in Chapter 6. Finally, the book concludes with a discussion of important issues just over the horizon.

Astrophysicist-turned science fiction writer, Alastair Reynolds, in his novel *Chasm City* and the *Revelation Space* trilogy, explores in great detail a world where cybermalware has taken over. Buildings are distorted, while one of the lighthugger spaceships, a big part of the trilogy, is filled knee-deep in ship slime as malware eats away at the self-repairing mechanisms of the vast ship's structure. It's a horrific view of the extreme outcomes of ascendent malware. We hope that this book may go a small way towards reducing the prevalence and damage caused by cybersecurity failures.

Chapter 2

Case Studies

This chapter presents a series of case studies and examples of cyberbreaches and attacks. The examples serve as a basis for the discussion of the later chapters and provide the context of why human dimensions in cybersecurity are so important. The cases deal with issues ranging from types of attacks (Distributed Denial of Service (DDoS) Sections 2.1 and 2.2, and business email compromise (Business Email Compromise (BEC)) (Section 2.3)) to issues of insider threats, misuse of private information (such as Cambridge Analytica in Section 2.8), and technical issues such as Transport Layer Security (TLS) weaknesses Section 2.9 (beware the use of web filters). We also examine how certain states have an activist role in cybersecurity, which matches that of state security and how this may affect companies wishing to business therein. There is also a situation that if the public becomes too concerned about cybersecurity and privacy they may drop out of digital engagement, even with their own online health records, which can help them and save both them and the state considerable money. We also discuss the various methods used by hostile states, cybercriminals, and activists to gain access to crucial systems and data. Our first case study deals with an increasingly common and disruptive attack, used by states, DDoS, Hacktivists, and other cybercriminals and possibly rogue states.

2.1 Denial of Service

The way web servers work, along with other server systems, is by listening on one or more ports (Section 7.8.2) for incoming requests. For a website, the two main ports are typically 80 for HyperText Transfer Protocol (HTTP) and 443 for

HyperText Transfer Protocol Secure (HTTPS). Many of us will be familiar with cases where a website goes down because it is overloaded. This typically happens when some eagerly awaited publication is set to be released on a particular day at a particular time and everybody tries to download it at once at the same time. A web server can get overloaded because either it does not have the necessary computing grunt to handle all the requests or because its internet bandwidth is not great enough.

If its bandwidth is too small, then users will experience frustration at very slow access. But in the first case, when the web server gets really overloaded, it may crash or shut down. This creates the opportunity for malware to attack a server, by flooding it with internet packets. This is referred to as a Denial of Service (DoS) attack.

DDoS attacks comprise attack where the attackers (hackers) attempt to prevent legitimate users from accessing the service. In a DDoS attack, the attacker usually sends excessive messages asking the network or server to authenticate requests that have invalid return addresses. Increasingly, botnets are used in such an attack. DDoS attacks may be used to deliberately cause disruption, test the cyberdefenses of critical infrastructure, or increasingly as a decoy, designed to knock an organization offline, meaning the system administrators are too busy trying to stem this attack than to notice other suspicious activity.

For a single machine to send out packets at a rate great enough to crash a web server would typically require a very powerful machine. Hence, these attacks usually result from lots of machines sending packets at the same time. This multipronged attack is called, unsurprisingly, a DDoS variety of different types of attack. The Arbor website[1] provides a good taxonomy across the different network layers (Section 7.7.1): Layer 3 (Network); Layer 4 (Transport); Layer 5 (Session); Layer 6 (Presentation); and Layer 7 (Application). One of the biggest DDoS attacks on record was the Mirai attack on DYN in October 2016 (Section 2.1). As we saw in Chapter 7, IP addresses comprise a series of numbers, which are hard to remember and use. Thus, the internet uses domain names, such as google.com, that map to these numbers. The mapping is done by a *Domain Name Server (DNS)* (Section 7.7.3). This can be a complicated affair, particularly for large, global organizations. As such some companies provide a Domain Name System service, and one of the largest such companies is DYN. The DoS impacted a lot of big internet providers. At the time of writing, Wikipedia lists about 70, including

Airbnb; Amazon.com; Ancestry.com; BBC; The Boston Globe; Business Insider; CNN; Electronic Arts; Fox News; The Guardian; GitHub; Netflix; The New York Times; PayPal; Pinterest; PlayStation Network; Second Life; Shopify; Spotify; Starbucks; Swedish Government; Twitter; Verizon Communications; Visa; The Wall Street Journal; Xbox Live; Yammer; Yelp.

[1] How do you protect against DDoS attacks? www.arbornetworks.com/research/what-is-ddos *Accessed:* 21 Feb 2018.

This is a formidable list, and the consequences, economic and social, would have been huge.

Now, considering the scale of DYN's operation and the computing hardware they have at their disposal, mounting an attack was not easy, but the attackers managed to get a flood of internet traffic of almost one terabyte per second (990 Gbps). Since it would take several minutes to copy a one terabyte portable hard drive, achieving this traffic level is mind boggling. How was it done?

Just like the human brain, which has very slow computing elements (neurons), but lots and lots of them (10 billion), the attack software, Mirai, used a botnet of 100,000 little computers, exploiting a vulnerability in the Internet of Things (IoT) Section 7.9.1. Many household devices are now connected to the internet. For example, now downloading images from a digital camera is often done, not with a cable, but using WiFi, very convenient, since there is no longer a cable to carry around (and lose).

One tends to think of viruses coming via software such as Microsoft Office, but Mirai in fact attacks Linux. It is not Linux, per se, which is vulnerable, merely that through oversight, or convenience, the IoT products targeted have easily accessed logins. Other Mirai attacks include a popular security website, *Krebs on Security*, at 620 Gbps and on *Ars Technica* at 1 Tbps [18].

Many users will not realize just how much computing is going on inside these devices. They certainly may not know how to go in and change the usernames and passwords, by which these devices use WiFi. What's more, it may be a pain to do so, requiring fiddling around with little touchscreens or some joystick to navigate around a menu of letters and numbers. The bottom line is that people don't bother, and these devices are left with factory security settings, and, up until very recently, usually a simple, obvious phrase for each: username—admin; password—password.

Mirai used a worm to search out poorly secured cameras and other devices and install its bot software. This would have happened sometime before the attack. The bots would have just remained asleep on their host, a bit like the herpes virus hides in the trigeminal nerve, waiting for an opportunity to pop out. When the attack time came, each little bot, itself a squib in the computing world, woke up and joined with many others to launch a devastating flood of packets at the target.

It would have taken a bit of effort to write Mirai. But future users didn't need such an effort. It became available on the Dark Web and DoS attacks are now widespread. The perpetrators often go unidentified for years. Skilled practitioners are good at hiding their tracks. Satoshi, the patronym of the inventor of bitcoin, is still unidentified, despite his achievement in 2009 of one of the greatest discoveries in computing in the millennium so far. Yet, the inventor of Mirai, Paras Jha, was ultimately tracked down and charged by the FBI. He had been a Rutgers student, and Rutgers has suffered $300 K cyberconsultancy costs and committed US $1 million to cybersecurity in 2014–2016.

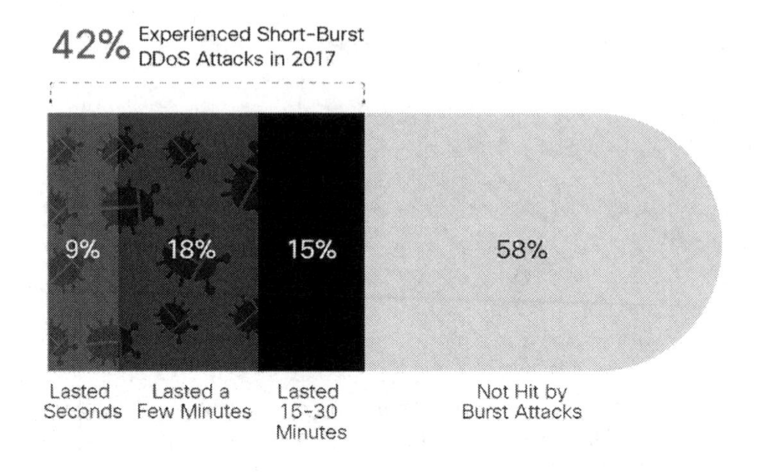

Figure 2.1: Attacks. Source: CISCO 2018, p. 32 (with permission).

Although the number of hackers is huge, there is a band of volunteers seeking to make the web a more secure place, dubbed the white hat vigilantes by Darren Pauli.[2] Some, known by their handles, such as Xylitol and Kafeine, according to Pauli, have diverse day jobs, but destroy malware in their spare time. Others, such as Henrik Adrian, known on Twitter as @unixfreaxjp, was head of Kapersky, Japan[3] but now participates in Malware MustDie,[4] a Not-For-Profit organization, with a number of malware scalps to its credit.

2.1.1 Motivation and Frequency of DoS Attacks

It is likely that the use of DDoS attacks will increase because of the rise of IoT. This because IoT devices are less resource dependent as computer botnets, and also IoT devices within the target organization are often weak points in their network. DDoS is becoming increasingly common, CISCO estimates that around 42% of all attacks in 2017 were based on DDoS attacks. While most of these attacks as shown in Figure 2.1 lasted only for a few minutes, these burst tactics can be costly than when targeting gaming websites and service providers, where even a short disruption can cause an economic loss.

The reasons for such an attack are diverse, ranging from ransomware to some idealogical or political reason for compromising a website: DoS attacks, unlike

[2] www.itnews.com.au/news/the-rise-of-the-white-hat-vigilante-356543/page0 *Accessed:* 11 June 2018.

[3] Eugene Kapersky established the eponymous security software company in 1997, now with products used by 400 million people, with 270,000 corporate clients, according to their website, www.kaspersky.com.au *Accessed:* 11 June 2018.

[4] www.malwaremustdie.org

ransomware for data theft, have unclear, motivations, sometimes never established.

- Intercompany rivalry to reduce service of competitors.
- Hacktivists, who attack a company, because they are opposed in some way to what it does.
- Nation state attacks on critical infrastructure.
- Blackmail, a similar motivation to ransomware.
- As a decoy to divert cybersecurity resources from the real attack, which might be, say, data theft.

However, a recent report by Telstra in Australia[5] suggests they are widespread problems, with 54% of Australian organizations experiencing DoS attacks weekly, monthly, or quarterly.

Criminals are using large botnets to carry out sophisticated attacks. An example is the Necrus botnet. The Necrus botnet is a cybercrime botnet that consists of some 6 million zombie computers, which delivers some of the worst banking Trojan horses and ransomware threats in batches of millions of emails at a time, and it keeps reinventing itself, linked with the spam distribution of the Dridex gang. The Dridex group has existed for some years, targeting financial institutions, using viral spyware to enable the authorization of fraudulent transfers from their corporate accounts.[6] It is used to spread one of the world's most nefarious banking Trojan horses. It also moved to mass distributing Locky, a Dridex ransomware child and then added DDoS attacks. Locky ransomware uses sophisticated techniques to infiltrate computers and hide from its victims.[7]

2.1.2 Preventing and Countering a DoS Attack

There are two components to countering a DoS attack: recognize it quickly; block the attackers, and have mirror servers ready to take over if the primary server crashes. The difficulty faced by defensive software lies in the huge range attack devices. They might be anywhere in the world, thus blocking a particular country or domain won't work. Shutting down a server is only a short-term solution.

In other words, sophisticated software is needed to recognize each and every attack bot and block it. Examples include CISCO CheckPoint and its Anti-Bot Software Blade.[8]

---

[5] Telstra Security Report.

[6] www.forbes.com/sites/geoffwhite/2018/09/26/how-the-dridex-gang-makes-millions-from-bespoke-ransomware/ *Accessed:* 31 Jan 2019.

[7] *Accessed:* 31 Jan 2019.

[8] https://learn-umbrella.cisco.com/malware-protection/check-point-integration *Accessed:* 21 Feb 2018.

In some ways, marketing, advertising, and convenience have increased our vulnerability. Take email. In principle, the mail client on your computer, tablet, or phone only needs to connect with the web server. All other communication could be blocked. But email now contains dozens of links within a message, which link to images, adverts, and, sometimes malware. Here, as an illustration, is a list of *blocked* mail client requests outside of the corporate web server made in the first nine days of June 2018.

```
action: deny
direction: outgoing
 On 9 Jun 2018,    images.springer.com on port 80
                   (http). denied
 On 8 Jun 2018,    pixel.monitor1.returnpath.net
                   on port 80 (http). denied
 On 8 Jun 2018,    image.info.liquidlearning.com on
                   port 80 (http). denied
 On 8 Jun 2018,    gen.sendtric.com on port 80 (http).
                   denied
 On 8 Jun 2018,    image.s10.exacttarget.com on port 80
                   (http). denied
 On 8 Jun 2018,    click.info.liquidlearning.com on
                   port 80 (http). denied
 On 8 Jun 2018,    edmsys.jgbm.org on port 80 (http).
                   denied
 On 7 Jun 2018,    alerts.staysmartonline.gov.au on
                   port 80 (http). denied
 On 7 Jun 2018,    crm.agilescrumsmails.com on port 80
                   (http). denied
 On 7 Jun 2018,    www.amms2018.org on port 80 (http).
                   denied
 On 7 Jun 2018,    news.acrf.com.au on port 80 (http).
                   denied
 On 6 Jun 2018,    click.media.ieee.org on port 80
                   (http). denied
 On 6 Jun 2018,    www.globalspec.com on port 80 (http).
                   denied
 On 6 Jun 2018,    oap-journals.com on port 80 (http).
                   denied
 On 6 Jun 2018,    s1595419559.t.en25.com on port 80
                   (http). denied
 On 6 Jun 2018,    www.educaloxy.com on port 80 (http).
                   denied
 On 6 Jun 2018,    bleztechdelivery.in.net on port 80
                   (http). denied
```

```
On 6 Jun 2018,   email.house.com.au on port 80
                 (http). denied
On 6 Jun 2018,   imagesak.secureserver.net on port 80
                 (http). denied
On 6 Jun 2018,   cdn.ksrinc.com on port 80 (http).
                 denied
On 6 Jun 2018,   email.develop-online.net on port 80
                 (http). denied
On 6 Jun 2018,   edna.ientry.com on port 80 (http).
                 denied
On 6 Jun 2018,   gs.apple.com on port 80 (http).
                 denied
On 5 Jun 2018,   s1814406654.t.en25.com on port 80
                 (http). denied
On 5 Jun 2018,   img03.en25.com on port 80 (http).
                 denied
On 5 Jun 2018,   email.cebit.com.au on port 80
                 (http). denied
On 5 Jun 2018,   mitpune.com on port 80 (http).
                 denied
On 5 Jun 2018,   www.movable-ink-6437.com on port 80
                 (http). denied
On 5 Jun 2018,   f.h1.hilton.com on port 80 (http).
                 denied
On 5 Jun 2018,   h1.hilton.com on port 80 (http).
                 denied
On 5 Jun 2018,   home.neustar.biz on port 80 (http).
                 denied
On 5 Jun 2018,   na-sjh.marketo.com on port 80
                 (http). denied
On 5 Jun 2018,   www.polytechnicpositions.com on
                 port 80 (http). denied
On 4 Jun 2018,   media.journals.elsevier.com on
                 port 80 (http). denied
On 4 Jun 2018,   csemails.elsevier.com on port 80
                 (http). denied
On 4 Jun 2018,   communications.elsevier.com on
                 port 80 (http). denied
On 4 Jun 2018,   content.elsevierjournals.intuitiv.net
                 on port 80 (http). denied
On 4 Jun 2018,   d3cxckyc3pu9pz.cloudfront.net on
                 port 80 (http). denied
```

```
On 4 Jun 2018,    i5\glsg{cma}il20.com on port 80
                  (http). denied
On 2 Jun 2018,    tradebriefs.com on port 80 (http).
                  denied
On 2 Jun 2018,    authorconnect-thomsonreuters.com on
                  port 80 (http). denied
On 2 Jun 2018,    ib.adnxs.com on port 80 (http).
                  denied
On 2 Jun 2018,    www.linkedin.com on port 80 (http).
                  denied
On 2 Jun 2018,    loyalty.qantas.com on port 80
                  (http). denied
On 2 Jun 2018,    i.transact.thegoodguys.com.au on
                  port 80 (http). denied
On 2 Jun 2018,    f.email.thegoodguys.com.au on
                  port 80 (http). denied
On 2 Jun 2018,    l.email.thegoodguys.com.au on
                  port 80 (http). denied
On 1 Jun 2018,    worldconf.benchurl.com on port
                  80 (http). denied
On 1 Jun 2018,    click.e.newscientist.com on
                  port 80 (http). denied
On 1 Jun 2018,    image.e.newscientist.com on
                  port 80 (http). denied
On 1 Jun 2018,    ajax.googleapis.com on port 80
                  (http). denied
On 1 Jun 2018,    msmedia.morningstar.com on port
                  80 (http). denied
On 1 Jun 2018,    mmactiv.in on port 80 (http).
                  denied
On 1 Jun 2018,    click.icptrack.com on port 80
                  (http). denied
On 1 Jun 2018,    staticapp.icpsc.com on port 443
                  (https). denied
On 1 Jun 2018,    staticapp.icpsc.com on port 80
                  (http). denied
On 1 Jun 2018,    cvc0274.chepdev.com on port 443
                  (https). denied
On 1 Jun 2018,    ib.adnxs.com on port 443 (https).
                  denied
On 1 Jun 2018,    tags.bluekai.com on port 443 (https).
                  denied
```

```
On 1 Jun 2018,   e.coles-liquor.com.au on port 443
                 (https). denied
On 1 Jun 2018,   e.coles-liquor.com.au on port 80
                 (http). denied
On 1 Jun 2018,   d39ttiideeq0ys.cloudfront.net on
                 port 80 (http). denied
On 1 Jun 2018,   o9787j9z.emltrk.com on port 443
                 (https). denied
On 1 Jun 2018,   nl2.bdcdn.net on port 80 (http).
                 denied
On 1 Jun 2018,   d1w7fb2mkkr3kw.cloudfront.net on
                 port 80 (http). denied
On 1 Jun 2018,   email.robinskitchen.com.au on
                 port 80(http). denied
On 1 Jun 2018,   t.e.st\glsg{rw}oodhotelsemail.com on
                 port 80 (http). denied
On 1 Jun 2018,   click.e.economist.com on port 443
                 (https). denied
On 1 Jun 2018,   tapestry.tapad.com on port 443
                 (https). denied
On 1 Jun 2018,   cdn.static-economist.com on port 80
                 (http). denied
On 1 Jun 2018,   image.e.economist.com on port 80
                 (http). denied
On 1 Jun 2018,   www.economist.com on port 443
                 (https). denied
On 1 Jun 2018,   pubads.g.doubleclick.net on port 80
                 (http). denied
On 1 Jun 2018,   d1lggihq2bt4jo.cloudfront.net on
                 port 443 (https). denied
On 1 Jun 2018,   comm100edm4.com on port 443 (https).
                 denied
On 1 Jun 2018, Mail via com.apple.WebKit.Networking.xpc
               tried to establish a ajax.googleapis.com
               on port 443 (https). denied
```

Cyber Nugget 3: *Opening a web page may generate many extra page requests.*

2.2 Ransomware

Malware, like most computer programs, is often based on previous versions which are updated, improved on, and used for different kinds of attacks. This significantly changes and magnifies the risk. The malware attacks of **Wannacry, Petya, NotPetya**, and **BadRabbit** are all related to each other in terms of original code, but with slight variations have been used for different purposes. Because of the weaknesses of human behavior in terms of lack of updating operating systems and being tricked to download malicious software via social engineering (see Section 5.3.2.4), these types of attacks are likely to continue and evolve.

2.2.1 WannaCry

Wannacry malware was based on an exploitation of Microsoft Windows called EternalBlue, which was developed by the National Security Agency (NSA), which was then leaked by a hacker crew called the Shadow Boxers on the dark web, according to Brewster.[9] There is evidence that the EternalBlue Exploit on unpatched Windows systems was updated further by cybercriminal and/or state organizations operating out of North Korea[10] Wannacry used a worm that spread by exploiting vulnerabilities in the Windows operating system, mainly if older versions have not been patched or updated. Once installed, it then encrypted files and demanded payment to decrypt them. This attack earned more than US $143 billion through bitcoin payments according to CISCO'S 2018 cybersecurity report. In 2017 security firm Symantec reported in 2018 that 5.48 billion attacks by Wannacry were blocked Wannacry was spread by social engineering by the use of SPAM emails such as fake invoices, job offers, and other lures being sent out to random email addresses. Within the emails is a *.zip file* (archive), and once clicked, it initiates the Wannacry infection.[10]

The Wannacry attack (Figure 2.2) was particularly effective in attacking the National Health Service, UK (NHS) in the UK with multiple hospital reporting closures of entire wards, patients being turned away, and some staff being sent home. Barts Health, a central London NHS trust, advised patients to look for support elsewhere and said ambulances were being diverted, while another NHS organization said it had to turn away outpatients and limit its radiology services. In the Essex town of Colchester, the hospital decided to close much of its A&E department to accept only those in "critical or life-threatening situations".[9] Figure 2.3 shows the time course of the outbreak.

[9]An NSA cyberweapon might be behind a massive global ransomware outbreak `www.forbes.com/sites/thomasbrewster/2017/05/12/nsa-exploit-used-by-wannacry-ransomware-in-global-explosion/#647b799fe599` *Accessed:* 21 Dec 2018.

[10]Cybersleuths unearth more clues linking Wannacry to North Korea. www.healthdatamanagement.com/news/cybersleuths-unearth-more-clues-linking-wannacry-to-north-korea *Accessed:* 25 July 2018.

Figure 2.2: A screenshot from a Wannacry attack.

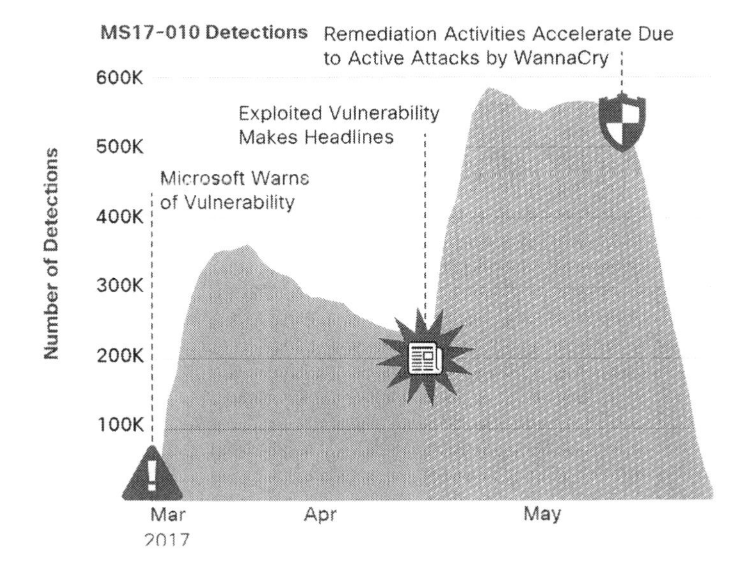

Figure 2.3: Time course of Wannacry.

Luckily, a kill switch was found by accident to prevent the spread of this malware tracking it back to its internet protocol (IP) address of origin, a possible artifact of its design as spyware for the NSA according to Kan.[11] Yet the difficulties of Wannacry could have been avoided. The NSA, when it became aware that EternalBlue had been leaked to the dark web, did alert Microsoft about the need to patch its operating systems according to Sean Kerner.[12] In March 2017, Microsoft issued a security update altering users to patch their system; however, a significant number of devices remained unpatched by April 14, 2017, when the attack occurred as discussed in the CISCO 2018 annual cybersecurity report (p. 41).[13] What was required was a major event to change behavior rather than knowledge of a weakness. As we will see in Chapter 4, the delay in patching and updating systems can be explained by the Motivation To Avoid Harm (MTAH). As many computer users have no experienced adverse events or could understand the risk, they were unlikely to act. This changed once the knowledge of Wannacry malware became more common. Also in the NHS, there was lack of IT support, meaning many users would have to find the time and ability to patch operating systems. As we will see in Chapter 4, this can also be explained by MTAH; as they lack self-efficacy or belief, they can do much to prevent these types of attacks.

Cyber Nugget 4: *Patching of operating systems is paramount in reducing vulnerabilities.*

Backups of data offline should occur, and training in avoiding social engineering attacks (Section 5.3.2, Cyber Nugget 27) is a must for all employees.

2.2.2 Petya and NotPetya

Petya, like Wannacry, is also in the family of encrypting ransomware. The malware targets Microsoft Windows-based systems, infecting the master boot record to execute a payload that encrypts a hard drive's file system table and prevents Windows from booting. It subsequently demands that the user make a payment in bitcoin in order to regain access to the system. The name derives from a satellite that was part of the sinister plot in the 1995 James Bond film *Golden Eye*; a Twitter account suspected of belonging to the malware's author used a picture of actor Alan Cumming, who played the villain, as its avatar. Unlike, its predecessor

[11] A "kill switch" is slowing the spread of Wannacry ransomware: A security researcher may have helped stop the spread of the ransomware, which hit tens of thousands of PCs worldwide. www.pcworld.idg.com.au/article/619237/kill-switch-slowing-spread-wannacry-ransomware/ *Accessed:* 21 Dec 2018.

[12] A year after wannacry, what lessons have been learned? www.eweek.com/security/a-year-after-wannacry-what-lessons-have-been-learned *Accessed:* 21 Dec 2018.

[13] www.cisco.com/c/en/us/products/security/security-reports.html *Accessed:* 21 Dec 2018.

Wannacry, the kill switch option linked to the IP source had been removed in the code. The business model around Petya was based on ransomware as a service, where distributors get 85% of the paid ransom amount and the authors the remaining 15.[14]

The Petya attack of June 26, 2017, some 3 months after the Wannacry event, affected many companies across Europe reported including UK-based advertising and public relations firms WPP, Ukraine's state-run power company Ukrenergo, Russian oil producer Rosneft, and global transport company Maersk (see Andrew Greenberg's detailed account in Wired,[15] the subject of his forthcoming book, *Sandworm*. Petya was spread originally by users downloading and using a Trojanized Ukrainian accounting software download (M.E.Doc), so it may have also been a political target of Russian hackers on the Ukrainian supply chain.

The NotPetya virus superficially resembles Petya in several ways: it encrypts the master file table and flashes up a screen requesting a ransom to restore access to the files. But there are a number of important ways in which it's different and much more dangerous:

1. NotPetya spreads on its own.
2. NotPetya encrypts everything.
3. NotPetya isn't ransomware, since it didn't actually ever provide a decryption key.
4. NotPetya damages the data beyond repair by encrypting it and, as they say, throwing away the key.

It is possible the motive for NotPetya, like Petya is cyberwarfare, as attacks focused on Ukraine and emanated from Russia. Importantly, the motivations for attacks of NotPetya were more diffuse and include state actions as well as criminal activity. NotPetya had also evolved to infect all platforms from Windows XP to Windows 10. Interestingly, the NotPetya malware was present at the same time as the Petya attack, which showed how quickly the means of attack and code can improve from one attack to another. According to Greenberg,[15] the White House estimated the cost of NotPetya at US $10 billion, the most costly such attack to date, while the Ukraine had a taste of cybergeddon

> On a national scale, NotPetya was eating Ukraine's computers alive. It would hit at least four hospitals in Kiev alone, six power companies, two airports, more than 22 Ukrainian banks, ATMs and card

[14]Petya Or NotPetya: why the latest ransomware is deadlier than Wannacry. Forbes.com, 14-14. at www.forbes.com/sites/thomasbrewster/2017/06/27/petya-notpetya-ransomware-is-more-powerful-than-wannacry/#4b9ca114532e *Accessed:* 21 Dec 2018.

[15] www.wired.com/story/notpetya-cyberattack-ukraine-russia-code-crashed-the-world/ *Accessed:* 24 Apr 2019.

> payment systems in retailers and transport, and practically every federal agency. "The government was dead," summarizes Ukrainian minister of infrastructure Volodymyr Omelyan. According to ISSP, at least 300 companies were hit, and one senior Ukrainian government official estimated that 10% of all computers in the country were wiped. The attack even shut down the computers used by scientists at the Chernobyl cleanup site, 60 miles north of Kiev. "It was a massive bombing of all our systems," Omelyan says.

As noted in Section 2.2.1, NotPetya exploited a vulnerability, which had already been addressed in Microsoft patch, MS17-010.[16] Microsoft now provides a checklist to ensure that this patch is installed.[17] Unfortunately, not enough people had installed this patch (Cyber Nugget 4).

A suspected variant of Petya, BadRabbit is a malicious software that infects a computer and restricts user access to the infected machine until a ransom is paid to unlock it. BadRabbit spreads via fake Adobe Flash updates, tricking users into clicking the malware by falsely alerting the user that their Flash player requires an update. This was and is a much improved version of previous sets of ransomware.

An interesting footnote to Wannacry and its ilk was reported by Charlie Osborne on ZDNet in early 2019.[18] Insurance companies are resisting paying out on insurance claims on NotPetya. This recalls the issues of subtle changes in terms and conditions in Section 3.4.3.1.

2.3 Check Before You Send: Business Email Compromise (BEC) Attacks

One of the fastest growing cybercrimes is BEC, a scam of targeting business working with foreign suppliers or businesses that regularly perform electronic transfer payments [73]. These crimes are carried out by compromising legitimate business email accounts through social engineering or computer intrusion to conduct unauthorized transfers of funds. As will be discussed in Chapter 4, these type of attacks are more likely to succeed when people are stressed or short of time. As is often the case with senior management or overworked staff on a Friday morning.

BEC attackers engage in spoofing by sending emails that appear to be from a legitimate source. By studying posts on social media before launching a scam,

[16] www.csoonline.com/article/3233210/petya-ransomware-and-notpetya-malware-what-you-need-to-know-now.html *Accessed:* 23 Apr 2019.

[17] support.microsoft.com/en-us/help/4023262/how-to-verify-that-ms17-010-is-installed *Accessed:* 24 Apr 2019.

[18] www.zdnet.com/article/notpetya-an-act-of-war-cyberinsurance-firm-taken-to-task-for-refusing-to-pay-out/ *Accessed:* 14 Jan 2019.

fraudsters are able to identify which individuals and protocols are necessary to perform fund transfers [73]. Often such emails will ask users to click on a link and change their password because of security concerns. An example is shown in Figure 2.4.

Once the link is clicked, the users are sent to a fake domain, very similar to a legitimate source, where the attackers can gain access to the email system by recording the new password for that email account. Such an approach was used to hack into the Democratic email server of Hillary Clinton campaign in 2016, with the email being personally addressed to her chief of staff John Podesta [73, p. 29]. This breach then led to the leaking of some 60,000 emails relating to the Clinton campaign, from his Gmail account.

In 2014 the FBI estimated that US companies had lost US $179 million in such scams! [156] rising to US $5 billion by November 2017 [35]. The rate of growth of such crimes being some 2,370% from 2015 to 2017 [35]. Even internet companies such as Google and Facebook have been duped by such a scam losing US $100 million between them [38].

The attacks are particularly targeted at CEO and CFOs who often have access privileges to transfer large amounts of money, and such a scam is often called *whaling* [109,149].

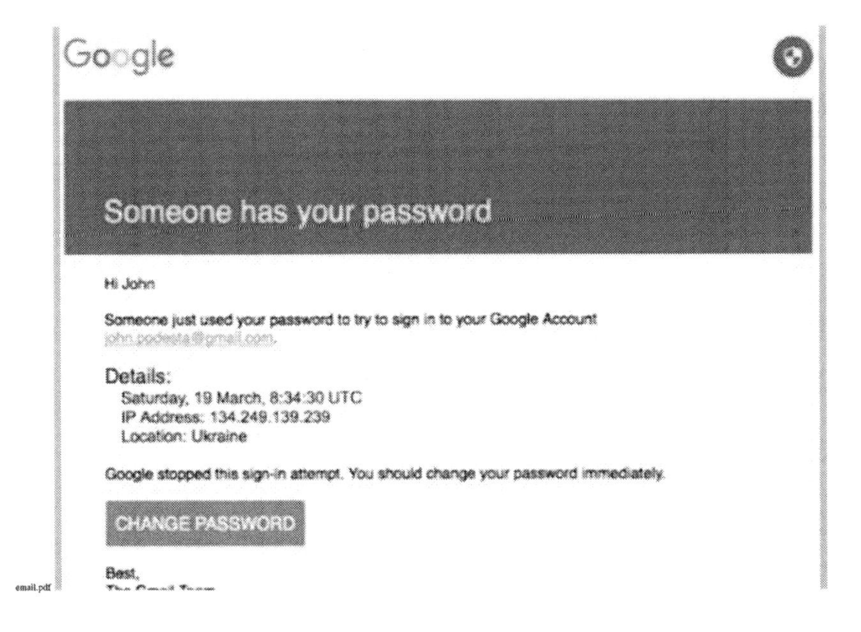

Figure 2.4: Scam email as part of a BEC attack. (Source: Katz [72], p. 29 (with permission).)

A compromised email account may also be infected with spyware, which records the location of the CEO or CFO, since a scam of someone impersonating them is then more likely to succeed when they are out of the country [49]. Another avenue for this type of crime is to intercept a real estate payment during a transfer of title or completion of a transaction [147]. The fraudster with access to an email account simply asks the money be deposited in a different bank account.

Cyber Nugget 5: *Raising awareness of the myriad of ways criminals can get email information and using double sign-offs on large money transfers can reduce the risk of Business Email Compromise.*

2.3.1 Blockchain Land Titles

In the Western world, we take land ownership for granted and have effective central registers of land titles. In the developing world, land title is often much less secure. The infrastructure for a central register may not be strong enough and corruption can imperil its validity. Thus blockchains are an appealing solution. Every land sale transaction is recorded in the blockchain. The record is immutable and a copy is owned by everybody. A number of trials are underway. The Sweden Land Registry and the Republic of Georgia are piloting land registry schemes. India is trying to avert land fraud with blockchains (Section 7.14).

In Australia, NSW has moved in 2018 to electronic storage of land titles with transfer done digitally. However, it is essential to ensure that funds are not intercepted during transfer.

2.4 When Too Much Concern over Cybersecurity Is Too Much: Opting Out of My Health Records in Australia

While being risk adverse in cybersecurity is a good thing, a public lack of trust and fear that no information is secure and private may become a problem for government. A good example when a lack of public faith in the security of personal information may actually make the delivery of government services more inefficient and costly is the My Health Debacle in Australia,[19] according

[19] Australian Broadcasting Corporation: My Health Record races to save face by closing loopholes with partner apps. www.abc.net.au/news/2018-07-24/digital-health-agency-changes-my-health-record-app-contracts/10026644 *Accessed:* 25 July 2018.

to Dana McCauley in the Sydney Morning Herald.[20] The My Health Record as the name implies, is an online health record of Australians, which allows medical services to be better delivered across locations and specialists for patients. Digitized health records also help avoid medication errors and help patients transition from hospital to home. The system was launched in 2018, after a trial in 2017 showed its potential for better and targeted treatments in 15 test sites across Australia [100].

My Health Record was based on an opt-out system, that is all Australians were all originally included in the database, but could opt out or leave the system. My Health data had access controls set by the user and the access to the system was by two factor identification. Users also received an SMS or email validation if a healthcare provider accessed their records.[21] Despite these safeguards and with advent of mandatory data breach reporting in February 2018, there was much public disquiet.

The Australian government's track record on data privacy in this area was not good. The Federal Department of Health published the so-called deidentified dataset from the Medicare Benefits and the Pharmaceutical Benefits Scheme of some 2.5 million Australian. Researchers, though were able to reidentify the data, and a subsequent investigation by the Privacy Commissioner found that the Privacy Act had been breached three times, according to Cross.[22] Human error was largely to blame for these breaches. Data breaches in other countries were also becoming more common, with hackers in Singapore stealing 1.5 million health records in 2017, including those of the Prime Minister Lee Hisen Loong.[22]

The Australian Human Rights Commissioner also expressed concerns about the data being able to be hacked or led to being misused.[23] The increased media reports concerns about security of the data and it being used for purposes other than medical treatment led many Australians to opt out of the system [89]. This led to new legislation that users could opt out permanently and that other authorities could not access this data without a warrant. The My Health Record changes were also not communicated well to the public in the first place, and the benefits of the system were not well explained. In the absence of evidence of good privacy and cybersecurity practices, the public are not likely to trust government with their information, even if it benefits their health and well-being.

As will be discussed in Chapter 4, the public of Australia had a high level of MTAH (data breaches and privacy violations) in this case, but in the absence of

[20] www.smh.com.au/politics/federal/millions-to-opt-out-of-my-health-record-as-backlash-builds-20180724-p4ztb0.html *Accessed:* 27 May 2019.

[21] Australian Digital Health Agency: What Is My Health Record? www.myhealthrecord.gov.au/for-you-your-family/what-is-my-health-record *Accessed:* 25 July 2018.

[22] http://theconversation.com/what-could-a-my-health-record-data-breach-look-like-100090 *Accessed:* 25 July 2018.

[23] Australian Broadcasting Corporation: Human Rights Commissioner tells Government to fix My Health Record problems. www.abc.net.au/news/2018-07-24/my-health-record-human-rights-commissioner-wants-changes/10028618 *Accessed:* 25 July 2018.

communicated safeguards, were not told how they could also help protect their information. Also as discussed therein, the social norm of a lack of trust in the government in Australia meant that significant resources should have been spent on outlining the benefits and safeguards of the My Health system. The social norms of a lack of government trust, in this case, was consistent with a lack of belief in security of their information.

Cyber Nugget 6: *Government data programs need tight cybersecurity standards to ensure user engagement.*

The benefits of the need for personal information must be clearly laid out against any risks of breaches.

Cyber Nugget 7: *Government and corporations should adhere to the privacy principle that the data can only be used for clearly defined purposes.*

2.5 Corporate Data Breaches

We can distinguish two types of data leak:

1. A flood (Section 2.5.2): a large number of files or databases are all stolen in one single hit, either as a hack, say through a weak password, or from a rogue individual loading up a USB drive.
2. A stream (Section 2.5.1): where a hacker installs some sort of malware that harvests data over a period of time, this is usually known as a *supply chain attack.*

2.5.1 Supply Chain Attacks

The Ticketmaster breach was a stream, which continued to flow for a couple of months after the first hint of its existence, affecting 40,000 customers in the UK.[24]

Richard Priday[25] in Wired describes how bank Monzo noticed a huge bias of fraud reports towards Ticketmaster. It took another couple of months to find out what was happening and to plug the leak. It transpired that complexity was at work. A contractor, Inbenta Technologies, operated a chatbot on the Ticketmaster site. However, somehow this ended up on the Ticketmaster payment page. Hackers were then able to access and harvest payment details.

[24]www.wired.co.uk/article/wired-awake-280618 *Accessed:* 4 July 2018.

[25]www.wired.co.uk/article/ticketmaster-data-breach-monzo-inbenta *Accessed:* 4 July 2018.

Cyber Nugget 8: *Beware adding modules, agents, or bots of any kind from other companies to your website.*

In 2018 personal information was stolen from recruiting firm PageUp, which provides services to many large Australian companies such as Telstra, Australia Post, and Jetstar, with a claimed 2 million users worldwide.[26]

2.5.2 Illustrative Floods

It may not be always clear when data theft is a single event, a flood, but the following seem to be examples.

2.5.2.1 Guard Your CV

PageUP[27] suffered a major flood in May 2018 according to Yoland Redrup in the Australian Financial Review.[28] She described it as possibly being *Australia's Equifax* (Section 2.5.2.2), in which hackers stole personal data from 147 million customers in North America and the UK,[29] and is expected to cost the company close to half a billion dollars. PageUP may be the target of a class action, and its plans for a public offering may be in jeopardy as a result of the breach.

An interesting aspect of the security analysis PageUP went through following the breach was identification of a risk from failed password attempts. Such passwords appeared unencrypted in log files (from before 2007) and fell prey to a common human failing—using simple variations on the same password, Fido1, Fido2, Fido3... (Cyber Nugget 42)

2.5.2.2 The Equifax Hack

Equifax, Inc. is a credit reporting agency that lost data from 147 million customers, including names, birth dates, and social security numbers. It resulted in a £500,000 fine in the United Kingdom. Reuter claimed in March 2018 that it might (then) be the costliest data breach in history.[30]

---

[26] www.abc.net.au/news/2018-06-06/australian-data-may-be-compromised-in-pageup-security-breach/9840048 *Accessed:* 13 Aug 2018.

[27] www.pageuppeople.com/unauthorised-activity-on-it-system/ *Accessed:* 5 July 2018.

[28] www.afr.com/technology/pageup-to-faces-customer-loses-law-suits-after-data-breach-20180607-h112y4 *Accessed:* 4 July 2018.

[29] www.nytimes.com/2017/09/07/business/equifax-cyberattack.html *Accessed:* 8 Jan 2018.

[30] www.reuters.com/article/us-equifax-cyber/equifax-breach-could-be-most-costly-in-corporate-history-idUSKCN1GE257 *Accessed:* 8 Jan 2018.

2.5.2.3 Don't Organize an Affair Online

Adultery is frowned upon throughout most of the world, in some places attracting harsh penalties. Thus the website Ashley Madison, a site to foster extramarital affairs, was always somewhat risky and, it turned out risky too. The site was hacked in July 2015, and the members' details were stolen. Rick Thomas describes in the *LA* Times[31] how he was subsequently blackmailed by the hackers. Two years later, in July 2017, the parent company Ruby Corporation agreed to settle a class action for US $11.2 million.

The theft of personal information has been going on for years and still continues. In April 2011, Sony suffered a massive loss of 77 million personal records, according to the *Guardian*.[32]

2.5.2.4 Flood Prevention

There is absolutely no reason why all personal data should be encrypted, thus why are these breaches still continuing. As always with cybersecurity, there are both human and technical factors.

The technical factors often arise from the complexity of modern large- scale data storage. Often organizations now host data in the cloud or some other managed service, and proving the absolute robustness of such systems is proving difficult. Compounding the difficulty is that when data is used it may be stored temporarily in a cache somewhere (a technical factor) and for one reason or another, this data may be left lying around (a human factor).[33] CQR, a security consultancy, reports other examples of leakage of S3 (basically, the chunks of data which Amazon uses in its cloud storage system, see Section 7.12) through poor privacy configuration.[34] Another example was reported on ZDNet in 2017,[35] where

> As many as 14 million records of subscribers who called the phone giant's customer services in the past six months were found on an unprotected Amazon S3 storage server...The customer records were contained in log files that were generated when Verizon customers in the last six months called customer service.

These issues can be hard to deal with, since it may not be clear which software (and hence which company) has the problem.

---

[31] www.latimes.com/home/la-hm-la-affairs-rick-thomas-20170111-story.html *Accessed:* 13 Aug 2018.

[32] www.theguardian.com/technology/2011/apr/26/playstation-network-hackers-data *Accessed:* 13 Aug 2018.

[33] `www.itwire.com/security/84003-godaddy-data-found-exposed-in-unsecured-amazon-s3-bucket.html` *Accessed:* 15 Aug 2018.

[34] `www.cqr.com/insecure-s3-buckets-expose-australian-government-data/` *Accessed:* 15 Aug 2018.

[35] `www.zdnet.com/article/millions-verizon-customer-records-israeli-data/` *Accessed:* 27 Apr 2019.

2.6 The Nation State and CyberSecurity: Firewalls, Friends, and Enemies

In this case study, we consider the good and the bad of national internet filters and control.

2.6.1 The Great Firewall, Golden Shield, and the Great Cannon of China

Actions by the Chinese state have the capacity to move cybersecurity from a means of the prevention of crime and disruption in the internet, to the tools of censorship, state control, and the weaponization of the internet. Indeed, it is argued by some quarters that the approach taken by China may lead to a splintering of the internet into different geopolitical blocks [13,28].

The centerpiece of state control of the internet for its 649 million users is the Great Firewall of China (GFW). This is essentially a filter and a block to Western internet companies such as Google, Facebook, Twitter, and Instagram, though it is often extended to media outlets [45]. It can also make more sluggish or throttle websites, such as the Google search engine. The estimated cost of establishing the GFW in 2003 was US $60 million, which has now grown and is supplemented by an army of 2 million censors [13], including some 20,000 internet police [46]. Often, these censors are employed within Chinese tech companies, such as Sina Weibo , the country's main microblog company that employs 4,000 of these government officials.

The impact of these controls limits access and speed to internet sites outside China and significantly slows internet speeds. Only 1.6% of the Chinese population enjoy connections that run faster than 10 Mbps, with the average internet speed being 3.7 Mbps [81]. On the other hand, such controls have created barriers for entry into the Chinese 2 trillion digital dollar economy, and greatly favored compliant Chinese companies. There has also been with such slower speeds, something of a move to mobile commerce. Chinese consumers are more likely to use their phone as the way they make purchases (55%) compared with 29% for the rest of the world [81, p. 109].

It is possible for users within China to evade such controls temporarily by use of VPN services, and there is evidence that the use of such services provides a gateway service to discover coincidently other banned websites and services [61]. The Chinese government also seeks to block access to VPN (Section 7.9) service providers as well [45]. From *The Economist*

> It is generally senior bureaucrats, not engineers like Mr Fang, who decide what foreign sites are unfit for Chinese users, such as YouTube (blocked permanently in 2009), Facebook and Twitter (blocked since riots in Xinjiang in 2009) and *Bloomberg* and the

New York Times (blocked in 2012, after publishing detailed reports on the finances of Chinese leaders' families).

The other aspect of State control is internal, and is called *The Golden Shield*. This area of internet control concerns itself with containing threats from within and is spread across the provinces of China, although the censors employed in the provinces may have differing issues of cause of concern and interpretation when it comes to censorship. The Chinese government, though is concerned about foreign powers and about subversive elements, has recently developed a cyber-weapon based on this large base of internet users and therefore computers [58].

Dubbed *The Great Cannon of China*, it is alleged that the Chinese state has organized DDoS attacks using its large number of computers by redirecting internet traffic from the Chinese search engine *Baidu*. Such an approach was allegedly used in an attack on *GitHub*, because the site hosted pages fostering links to content restricted in China [58]. The approach only seems to target unencrypted HTTP and not the more secure HTTPS sites.

The tools of state control in such a big market create incentives for many western companies to comply or provide software that helps such compliance. *The Economist* [46] reports Hewlett-Packard devised an online public monitoring system for the Chinese market in 2006. This is not surprising, since according to a Chinese government register, there are an estimated 100 Chinese companies that have 125 products for monitoring and filtering public opinion [46]. It may be possible for other regimes to tighten controls over their population, given China's example as is the case in Vietnam and Thailand [28]. It would also seem reasonable that this would provide export opportunities for Chinese companies already assisting with the GFW.

Cyber Nugget 9: *Greater state controls of business conduct are coming to China.*

2.6.2 Social Credits Anyone?

The Chinese government is instituting a *social credit system*, whereby each citizen is given a trustworthy rating based on "anything from shopping habits to choice of friends" [64, p. 42]. This also applies to businesses in China. Having a bad social credit can place you on a blacklist, denying government contracts, employment, or for Chinese citizens a ban of 1 year from traveling on fast trains or overseas [96]. The social credit system is seen very much as an outcome of Confucian values, which promote social harmony, piety, and order [64]. You can get bad social credit for dishonest dealings, not visiting your parents within 60 days, and nonpayment of fines or being on "a judgment defaulter list," whereby a party defaults on payments from Court orders. There is an estimated 3.1 million Chinese people on such lists [47].

Other things that could get you in trouble may be building shoddy or unsafe products or any conduct undermining the social order. Those blacklisted may be socially outed, having, for example, their names placed on billboards [144]. This method of social credit has also been considered for foreign businesses in China. These include the Beijing Foreign Enterprise dual points system that monitors foreign investors with positive and negative points. Based on this, the system categorizes companies and provides green pass credit to companies with good credit.

Cyber Nugget 10: *Be wary of social credit scores for work in China.*

2.7 Encryption: The Government Is Your Friend but Not Always Your Best Friend

Many governments worldwide (such as the USA, UK, and Australia) are seeking powers to gain access to encrypted information for national security and crime prevention reasons. Often, this needs to be done with legal and legislative powers, either backed by agency powers or, in some cases, by court orders though it is argued that intelligence of national security and egregious crime (child pornography and exploitation) requires constant agency surveillance. So while governments, as discussed in Chapter 5, have developed laws and codes of practice to ensure greater protection of data and cybersecurity, there is nevertheless an interest to bypass these mathematical safeguards on data such as encryption. An example of the former is that the UK data protection act, developed from its European act of a similar, makes exemptions for data privacy for information required that is in the national interest or for security reasons.

It should also be realized that there are always trade-offs in the area of cybersecurity, as change in one area (reducing the use of encryption to hide malicious activities by terrorists), may weaken other areas (the overall strength of encryption is thus reduced, and the internet becomes more vulnerable, so cybercrime increases).

2.7.1 Can the Law of the Land Defeat the Law of Mathematics?

Unfortunately, it is worse than that. The cornerstone of security of HTTPS, e-commerce, and the digital economy is built on the bedrock of encryption, and the only legal way for governments to gain backdoor access is to outlaw or constrain, if possible, the use of certain encryption technologies. However, compelling platform providers to provide encryption keys or somehow intercept messages after encryption is not really possible.

The Diffie–Hellman approach, discussed in Section 7.2.2, allowing new keys to be developed on the fly, presents difficulties for government. How can government gains access to encrypted information if the key randomly changes every time a message is sent. The answer is they can't mathematically, or at least, not within current computational constraints. The government could legislate what is acceptable in terms of encryption, but this could weaken cybersecurity for everyone and could threaten Australia's $79 billion digital economy. It could force providers to install spyware on devices to view an unencrypted message when it is briefly opened by another application, but if users only view messages with their own private key this may not be possible either.

Another option, asking platform providers to include spyware in updates, may also not be a good idea, as people will be less likely to patch applications if they become aware of this, and criminals may simply not update their software. So, the installation of a spyware malware by deception would weaken cybersecurity and not really catch those in dark places.

While many of us are not privy to the machinations of the security *five eyes* services, comprising Australia, the United States, the United Kingdom, New Zealand, and Canada, we can by a reasonable amount of knowledge work out what is possible, given an understanding of computing and mathematics in this area. Complicating this, however, is how human behavior changes as a result of government policy and regulation in cybersecurity. There are two possible means by which law enforcement can gain access to encrypted information, forcing exceptional access

1. to globally distributed, encrypted message applications.
2. plaintext on encrypted devices such as smartphones.

Forcing exceptional access to allow law enforcement may be done, it has been suggested, by adding an agency key that is held by a law enforcement that can be used along to decrypt the data, via accessing the private key. The problem, though the use of agency keys makes the internet security for all much weaker. It is also possible that if private keys are somehow breached, then the public keys themselves become vulnerable and the data collected via them is compromised. Also disclosing private keys, which usually change at each transaction, fundamentally weakens the security of internet, and it is even possible that with access to private keys that third parties may forge internet traffic. Procedurally, who would control these public keys? There would be a need for complete the global agreement for it to be effective, and would nations trust each other to allow others to have access to their encrypted information? We return to this issue in the final chapter.

2.7.2 *Who Watches the Watchers and the Impact on the Economy*

Providing law enforcement agencies with significant new powers and access does not mean they will use them correctly, or that all who work for them will act ethically and responsibly. The recent Wannacry attack was based on the malware software developed by the NSA, which was leaked to the dark web by a contractor. There have been examples of unauthorized access to the cell phone members of senior representatives to the Greek government between 2004 and 2005 and unauthorized wiretapping of some 6,000 people in Italy, including business, financial, judges, and political leaders between 1996 and 2006 [1], not to mention the recent Snowden revelations. There is also the cost to the economy of weakening the encryption regime, making the internet less convenient and slowing devices. Trust of secure transactions and communications one could argue is the bedrock of e-commerce and the global economy.

Cyber Nugget 11: *Governments modifying encryption in the cause of crime prevention and national security could have damaging consequences for cybersecurity.*

2.8 Cambridge Analytica

One of the more sensational scandals of the Trump election campaign was the mischief caused on Facebook by an artificial intelligence firm, Cambridge Analytica (CA). After some dubious practices were revealed, the CEO resigned and, not long after, the company folded. The Guardian has a comprehensive website on the many twists and turns of this saga.[36]

There were issues related to underhand manipulation, gaining material for blackmail and so on, but what started the ball rolling was a cybersecurity issue, which is what concerns us here. The acceptance of social network and app technology (Section 4.5) is very high. Much work has gone into making them easy to use and the huge update around the globe points to their Perceived Usefulness (PU). The MTAH is too low, however. People do not see the risks associated with not changing the privacy settings from their (usually open) defaults. As we point out in the Bose example Section 3.3.3, the voluminous and inpenetrable terms and conditions required by many companies contain hidden permissions for use of data collected during legitimate use of the software. In fact, the Facebook

[36] `www.theguardian.com/news/series/cambridge-analytica-files` *Accessed:* 20 Nov 2018.

business model depends, at least in part, on focused advertising through data mining user data.

A recent egregious example was reported in *The Washington Post* (behind a paywall)[37] by Sam Schechner and Mark Secada. According to a commentary on the article by Karissa Bell,[38] a period tracking app, Flo, had come to the view that a woman's menstrual period was just simply too interesting to be kept private and secretly uploaded it to Facebook.

CA sets out to influence people by campaign ads constructed to meet individual attitudes, preferences, and prejudices. To begin with, they had a huge chunk of accounts, to which they had semilegitimate access. By this we mean that people had not prevented use of their data, but perhaps more through ignorance or idleness than subterfuge. The data mining algorithms they used don't really concern us here. It is the access that matters.

Cyber Nugget 12: *Always check social media preferences. The defaults may not be what you need.*

This was a good start. But CA went a lot further by using social networks. As discussed in Chapter 3, small world networks have a very low distance between any two nodes in the network, Milgram's six degrees of freedom idea [92]. Thus from this chunk of nodes, they already had, the initial nodes, they could reach a huge number of additional nodes, thought to be around 50 million.[39]

They had two possibilities with these additional nodes:

1. the new node had agreed, by accident or design, to share Facebook material, photos, and whatever, with the initial node. This of course was the jackpot.

2. there was not much new information accessible in the new node, but here metadata comes into play.

In the second case, just knowing the connections provides quite a lot by inference, based on the common social network property of *homophily*, Section 3.3.2.1. Thus if Alistair and Bob both like horror movies, then there is an increased chance that their mutual friend, Cleopatra, also likes horror movies. It's easy to see how such a relationship would arise. Friends go to see movies

[37] `www.wsj.com/articles/you-give-apps-sensitive-personal-information-then-they-tell-facebook-11550851636` *Accessed:* 24 Feb 2019.

[38] `https://mashable.com/article/flo-period-tracking-app-will-stop-sharing-data-with-facebook/?geo=AU&utm_campaign=mash-prod-nav-geo&utm_source=internal&utm_medium=onsite#c9Wcok4Aisqp` *Accessed:* 24 Feb 2019.

[39] `www.theguardian.com/news/2018/mar/17/cambridge-analytica-facebook-influence-us-election` *Accessed:* 20 Nov 2018.

together, and they would only go to a horror movie if they all liked the genre. Figure 2.5 shows how networks may aggregate in this way.

Thus, working out the connections (what we often call the metadata) gives good inferences about the new nodes, based only on the initial nodes, and the nodes that have provided extensive information.

CA got a lot of bad press for this, since it was considered to be underhand if not illegal in the electoral process. However, the same sort of things go on all the time with the data we surrender everyday. Where it is possible to link retail data with social networks, then targeted advertising, from a weekly special on Mars bars to big discounts on giant TVs.

It is even possible to go the other way. If two people have a cluster of similar preferences and, maybe, a shared geographic location, then they may well know each other. In earlier times, if two people in a town were say, competition chess players, then it would be a good bet that they would get acquainted. The era of big data takes us one step beyond a specific pursuit, to a mix of diverse attributes.

Cyber Nugget 13: *Beware of the information to which you give access to your friends. They may move it on.*

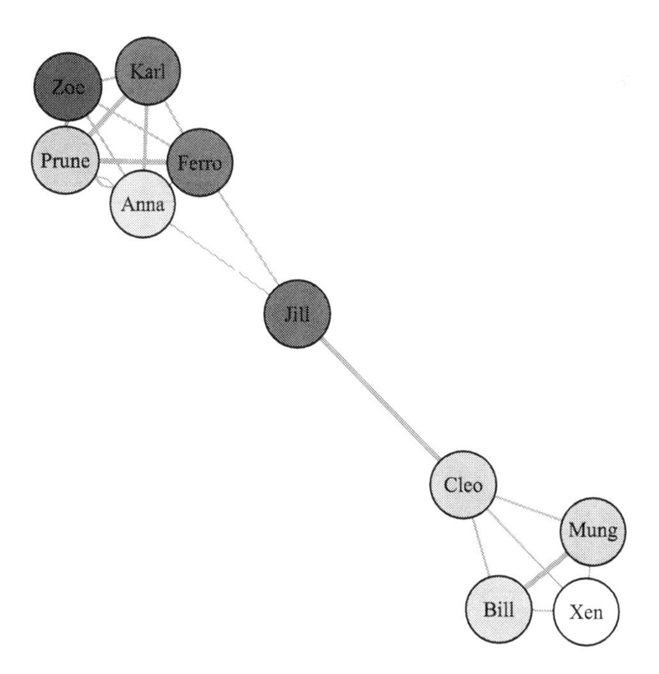

Figure 2.5: Social network with gray level representing preferences. (Xen, shown as white can be inferred to be largely mid-gray (Cleo, Mung, Bill) in preferences.)

CA is no more, but the unraveling of its activities continues. The New Yorker reports in November 2018 that there are indications that it was active in the Leave.EU campaign for Brexit.[40]

Facebook again faces challenges of interference through the spread of fake news in the European elections in May 2019.[41] It is now being much more proactive, taking down *2 billion* fake accounts within a year. Yet, there are still numerous other accounts spreading nonsense, intending to influence elections.

2.9 Trampling over Transport Layer Security

We saw in Section 7.4.1 that HTTPS is the workhorse of e-commerce, and is becoming the default for many websites. It uses TLS to provide secure, top-level encryption of traffic to a website, thus supposedly keeping your bank details and login secure. Or does it? There is a range of software people regularly install and use to carry out TLS-inspection.[42]

Simplistically, what happens is this software, a *middlebox*, intercepts the *HTTPS* request and replaces the real certificate, say for Piggie's Bank, with a fake, in a classic Man in the Middle Attack (MITM) manner. This in itself is not a cyberattack. The software may have honorable goals. But it creates unexpected vulnerabilities. It should send shivers down your spine: when you log into Piggie's, carefully using your two-factor identification, you kind of assume that only Piggie will see your authentication details.

First we'll look at the two cases, which brought this practice to light, *Superfish* and PrivDog. *Superfish* costs Lenovo US $10.8 million.[43] *Superfish* is at best crapware, faking certificates (Section 7.12) in order to insert ads into secure HTTPS streams. Lenovo's fall from grace was to ship laptops with *Superfish* preinstalled[44] in 2014.

Superfish didn't actually write the malicious component. They used a library from *Komodia*, unashamedly called SSL-hijacker.[45] Despite endless rants about using unique passwords[45]

> Komodia used the same private key for every machine running Superfish. It didn't take long for security researcher Robert Graham to crack the password for the private key (hint: it was "komodia").

[40] `www.newyorker.com/news/news-desk/new-evidence-emerges-of-steve-bannon-and-cambridge-analyticas-role-in-brexit` *Accessed:* 20 Nov 2018.

[41] `www.theguardian.com/technology/2019/may/05/facebook-admits-huge-scale-of-fake-news-and-election-interference` *Accessed:* 23 May 2019.

[42] `https://tlseminar.github.io/tls-interception/` *Accessed:* 28 Dec 2018.

[43] `www.theregister.co.uk/2018/11/30/lenovo_superfish_superloss/` *Accessed:* 27 Dec 2018.

[44] `www.theregister.co.uk/2015/02/19/superfish_lenovo_spyware/` *Accessed:* 28 Dec 2018.

[45] `https://tlseminar.github.io/tls-interception/` *Accessed:* 28 Dec 2018.

PrivDog was an ad filtering system from *AdTrustMedia* (which doesn't seem to have a website, although there are numerous sites offering ways of removing its software), intended to clean ads on HTTPS sites, supposedly bundled with some Comodo security software, but no longer visible on their website.[46] The way it went about doing this was insecure. PrivDog was in some ways worse than Superfish. It replaced certificates without validating the certificates of the target website. Thus, suppose, Piggy Bank was masquerading as Piggie Bank, but did not have the signed certificate. PrivDog would just go ahead with the connection to Piggy Bank, without any checking.

In 2015 Apple took the security step of removing a number of ad blockers, because they installed their own root certificates.[47]

Cyber Nugget 14: *Beware ad blockers, spyware, and software which might intercept and compromise secure transport protocols with supposed end-to-end encryption such as HTTPS.*

2.10 Beware the Insider

One of the biggest risks in cybersecurity is not from the hostile outsiders but from careless or malicious insiders. It is believed that some 44.5% of all cyberattacks are caused by insiders [155]. while human error has been known to account for 20% of the 2 billion records leaked in 2017.[48] Those inside organizations are often the targets of outside attacks, with the aim of persuading them to click on malevolent links. These type of attacks made up 30% of all cyberattacks in 2017. It is suggested that while inside threats are not as common as outside attacks, they cost more per incident at an estimated $412,000 in the US alone, and in several incidents, these costs have been more than 1 billion dollars [48, p. 65].

Inside attacks or risks are particularly hard to prevent using technological means as Elifoglu et al. [48, p. 61] note. Contrary to popular belief, most insider incidents are not based on sophisticated hacker tools. Most insider threat incidents are the consequences of human actions, such as mistakes, negligence, greed, or reckless behavior. Hyman [68] suggests that there are three types of insider threats:

---

[46] `www.comodo.com/home/internet-security/free-internet-security.php` *Accessed:* 28 Dec 2018.

[47] `www.theguardian.com/technology/2015/oct/09/apple-removes-iphone-adblockers-facebook-third-party-apps` *Accessed:* 12 Jan 2019.

[48] IBM-X Force threat intelligence index 2018, p. 5 www-01.ibm.com/common/ssi/cgi-bin/ssialias?htmlfid=77014377USEN *Accessed:* 18 Dec 2018.

1. Negligent employees.
2. Disgruntled employees.
3. Malicious employees who join the organization with the intent to defraud them.

Further details about what may cause employees to be negligent in a cybersense are covered in Chapter 4 on consumer choice and in Chapter 5 on risk. But even in sophisticated organizations such as banks, mistakes may still happen. In 2016, for example, the Commonwealth Bank of Australia leaked some 20 million customer records when it failed to destroy old backup magnetic tapes of data, according to Noyes in *The Sydney Morning Herald*.[49] Other examples of foolish behavior by employees include the following:

- Lost equipment such as laptops, tablet, or data disk with sensitive information.
- Unauthorized setup of modems or remote access from wireless access points.
- Use of corporate computing devices for nonbusiness purposes.
- Use of personal email accounts for business.
- Deletion of data files or accidental disclosure of sensitive material using email.
- Use of business email for personal correspondence.
- Non-work-related web browsing [48, p. 62].

These are not necessarily examples of extreme carelessness, but collectively these expose the organization to a greater chance of a successful cyberattack.

Disgruntled employees are another area of concern. Perhaps the most famous is Edward Snowden , who while working as a contractor for the NSA copied up to 1.7 million documents and distributed some 200,000 of these to the press [140]. Part of Snowden's job was to transfer large amount of data between computers at the NSA. Snowden merely copied the data onto USB sticks and smuggled the data out of the organization. A simple 1 min scan on the way out by a metal detector could have prevented this loss [140, p. 48]. Snowden took advantage of

[49]Almost 20 million bank records lost by the Commonwealth Bank, *The Sydney Morning Heraldwww.smh.com.au/business/banking-and-finance/almost-20-million-bank-account-records-Accessed: 17 Dec 2018.*

a number of security flaws in the NSA. He used a lack of two-factor identification to impersonate those in higher levels of management. The systems at the NSA had common root passwords, without encryption of traffic, making data theft more likely. Simple prevention of access to NSA computers to USB or portable hard drive, cell phones, or other devices would have also prevented copying of data. The use of administrator passwords and the high level of access provided across the NSA was another weakness Snowden exploited [140]. What is surprising is that protocols existed within the NSA, called The Orange Book, which had been in practice with the US security establishment for around 30 years could have prevented Snowden from leaking the data to the press. As will be discussed in Chapter 6 on governance, it is important not only to have good policies but also to have practices that maintain them.

It is not only lone wolves but also actors in the security establishment that are of concern. Disgruntled employees have allegedly, as a result of a frustrated industrial actions, interfered with traffic control systems in Los Angeles in August 2006 [68]. In cases of theft of intellectual property, there have been a number of serious documented incidents where insiders have sold out the trade secrets of their organizations [48, pp. 63–64]:

- In Waymo (v Uber), it was claimed that an engineer downloaded files about self-driving technology and shared them with Uber's Autonomous driving unit.
- A Ford employee copied proprietary documents of design to an external hard drive and was arrested shortly before applying for a new job in China with a competing firm.
- Two longtime employees of DuPont stole data for manufacturing titanium dioxide paint.
- A former Fame Mae employee installed a logic bomb that if not discovered would have shutdown the information system by disabling thousands of servers.

Jaeger [72] notes that the risk of the disclosure of trade secrets or access to critical infrastructure was found in a number of studies to occur within 30 days of employees giving their notice. There are also reports that organized crime, through the dark web is now seeking to recruit insiders to gain access to payment systems and information of large organizations [68] According to Hyman [68, p. 24], inside attacks can be minimized by

1. Deterrence controls, such as encryption, access management, endpoint security, mobile, and cloud security.
2. Detection controls, such as log management, security information, and event management and predictive analytics.

3. Inventories and audits for computers, mobile devices, and external hard drives and USBs both during and postemployment.
4. Pre-employment background checks to screen out problem employees.
5. Policies and procedures that help with the resolution of employee grievances and protect whistleblowers.
6. Termination processes that remove access as early as possible for a terminated employee.

Chapter 3

Networks and Norms

The social network behavior of humans is important to our understanding of how viruses and malware spread and how changes in a social network can occur to respond to this. Social networks can spread information at unprecedented speeds, and can help to reduce the impact of a large-scale cyberattack. They can also be used for nefarious purposes, as in the Cambridge Analytica scandal discussed in Section 2.8. On the other hand, by providing so much public information about individuals, they can be used as a means for designing and launching attacks. Social normsare both ubiquitous and resilient. Unfortunately, the time frame over which they change may be greater than the rate at which technology changes, increasing vulnerability to cyberattack. Cyberattacks are also mutating through the dark web, via access to malware at falling prices and by the sharing of intelligence and expertise, which means even unsophisticated novices can create havoc in cyberspace. Borrowing Nobel Laureate Richard Thaler's [139] phrase, we look at ways of nudging social networks into more secure practices.

This chapter develops two main ideas: social networks and, in simple, qualitative terms, the underlying graph theory; and social norms and how they impact cybersecurity. After a brief introduction, Section 3.2 considers mindsets, how we look at the world, through a somewhat inflexible lens. Section 3.3 goes onto consider social networks, a field of research that has grown explosively over the past decade. Section 3.4 now fuses mindsets with networks to consider social norms. Finally, we draw together some of the impact for cybersecurity in a discussion of modularity in Section 3.5.

3.1 Introduction

An important theme of this book is that human implementation of cybersecurity, often lags behind, sometimes way behind, the technology itself. We know how to make a strong password. We know how to estimate the amount of time required to crack it. Yet people persist in using weak passwords, where they have a choice, name of their dog, their favorite pizza, and so on.

Two factors stand out: the perception of risk, which is covered in Chapter 5; and a mixture of inertia and a (spurious) feeling of security (Chapter 4). Most people would not steal from supermarkets, kill their neighbors or start bushfires. On the other hand, many people ignore parking restrictions and speed limits, grizzle when they get a parking ticket or speeding fine, and carry on regardless. Unfortunately, cybersecurity seems to fall into this second, devil-may-care category.

Essentially, social norms, what one's friends and peers do, often transcend legal or other imperatives. One of the key factors in forming and maintaining norms is social influence, which, in turn is mediated by social networks. Thus we consider networks first in Section 3.3 and go on to consider norms in Section 3.4. But first we consider an important aspect of individual norms, what Snyder et al. [130] term mindsets. The norms we are interested in here are mainly *emergent*, that is they have appeared often without obvious cause, such as belching after eating, sanctioned in some societies but not others.

3.2 Mindsets

To make sense of the complex, changing world in front of us, we need to make some simplifications. We are dominated by concepts and ideas, *mindsets*, where we have thrown away a lot of details to keep just the general principles, a bit like the grin of the Cheshire Cat. By comparison, people with Asperger's are much more focused on specific details [129].

A simple example is proofreading. Read the following sentence and move straight on afterwards.

> The quick brown fox jumps over the the lazy dog

Many people miss the repeated *the* since they are reading for meaning [131]. (One might argue that French Connection UK (FCUK) has also benefited from this tendency).

This failure of attention to spelling detail can have a negative impact on cybersecurity. Suppose Alfonso receives an email from his bank, *milkywaybank.com*, announcing a new statement is ready. The email looks genuine, using the banks galaxy logo, the English is fine, and there is little that is suspicious. Alfonso clicks on the link and $10 K disappears from his bank account a microsecond later He just glanced at the URL, which was actually *millkyway.com/statements*, and didn't realize this was a phishing attack. Corporations can reduce the risk of such attacks by registering similar URLs and pointing them to the actual site. This could of course involve a lot of registration fees, thus its practicality will depend on organization resources.

Cyber Nugget 15: *Beware misspelt URLs and think of registering likely misspellings along with your domain.*

Mindsets are very hard to break. Not only does this occur at a very low knowledge level but also at the highest levels of expertise. The old phrase blinded by expertise has a basis in psychology, the so-called *Einstellung Effect*. Chess masters, for example, may miss an easy route to checkmate, because they are familiar with a nonoptimal alternative strategy [17]

> Inflexibility of thought induced by prior knowledge (i.e., the blocking effect of the familiar solution) was shown by experts...

A new 2018 discovery by David Levari and colleagues, published in the prestigious journal *Science* [84] has potential implications for cybersecurity mindsets. They demonstrated concept creep across a diverse range of concepts: dot color; hostile human faces; and research ethics. In a nutshell, if we have a belief that hostile human faces occur about, say 15% of the time, then if the occurrence drops, to say 10% after, say, legalizing cannabis, something surprising happens. People do not think the world a happier place. They now reclassify some faces as hostile, to keep the percentage at 15. Thus the concept of hostile face has crept to apply to additional faces.

As an illustration, consider dangerous emails, which contain malware of some kind. Now some unsolicited emails are really dangerous, but some may be useful, alerting the user to store sales, extended opening hours with discounts, and so on. It would be useful to open these emails and check out the offers.

First imagine that we have developed a mindset that 90% of unsolicited emails are safe. But over time some spam gets eliminated and phishing attacks can be blocked by Sender Policy Framework (SPF) and Domain-Based Message Authentication, Reporting and Conformance (DMARC) (Section 7.13.2). We don't see so many Nigerian lottery scams as we used to, where the email announces we have won a million dollars and just have to click on a link to collect our prize. Thus emails have got safer. To keep the percentage of safe emails at 90, the concept of safe shrinks, meaning that safe emails may be discarded. Alternatively, if a new spate of attacks occur, we may be unwilling at first to change our estimate of how likely something is to be safe, with unfortunate consequences. An egregious example is the trust people place in email (Section 3.4.3.5) and text messages, despite numerous politicians and celebrities suffering megaembarrassment.

Cyber Nugget 16: *Mindsets can cause us to overlook the obvious.*

3.3 Social Networks

Social networks have become part of everyday parlance. There is even an eponymous movie about Facebook . Understanding social networks will help us: first to understand the resilience of social norms in this chapter; and second to develop marketing strategies for improving cyber behavior in Chapter 4. To begin with, we need to learn a little about network structure.

3.3.1 Some Elementary Graph Theory

Back in 1967, Stanley Milgram came up with the famous conjecture of 6 degrees of separation [92]. But it was not until 1998 that Duncan Watts and Steve Strogatz [146] introduced the idea of small worldsthat interest in networks exploded. Amongst the vast range of theory and experiment now extant, we shall pick up just three concepts: small worlds; scale-free networks; and network motifs. These will suffice for studying social norms.

Following graph theory parlance, we shall speak of *nodes* and the *edges* that connect them. A node can be literally anything, from a house in a village to a person in a social network. An edge can be anything that connects nodes together, such as a road between houses. In the next two sections, we shall need the idea of *degree,* the number of connections a node has with its neighbors. These could be connections without a direction, or they could be directed, forming a so-called *digraph.* Thus sibling is a directionless connection, but father is directed.

3.3.1.1 Small Worlds

Snakes and ladders was a children's board game of yesteryear. The goal was to proceed along a path, with steps determined by the throw of the dice. But there were gifts and hazards along the way. Landing on a square with a ladder would enable one to take a big jump towards the goal; landing on a snake would have the opposite effect, taking the player back to near the beginning.

Small-world networks have a similar behavior. Nodes have locals connections, but some have a local connection replaced by a long-range connection, which jumps across the network (Figure 3.1). So, in a country village, everybody might know each other. But some people will know people in other villages. Thus if Fred knows Jill in Frogton, Jill knows Xen in Toadborough, and Xen knows Pip in Toadborough, then there are just three degrees of separation between Fred and Pip, even though they live in different villages.

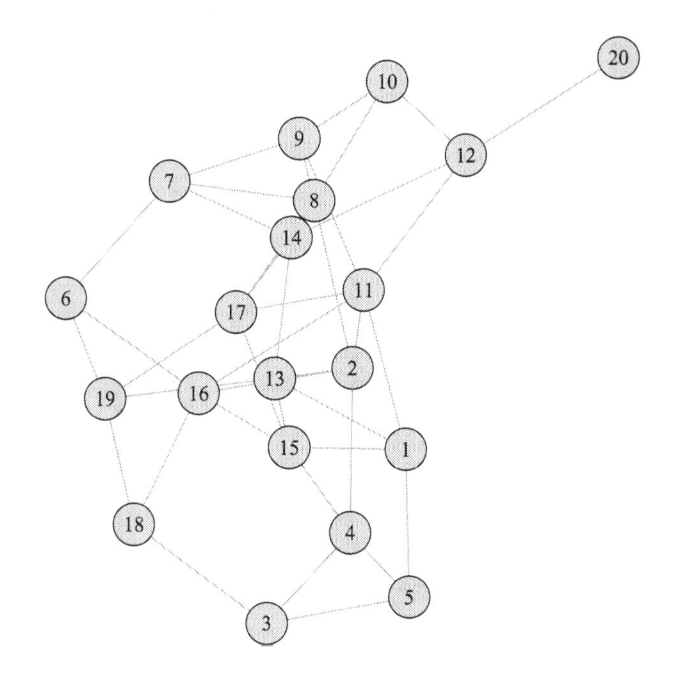

Figure 3.1: Small-world network with 20 nodes. Note the dense local clustering (nodes with sequential numbers still often connected) with occasional long range connections, such as between 12 and 20, or 1 and 11.

Thus in a small-world network, almost everybody is close to everybody else. A popular version of this was the idea of the Bacon number. Actor Kevin Bacon has a Bacon number of zero. A film star has a Bacon number of one, if they have starred in a film with Kevin Bacon, two if they have starred in a film with somebody who had starred with Bacon himself and so on. Most Bacon numbers turned out to be quite small.

In a small-world network, most nodes have roughly the same degree and the same number of connections, since the long-range behavior is created by the small number of distant links. On the other hand, there is a high clustering coefficient (Section 3.3.2.1). As a consequence, no node with a distant link is very much more important than any other. But not all networks are so uniform. The hacker network, shown in Figure 5.1 in Section 5.3.1, shows an example of a highly nonuniform social network.

3.3.1.2 Scale-Free Networks

Just 1 year after Watts seminal paper appeared in *Nature*, another seminal paper by Albert-László Barabási appeared in *Science* [11] (*Nature* and *Science* are the two top scientific journals). It introduced another network with short distances between nodes, but the structure was completely different. It was more like an airline network. Before the advent of budget carriers, such as EasyJet, airlines used to operate a hub and spoke model. To fly from Aberdeen to Albuquerque, you would fly Aberdeen to London Heathrow (British Airways hub), then to Denver (United Airlines hub) and on to Albuquerque. Heathrow and Denver would connect to many cities, whereas Albuquerque and Aberdeen connect to only a small number of cities, sometimes just the hub.

Barabási and Albert introduced the idea of scale-free networks (Figure 3.2), which have the same property as a hub and spoke network of some nodes with a lot of connections and others with few. In a scale-free network, there is a range of all possible node degrees, but with the frequency of occurrence going down as the degree goes up. Now take the Twittersphere. Katy Perry has the most followers, 108 million, with Barack Obama coming in at over 99 million at the time of writing. Leonardo di Caprio manages only 19 million, while *New York Times* columnist and Nobel Prize winner in economics, Paul Krugman, manages just 3.7 million. As the number of followers goes down, the number of people with that number of followers goes up. The precise relationship is something we leave to the range of excellent books on networks, such as Barabási's own book, Linked [10].

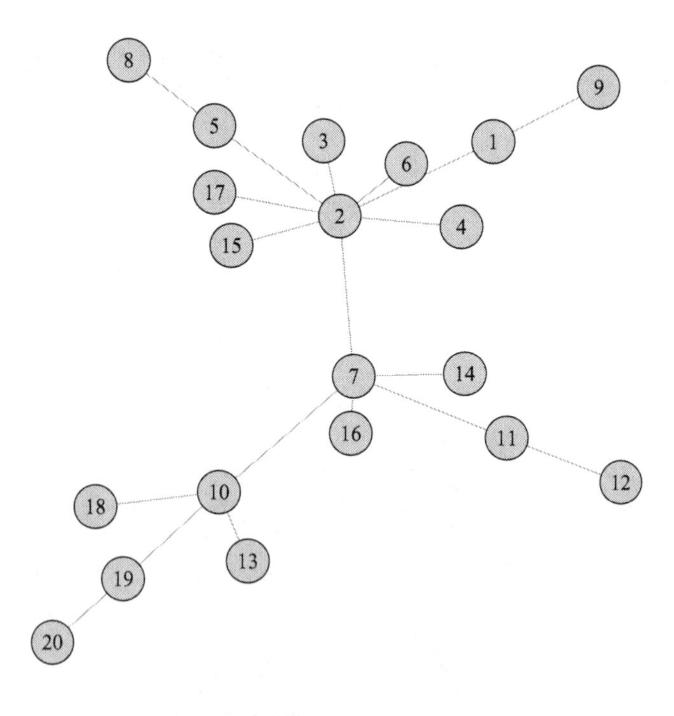

Figure 3.2: Scale-free network. Most nodes have a small number of connections, but there are highly connected nodes (2,7,10).

3.3.1.3 *Network Motifs*

Another direction in characterizing networks is to start not from the overall structure, such as the distribution of node degree, but to start from small network fragments and build up the network therefrom. Uri Alon et al. [93] have taken networks from very diverse systems, from biological cells to society, that certain network fragments were more common than others. The exponential random graph model [113] starts with graph structure components, such as say, triangles, which are used to define a model based on the likelihood of these substructures. Such methods have had considerable success, from the networks of bankers in 14th century Florence onwards.

3.3.2 Some Measures on Networks

Social network analysis has developed a range of methods for inferring structures. A range of graph- theoretic ideas can then be brought to bear on to indicate paths and modes of influence. In defining small-world and scale-free networks, we talked mainly about the degree and the number of connections coming in and out of each node. However, two graphs can have the same degree of distribution, yet be different in other ways, which require other metrics. A few which will prove useful are discussed in Sections 3.3.2.1 and 3.3.2.2.

3.3.2.1 *Clustering and Assortativeness*

Two properties important in social networks are clustering and assortativity. Clustering was used as a way of defining small-world networks by Watts and Strogatz [146]. In simple terms, this means that, if we take any node in a graph and look at its neighbors, those neighbors are likely to be connected. This is commonplace in social groups: your friends are likely to know each other, especially in smaller communities.

Assortativity also known as *homophily* measures the extent to which nodes that are connected are alike. This again is intuitive for society. People tend to hang out with people with similar interests or skills. This network parameter is important in so far as it dictates, whether, when traversing a network, we tend to get locked into a particular set of values and don't easily cross over to other domains of influence.

3.3.2.2 *Betweenness Centrality*

An important idea in graph theory, which turns out to be very useful in social networks, is the idea of centrality, notably *betweenness centrality.* This measures the fraction of shortest paths between any two nodes in the graph, which go along a particular edge, If this sounds a bit abstract, imagine we have two villages, Frogton and Toadborough, either side of the river Ouse. Each village has a number of houses (nodes) connected by roads (edges). On each side, any road will be part of the shortest route between some houses, but not very many. But to go from a house on the south side to one on the north side of the Ouse means going over the one and only bridge. Thus the bridge has a very high betweenness centrality, since all shortest paths between north and south have to pass along it.

Take the famous Champs d'Elysée in Paris. If you want to go from Place de la Concorde to the Arc de Triomphe, then your shortest path is along this grand avenue. But not many shortest routes between two places on the right bank will go along it. This is perhaps not such a bad thing, since the Arc de Triomphe roundabout is one of the scariest in Europe with an accident there every half hour. However, if you want to cross from the right bank to the left bank, then you have to go across one of Paris' 37 bridges across the Seine. Thus these bridges have very high betweenness centrality.

We can similarly define a centrality for the nodes themselves. If Bert is the local gossip, then a lot of rumors will pass through him.

3.3.2.3 Modularity

Since the huge growth in network science, beginning with small-world and scale-free networks, modularity has been of intense interest. A modular network is one in which the nodes form distinct clusters or communities, with weak connections to other communities. An obvious example would be clusters of friends, where students might have more friends within their college than within other colleges.

One of the leaders in modularity analysis is Mike Newman, and his original definition [98] is still in frequent use. The idea of Newman and Girvan [98] was to effectively count the number of edges inside each community and compare it with the number of edges going out. This led to

$$Q = \sum_i (e_{ii} - a_{ii})^2 \tag{3.1}$$

e_{ij} is the number of edges in community, i, connecting with community, j. This has to be normalized by the total number of edges coming out of any given community, $a_{ij} = \sum_j e_{ij}$. When $Q = 0$, there is effectively no modularity, and a large random network will give $Q \approx 0$. As $Q \to 1$ the network becomes more modular. We can see how this works with a simple example of the three-module network, shown in Figure 3.3.

Although there are numerous variations and improvements on this simple metric, it will suffice for this book. The importance of modularity to cybersecurity is discussed in Section 3.5.

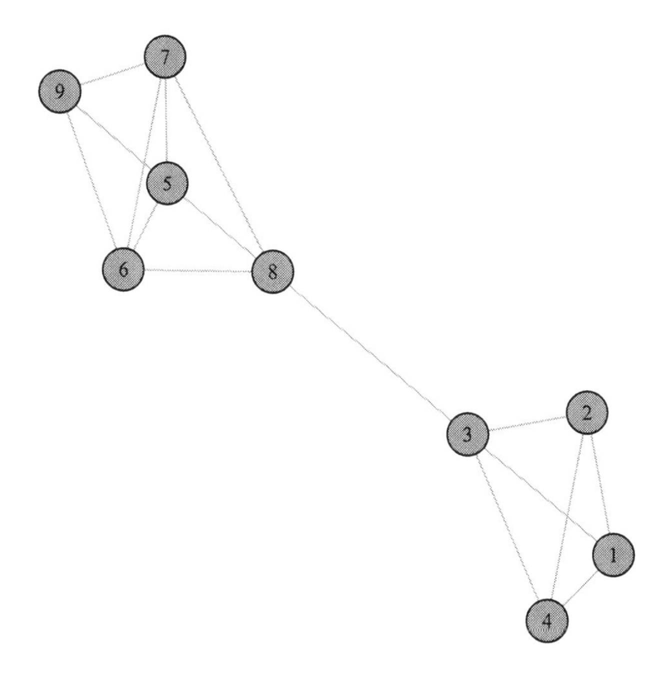

Figure 3.3: A simple modular network with two communities and a single tie between them.

3.3.3 Network Discovery

When the network revolution began 20 years ago, discovering social network structure was hard work. It relied on techniques, such as interviews and surveys, with all their associated limitations. Social media have transformed network discovery and made it much easier. However, there are ethical implications, which may lead to future constraints on how data may be used.

Metadata is very useful. Mobile phone calls, emails, and message apps all leave a trace of who communicates with whom. Corporations can to a large extent use the metadata within the organization as a condition of employment. When the links are outside, some degree of user consent is needed, as with Terms and Conditions. Here, though, an important norm, which we shall discuss later in the book (Section 3.4.3.1) is one of assuming Terms and Conditions, often lengthy legal documents are benign, an assumption, which may be false.

There are other ways of getting information surreptitiously and possibly illegally. Bose is being sued, at the time of writing, for collecting and selling data about users' musical preferences and practices, collected from its users via its app. Bose selling user music preferences via its app.[1] Users of its headphones

[1]http://forums.stevehoffman.tv/threads/bose-headphones-spy-on-listeners-says-lawsuit.665881/.

and other devices are invited to download its app for easier management of the music collection. This app then uploads all this information to a Bose website and to a secondary organization, **segment.io**, which collects and sells data. One of the issues in the lawsuit is whether or not the customer had agreed to this when she agreed to the terms and conditions. The data collection is certainly not transparent.[2]

Machine learning facilitates taking data such as this and transforming it into network information. One way to do this, for example, is by assuming homophily (Section 3.3.2.1). Customers with very similar musical tastes and geographic location may know each other.

3.3.4 Using and Transforming Networks

Knowing a social network structure has two big advantages: communicating with people and the new domain of social network marketing; and ways to modify the network.

If we know the nodes and edges of high betweenness centrality (Section 3.3.2.2), then they can be targeted not only for communication but also for breaking or disrupting communication. Similarly in a scale-free network (Section 3.3.1.2), the hubs, the high-degree nodes with lots of connections going in and out, have an enormous influence in the network. Removing them will seriously damage the network structure, whereas in a small-world network (Section 3.3.1.1) removing a single node is less destructive. Modular networks make it easier for a cyberbreach to be contained, much in the way that quarantine helps to halt the spread of an epidemic.

3.3.5 Friends of Friends

The power of social networks is extremely high. Christakis at the Harvard Medical School [32] has studied the network effects on various health conditions. It turns out that if your friends are obese, or if they smoke, you too are more likely than average to be obese or to smoke. What is even more remarkable is that this influence extends not just to your friends, but their friends and friends of friends. Thus, the increased likelihood of somebody being fat depends on whether people they don't know are fat, and people who even their friends don't know.

Cyber Nugget 17: *Remote social connections can have an influence on cybersecurity attitudes.*

[2] www.reuters.com/article/us-bose-lawsuit/bose-headphones-spy-on-listeners-lawsuit-idUSKBN17L2BT.

3.3.6 Secure Networks

Many cyberbreaches within organizations start from a single point of entry, a silly password, clicking on a bad link, and so on. The invader then moves laterally through the network looking for things it can use, particularly important servers or other central resources. CrowdStrike calls this the breakout time.[3] Different countries have cyberattack agendas, who they ranked in terms of breakout time, the time sometimes being under 20 min. This is in effect the time window in which an attack has to be contained to avoid major damage.

CrowdStrike makes these assessments through the use of graph theory applied to its *Threat Graph*, looking for suspicious network patterns in over a trillion events per week across its customer base spanning 176 countries.

Thus it's highly desirable to make networks as disjoint as possible. A small number of degrees of separation may make for communication speed, but it facilitates the movement of an invader through a network.

3.4 Social Norms

Social norms are codes of practice, which have come into place, but are usually not written down anywhere and do not have legal force. Burke and Peyton Young [27] describe them as

> We define a social norm as a standard, customary, or ideal form of behavior to which individuals in a social group try to conform...
>
> We would argue that there is a constellation of internal and external mechanisms that hold norms in place, and that the salience of these factors varies from one situation to another.

They can range from simple things such as dress codes or taking a gift to a dinner invitation, to more complex social protocols. Importance can vary from one society to another. In Japan, there is a very elaborate protocol surrounding the giving and receiving of gifts, whereas in Australia, it is more the thought that counts.

Although such norms may be of uncertain origin, they are nevertheless very powerful. They may also not be in the interests of individuals or society. Peyton-Young et al. have studied social norms from many aspects and shows, for example, that medical practice may be nonoptimal as a result of local norms. One thinks of medicine as objective or evidence based, but they found that this is not necessarily true [27]:

> ...such choices may entail welfare losses for patients as a result of "conformity warp." Consistent with the model's predictions, we

[3] www.crowdstrike.com/resources/news/crowdstrike-annual-threat-report-details-attacker-insights-and-reveals-industrys-first-adversary-rankings/ *Accessed:* 12 Mar 2019.

> observe that a 75 year old heart patient is more likely to receive an invasive treatment—either coronary angioplasty or bypass surgery in Tallahassee, a city with a relatively high proportion of younger cardiac patients (62 and under), than in Fort Lauderdale, a city with a comparatively older patient population. Since surgery becomes riskier with age, 75 year-olds in Tallahassee are likely to have worse outcomes than 75 year-olds in Fort Lauderdale, even with no differences in the average competence of physicians or other quality factors across the locations.

Network effects are extremely important in determining norms as we discuss in Section 3.3.5. We conclude this discussion of norms with some examples in the cyberworld.

3.4.1 Emergent versus Agreed Norms

Our definition of norms is slightly different, focusing as it does on their emergent character, to some initiatives to describe cyber norms. The Global Commission for the Stability of Cyberspace has recently proposed the following set of cyber-norms,[4] but these represent more aspirations than actuality:

- Norm to Avoid Tampering
- Norm against Commandeering of ICT Devices into Botnets
- Norm for States to Create a Vulnerability Equities Process
- Norm to Reduce and Mitigate Significant Vulnerabilities
- Norm on Basic Cyber Hygiene as Foundational Defense
- Norm against Offensive Cyberoperations by Nonstate Actors

Milton Mueller at the Internet Governance Project at Georgia Tech[5] offers a polemical view of these issues,[6] noting

> One is that we see too much public posturing, more interest in running out in front of a parade as "leaders" and getting publicity than in doing the real work it will take to achieve effective global governance in cyberspace...

[4] https://cyberstability.org/news/global-commission-introduces-six-critical-norms-towards-cyber-stability/ *Accessed:* 14 Jan 2019.

[5] https://www.internetgovernance.org/2018/09/04/a-farewell-to-norms/ *Accessed:* 14 Jan 2019.

[6] www.internetgovernance.org/2018/11/09/the-paris-igf-convergence-on-norms-or-grand-illusion/ *Accessed:* 14 Jan 2019.

> Another cause of uneasiness is the way in which national governments are gradually edging aside the multistakeholder community. The high-level panels, commissions, and norm proclamations are increasingly state-driven and state-aligned, even as they pay lip service to multistakeholder governance...
>
> These lists of pious do's and don'ts seem to assume that people don't already know it's harmful to make botnets or tamper with products and services. The problem is not that they don't know it's wrong, it's that they can still attain benefits from doing so. What are these norm packages doing to alter the incentive structure?

It is his last point, which is crucial. Norms emerge rather than being developed top-down.

3.4.2 Trends and Social Media Marketing

Although many social norms have been around for a long time and are quite resilient, an important feature of social media has been *trending* . Social media allows fads and fashions to spread rapidly and, in some cases, become established as norms. Marketers see this as an opportunity for low-cost, rapid dissemination of a corporate message.

Environmentalists are not overly positive towards bottled water. The plastic bottles are a waste nightmare, while the water is often not much better than filtered tap water (where the tap water is of drinkable quality of course). Yet when soap opera celebrities started drinking commercial bottled water, a craze took off, which has yet to abate. It is interesting, though, that although such a norm can spring out of a definable source, as perhaps in this case, it isn't easy to eliminate by the same mechanism.

3.4.3 Some Adverse Social Norms in Cybersecurity

Here we discuss a few adverse social norms: ignoring terms and conditions (Section 3.4.3.1); assuming data security (Section 3.4.3.2); personal cyber hygiene (Section 3.4.3.3); and one of the most interesting recent norms, distributed trust (Section 3.4.3.4).

3.4.3.1 Terms and Conditions

Most apps for mobile phones, tablets, laptops, and whatever usually come with a long list of terms and conditions. If one was buying a house or a car one would read these very carefully and negotiate. In the case of a house, one would normally use professional legal advice. But with apps we blindly agree and get to work. The prevailing culture is one of assuming that all will be well with the terms of service.

However, there may be hidden nasties. Almost all apps immediately phone home, in other words, contact their maker or vendor and upload information about the user. Very few people try to block phoning home. It can be beneficial to the user, in say, optimizing app performance, but can also be sinister and devious as we have already seen.

The iRobot vacuum cleaner was launched as a stand-alone device, but more recent versions are WiFi enabled. This enables the iRobot to transmit maps of peoples' houses back to the parent company, which may onsell them.[7]

> The company's terms of service appear to give the company the right to sell such data already, however. When signing up for the company's Home app, which connects to its smart robots, customers have to agree to a privacy policy that states that it can share personal information with subsidiaries, third party vendors, and the government, as well as in connection with "any company transaction" such as a merger or external investment.

However, a spokesperson said "iRobot would not sell data without its customers' permission, but he expressed confidence most would give their consent in order to access the smart home functions."

3.4.3.2 Data Security

Many corporations and government entities ask for a lot of personal information in order to sign up. There are two prevailing norms here: the first is to assume that the company needs/has a right to this information; the second is to assume that this data will be safe.

Australia has the Privacy Act 1988. This legislation applies to Commonwealth agencies and private sector bodies with annual turnover of $3 million or more as well as health providers regardless of turnover. Each state and territory (with the exception of Western Australia) has privacy legislation that applies to their own agencies. It also has a Privacy Commissioner to police it. Yet the Act is frequently abused, often without complaint. Assuming that data will be safe is naive and ostrich like, since breaches occur frequently.

These breaches can cost companies serious money, but the norm within the companies and the users is frequently to pretend it will not happen.[8]

> Reuters - Anthem Inc (ANTM.N), the largest U.S. health insurance company, has agreed to settle litigation over hacking in 2015 that compromised about 79 million people's personal information for

[7]www.theguardian.com/technology/2017/jul/25/roomba-maker-could-share-maps-users-homes-google-amazon-apple-irobot-robot-vacuum *Accessed:* 1 May 2019.

[8]www.reuters.com/article/us-anthem-cyber-settlement/anthem-to-pay-record-115-million-to-settle-u-s-lawsuits-over-data-breach-idUSKBN19E2ML *Accessed:* 5 Feb 2019.

> $115 million, which lawyers said would be the largest settlement ever for a data breach.
>
> The breach is one of a series of high-profile data breaches that resulted in losses of hundreds of millions of dollars to U.S. companies in recent years, including Target Corp (TGT.N), which agreed to pay US $18.5 million to settle claims by 47 states in May, and Home Depot Inc (HD.N), which agreed to pay at least US $19.5 million to consumers last year.

Uber got some bad press for uploading users' contact lists from their mobile phones, again something done covertly, although not necessarily outside their terms and conditions. They were in trouble again for a massive data breach[9]:

> According to Bloomberg, the breach occured when two hackers obtained login credentials to access data stored on Uber's Amazon Web Services account. Paul Lipman, CEO of cybersecurity firm BullGuard, said that the fact that the data was being stored unencrypted was "unforgivable."

So, here we also have a norm operating within a company, or just blatant disregard for risk. Section 2.4 discusses how data breaches can reduce interest and participation in important government initiatives.

3.4.3.3 Cyber Hygiene

Authentication to a computer system is one of the most important aspects of cybersecurity. Yet, prevailing social norms encourage all sorts of bad practices: password name of partner or dog; same password for multiple sites; password written on a post-it note; and so on.

There are two assumptions hidden within this norm: that if something goes wrong, say a bank account, somebody else will pay (the bank); and that you as the individual will be the only victim. The latter is particularly dangerous. Weak passwords or security practices can allow a hacker to gain entry and compromise an entire system, maybe thousands of users as we saw in the Anthem example.

Password safes (Section 7.5.3) (Cyber Nugget 41) are a simple and very effective solutions to good password hygiene. Yet few people use them at the time of writing. As with anything that doesn't seem to be absolutely necessary, it seems to be something one can get away without doing. This is probably a big factor in their lack of uptake. Another, though, is trust. Why trust the password safe, particularly if it stores everything in the cloud? Computer professionals can reassure themselves if the source code is available, but this is not possible for most people. Can one trust analyses and recommendations from computer professionals? This brings us to our last example, distributed trust.

---

[9] www.theguardian.com/technology/2017/nov/21/uber-data-hack-cyber-attack *Accessed:* 4 Feb 2019.

3.4.3.4 Distributed Trust

In a fascinating and thought-provoking book, Rachel Botsman discusses the idea of distributed trust [20]. A decade ago, it would have been unthinkable for a young woman to get into a car with a complete stranger (Uber). It would have been quite uncommon for somebody to take a complete stranger into their home (AirBnb). She argues that trust in organizations has been declining, such as loss of faith in banks after the Global Financial Crisis. However, a new phenomenon has emerged, *distributed trust.*

We increasingly rely on online reviews by other people in selecting online shopping sites, service providers such as Uber, and so on. It's easy to see how these reviews could be faked. But we have come to believe that there is somehow safety in numbers. The emergence of this norm has enabled a considerable number of very useful services to develop.

3.4.3.5 Slack Email

Of the billions of people who use email, only a small fraction are fully aware of its security limitations. There are just so many problems with email (and text messages). Some egregious failings:

- Sending credit card details. This is steadily becoming less common as banks ramp up publicity of the risks
- Sending confidential documents. All documents, which might in any way be sensitive, need to end-to-end encryption. (Section 7.4.1). Not all are. It is the view of the authors of this book that
    - All email should be encrypted in transit
    - Everybody should have an encrypted mailbox and should insist on using it for anything of a personal or confidential nature.
- Answering little, seemingly insignificant queries. This is still very common. Medical practitioners might ask for some follow-up information, date of surgery, or hospitals may send admission details. Such information could be misused.
- Personal information could facilitate identity theft, such as driver's license number.

3.4.3.6 Good and Bad Advice

Be wary of advice, on or offline. Some blogs are highly reliable. In Section 7.5.3 we mention TeamSilk from Fraunhofer. Symantec is one of the major players in cybersecurity, while Google has a good track record for detecting security flaws in external software. However, Butterfly may be alluring, and her blog very readable, but does Butterfly know anything about cybersecurity. She might. She might have a PhD in maths from Stanford. However, her credibility needs to be validated. With the advent of fake news, the situation may be even worse. Some blogs and websites may be *deliberately* misleading.

Cyber Nugget 18: *Blogs may be readable and entertaining but are not necessarily technically accurate.*

3.4.3.7 The Ups and Downs of Virtual Private Networks

VPNs (Section 7.9) have a number of downsides. Bouncing messages around en route consumes resources and reduces performance. The need of a VPN arises from

- Encryption of personal/business traffic;
- Stopping applications from collecting personal data, such as browsing preferences;
- Salacious or illegal activity.

The first of these does not need a VPN if the applications are themselves encrypted (such as using a *https* website). The second is something, which users can do something about, by setting appropriate privileges and by supporting initiatives such as the European General Data Protection Regulation (GDPR). The third is outside the scope of this book, but the first two are strongly dependent upon social norms and peer groups. A decreasing fraction of people are unaware of the risks of using public or hotel WiFi. Yet people press on regardless, largely because their peers don't worry either.

There are alternatives to VPNs as evidenced by Google's BeyondCorp initiative, discussed in Section 7.9.4

3.4.3.8 Data Fragility

The works of Shakespeare, written in analog on paper, can still be read and understood today, 500 years later. Yet we may have documents, written in obsolete software, which ran on hardware of yesteryear, which are no longer readable. This last section deals with an aspect of cybersecurity, which does not involve malicious attack—preserving data for the long term.

Many of us will have had the experience of looking at photos that have faded or lost their color with age. Yet, we assume digital will be pristine forever. It will not be without special care. The biggest danger is the very long-term stuff we keep but almost never access for decades at a time, time for hardware and software to change. Things we need to bear in mind include:

- Hardware and software changes. Vendors often do not help by not ensuring compatibility from one version to the next
- Hardware storage devices fail with time. Magnetic tape is notorious for its long-term failure rate. But discs fail too. SSD drives, which are now ubiquitous and desirable for the speed and low noise operation have finite lifetimes, based on the numbers of read-writes
- Optical media are not uniform in their archival quality. The authors still have playable music CDs from the 80s. CD was a breakthrough technology, but CD-Rs may be different. Music CDs are stamped, and the storage medium is aluminum with holes (bits) burned into it. Once the problems of wrapping the aluminum in a plastic film to protect it from moisture had been solved, the lifetime of the CD became very long indeed (in fact not yet reached in 2019). However, cheaper copies, or CDs burned in computers may actually not use metal at all, but a dye, since this can be bleached with a much lower power laser. The lifetime is measured in years rather than decades. Some companies, such as Kodak introduced writable gold CDs, for very long-term archiving. This is one of the best options available, but, as you might expect, it is somewhat expensive.
- Cloud backup looks secure, since the problem of backing up has been transferred to the service provider. But providers can be hacked or they may go out of business.

Since your grandchildren might want to look at your baby photos.

Cyber Nugget 19: *Make sure your data backup is good for the long haul.*

As one might expect, museums are putting more and more thought into how to preserve digital materials. The British Museum has an excellent website discussing challenges and solutions[10]

3.5 Modularity in Cybersecurity

We live in a connected world and are inundated by requests to form new connections, such as from social networks such as LinkedIn. The problem with high connectivity is that it can be difficult to contain a leak or stop an invader getting out. This is a core feature of epidemic spreading, where containing infected individuals is of paramount importance.

[10] www.bl.uk/digital-preservation/challenges *Accessed:* 5 Fen 2019.

The internet provides global connectivity, but from homes to firms and governments, firewalls are everywhere. They monitor and control traffic into the internet and thus act as a level of modularity. If malware effects a particular cluster of computers, then the sooner they can be isolated from the network the better.

Cyber Nugget 20: *The more firewalls the better, subject to the constraint of satisfactory performance.*

Keeping computers as separate as possible, while not impairing functionality, is sensible. But computer users need to be kept separate as well. There are two ways where separability can often be improved:

- System or high-level authorizations (passwords). In military and government security classifications, this is well understood. However, it is not always the case elsewhere, where some people may have passwords they don't need and are a potential risk of password compromise (Section 2.10).
- A trend over the past decade or so has been increased casualization of the workforce. Most casuals are probably trustworthy, but some are not. Yet the cost of adequate vetting impacts on the cost saving of casual employees in the first place. Thus, rather than the obvious reduction in short contracts, one solution is to ring-fence casual access, so that if somebody does go rogue, the damage they can do is limited (Section 2.10).
- VPNs (Section 7.9) should be used wherever there is a non-encrypted link in a communication path, but often are not.

3.5.1 Concluding Comments

The notion of cyber norms is now being actively pursued at an international level. The *cybertech accord*[11] comprises over 40 companies, including big tech players, such as Microsoft and Facebook *partnering on initiatives that improve the security, stability, and resilience of cyberspace.*

Returning to Peyton-Young [27]

> ...some norms are remarkably resilient under changing circumstances. Due to their longevity, such norms may come to be seen as right and necessary, though in fact they are the product of chance and contingency, and are sustained simply because they coordinate people's expectations about how to interact with one another.

Social networks provide a framework for understanding norms and how they may be modified. In the next chapter on consumer choice, Chapter 4), we look at how the understanding of individual behavior is also important to cybersecurity.

[11] https://cybertechaccord.org/about/ *Accessed:* 12 Jan 2019.

Chapter 4

Consumer Choice

This chapter provides an overview of the factors that affect consumer behavior in the area of cybersecurity. We examine how cybersecurity attitudes and behavior vary across the population and discuss the importance of social norms in this area. The motivational aspects of people changing their behavior are also discussed. Cybersecurity attitudes and behavior are also driven by personality, which means that changing behavior is not always based on rational arguments. The type of social network behavior of humans is an important to our understanding of how viruses and malware spread. The challenge presented here is that people may adopt attitudes and behaviors that make them less safe for seemingly understandable but irrational reasons.

The first part of this chapter focuses on core beliefs and Attitudes, as revealed by research from psychological experiments, social surveys, and qualitative research. Section 4.2 looks at the demographics of cybersecurity. We then look at several ideas from the social sciences and marketing: Theory of Reasoned Action (TRA) (Section 4.3); motivation to avoid harm (MTAH) (Section 4.4); and Technology Acceptance Model (TAM) (Section 4.5). Section 4.6 examines situational factors, and we conclude the chapter with ways of improving the security behavior of users, taking note of stress and information overload (Section 4.7) and how the adoption of better and more secure technologies can occur.

4.1 Introduction

Estimates of cybercrime are up to around $6 trillion in costs annually [95], with Dell reporting some 16 million types of malware (Section 7.11) programs present in its user base in 2013 [7]. A recent worldwide report by internet security software provider Symantec suggests that this occurrence is likely to increase owing to factors such as attackers gaining greater sophistication over their targets and leapfrogging of their defenses. Cybercrime data shows a greater focus on extortion of consumers and organizations, demonstrated in a worldwide increase of 113% on ransomware (Section 2.2) demands, and that such attacks are now moving to mobile devices, according to a Symantec threat report.[1]

For the digital economy worldwide, this is an issue of grave concern, as trust (Section 3.4.3.4) and dealing with perceived risk are the major pillars supporting use in this sector [94,145,151]. To reduce the threats of cybercrime and gain the trust of consumers, organizations have developed a range of security measures, most recently using biometrics, Section 7.6 techniques [76,107,141]. However, such technological innovations are only as good as company [99] and consumer practices [148] and do not take into account malware attacks, which occur in spite of diligent user behavior [36]. Authentication by traditional passwords suffers from several human factors: people have difficulty remembering a huge number of secure passwords. Often passwords are written down, reused, and recycled, meaning that they are easily compromised [108]; conversely, system administrators tend to see only the cryptographic strength and other risk factors and ignore the vital issue of human mnemonic frailty. If strong passwords are enforced, or frequent changes are required, users take shortcuts by writing passwords down or recycling them.

But strong passwords themselves may be stolen. Users may be induced to give them up to spam or or phishing attacks (Section 5.3.2.4), or their machines may get infected by malware such as keyloggers (Section 7.11) that grabs keystrokes and leaks passwords. Such attacks are considered further in the context of social engineering in Section 5.3.2.4. Biometrics (Section 7.6) can solve the first of these, but malware requires a different approach, with software agents designed to seek out and kill malware. Malware detectors, such as virus scanners, tend to look for common patterns in malware code. This works because such code usually shares a common base of code functions, sometimes described as code DNA [69,70]. However, malware is now more sophisticated, with some techniques to foil scanners [2,117]. Users are thus engaged unwillingly in an unseen protection war against malware, while engaging in risky security behaviors, exploited by others which compromises their authentication of passwords. It is then essential to develop better authentication and protection technologies with an understanding of the consumer, administrative and employee security

[1] www.symantec.com/content/dam/symantec/docs/reports/istr-22-2017-en.pdf *Accessed:* 27 May 2019.

behavior, and their acceptance of innovations in this area. Without such research and implementation of both an understanding of human behavior and advances in technology, it is likely we will fall further behind in the arms race with cybercriminals and online malicious malcontents.

There is therefore a need to develop a greater understanding of consumer security beliefs, practices, and how these can be improved not only by technological intervention but also by better education and the adoption of safer methods (Section 8.3). Only by merging both technological solutions to increase cybersecurity and an understanding of user behavior can advances in cybersecurity practices occur.

Cyber Nugget 21: *Understanding user security behavior and likely acceptance of new cyber norms is as important as any technological silver bullets in cybersecurity.*

Even if users are sophisticated and prudent, there is always the unseen danger of what lurks beneath the surface in software and security. Many popular programs may have deep structural flaws that make them and users vulnerable to hackers and criminals. The interconnected global digital economy means that our details are shared and processed by a number of agents, which may be benevolent in the case of Google, but may be nefarious by others. This all points to the need for research and practice in cybersecurity, which understands user behavior, educates them about the risks, and provides better safe solutions that are readily adopted. There is thus a need to convince as much as inform users. What then are some fundamental consumer behavior theories that may be suitable to guide research in this area? This chapter outlines some crucial contributions that marketing theory, in particular, can make to the emerging international area of the importance of cybersecurity. Figure 4.1 describes a consumer behavior model of choices and provides a basis for the discussion in this chapter.

4.2 Cybersecurity as Predicted by Demographics

Research shows that security behaviors differ across the population, with 54% of victims of cyberfraud being men, who report higher losses (some 69% higher) than women [52]. Older people are also more likely to share their passwords [148]. There are also generational differences in the use of online services, particularly banking (Gen Y uses online banking more than other generations), which needs to be taken into account as the risks for online banking are greater the younger the consumer [52].

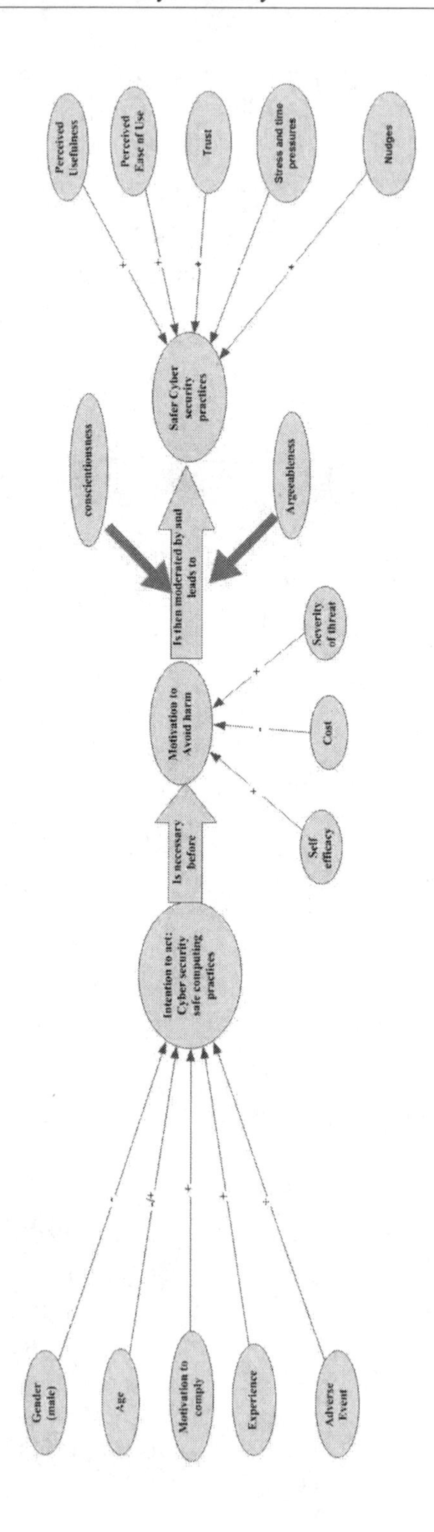

Figure 4.1: Consumer behavior model of choice.

Figure 4.2: Promoting a sense of responsibility for cybersecurity by influencing social norms. Source: www.fbi.gov/news/stories/national-cyber-security-awareness-month-2017 Accessed: 10 Sep 2018 (with permission).

4.3 Cybersecurity and the Theory of Reasoned Action

Early research in the field has noted that users are not the enemies of security, but instead are collaborators who need appropriate information and motivation to maintain system security [3,153]. Information and Communication Technology (ICT) research [6,116] suggests that there is scope to apply the TRA to understand user behavior in this area.

A number of studies show that the successful adoption of safer computing practices, such as not sharing passwords, frequently changing passwords, having passwords with mixed characters depends on the attitudes users have towards safety, threat appraisal, and subjective norms (Section 3.4), that of whether security requirements are compatible with the users' sense of convenience, or in the case of organizational settings, are seen as sensible [3,4,116,127].

Many public announcements by government authorities, for example, the FBI in the USA use appeals to social norms as a means of promoting safer behavior (Figure 4.2 Source: FBI[2]).

In some cases, users in organizations were found to deliberately circumvent security protocols, if they believed that, for example, password mechanisms were seen as pointless [3]. In other words, the motivation to comply with security

[2]www.fbi.gov/news/stories/national-cyber-security-awareness-month-2017 *Accessed:* 10 Sep 2018.

protocols is a strong predictor of the type of user behavior in this context. There are differences in attitude and behavior across users, depending on their expertise and experience. Duggan et al. [44] found that, in a university setting, scientists viewed information security as part of their tasks, and passwords provided a way of completing their work. By contrast, administrative and student groups saw passwords as a cost incurred when accessing the primary task. Other research has suggested that the attitude and behavior in computing practices depend on three factors: frequency in engaging in risky online behaviors; the experience of an adverse online event; and the disposition to be more or less trusting and cautious of others [31]. This discussion suggests the following are essential in the understanding of how to develop safer computing practices:

- The motivation to comply is clearly a major factor in cybersecurity. It comprises two elements: social norms of compliance level, which varies from culture to culture and country to country; and the transparency and intent of the security protocols imposed. Recalling the discussion in Section 3.3.5 of Christakis network effects, changing cyberculture through social networks requires only that good cyberpractices are at most three steps removed within the network.
- Expertise and experience influence the attitude towards the behavior of secure computing practices. Less experienced and novice users being more likely to engage in unsafe computing practices, because they are less aware of the risks.
- Experience, or experience of one's peers, of an adverse event online event, increases the attitude towards the behavior of secure computing practices.

It is not surprising that public campaigns to avoid unsafe or even criminal cyberbehavior focus on the motivation to comply. This is shown in Figure 4.3 (with permission from Australian Cyber Security Centre), which is an advertisement by The Australian Cyber Security seeking to persuade to consider that people on social media may not be who they say they are and may have malicious intent. (Figure 4.3 Source Australian Cyber Security Centre[3]).

Greater awareness also does not mean greater consumer action. Recent industry research from Acronis,[4] of computer users in the United States, shows that despite increased awareness of threats of ransomware, such as Wannacry and Petya rising 16%. Less than a third (27.8%) of users knew how to protect their data, photos, and files. This lack of precaution is explained by the nearly half (48.1%) not knowing that ransomware can wipe data or disable their computer

[3]https://www.staysmartonline.gov.au/partners/partner-resource-kits/national-scams-awarenessweek-resource-kit *Accessed:* 29 Aug 2019.

[4]www.acronis.com/en-us/blog/posts/acronis-global-data-protection-survey *Accessed:* 27 May 2019.

Figure 4.3: Targeting the motivation to comply rather than social norms. Source: Stay Smart Online (Australian Cyber Centre) https://www.staysmartonline.gov.au/partners/partner-resource-kits/stay-smart-online-week-2018-kit Accessed on September 10, 2019 (with permission).

and a further (43.7%) not thinking they need protection against ransomware. The Motivation To Avoid Harm (MTAH) and perception of threat is low in the world's largest economy, and this creates a challenge for security professionals and managers. There is, however, a field of research and practice that may be useful to consider in this situation.

4.4 Motivation To Avoid Harm (MTAH) and Cybersecurity

The MTAH is seen as an important predictor of purchasing ecofriendly products that do not harm the environment, [97]. As part of MTAH is ethical investing [122], which is seen as a key explanation of reciprocity in business relationships [104] and is an important determinant of consumers to accept products and services that reduce injury and risk, such as seat belts and airbags [78]. Research by Dang-Pham and Pittayachawan [36], on the behavior to avoid malware threats amongst 252 Australian university students, showed that perceptions of vulnerability and belief in self-efficacy had positive effects on the adoption of more secure use of own devices such as laptops, tablets, and mobile phones. This is a conclusion also mirrored in research on organizational computer users where threat appraisal, and information security self-efficacy had a positive effect on users' behavior [116].

Cyber Nugget 22: *The Motivation To Avoid Harm predicts the uptake of safer computing practices in the face of a clear threat if users have cost-effective self-efficacy.*

Figure 4.4, with permission from Australian Cyber Security Centre, shows a campaign to avoid a scam of people pretending be from the Australian Taxation Office, which can occur even by an attack on a mobile device.[5]

Huigang et al. [65] found that the motivation to avoid cyberthreats was predicted not only by the nature of the perceived threat and self-efficacy but also by the need to safeguard effectiveness and cost. When threatened, users were found to be more motivated to avoid the threat if they believed that the safeguarding measure was useful (safeguard effectiveness) and inexpensive (safeguard cost), and they have confidence in using it (self-efficacy). Huigang et al. [65] also found that perceived threat and safeguard effectiveness have a negative interaction on avoidance motivation so that a higher level of perceived threat is associated with a weaker association between safeguard effectiveness and avoidance motivation, or a higher level of safeguard effectiveness is associated with a weaker relationship between perceived threat and avoidance motivation. This suggests that higher safeguards may lead users to believe that cyberattacks they may encounter are unlikely, hence the low motivation here to avoid harm. The overall perception of risk (Chapter 5), or likelihood of harm, has also been shown to be a significant predictor of the adoption of email authentication services [60]. Likewise, users are motivated to engage in bad password-management behaviors because they do not see any immediate negative consequences to themselves [137]. This suggests that cybersecurity professionals and managers should consider the following:

Cyber Nugget 23: *Even if the threat of a cyber breach is perceived as severe, avoidance motivation will be low if users have low self-efficacy and the perceived avoidance costs are too high.*

[5] https://www.staysmartonline.gov.au/partners/partner-resource-kits/national-scams-awarenessweek-resource-kit *Accessed:* 29 Aug 2019.

Figure 4.4: Increasing perceived threat appraisal by advertising. Source: Stay Smart Online (Australian Cyber Centre) https://www.staysmartonline.gov.au/partners/partner-resource-kits/stay-smart-online-week-2018-kit Accessed on September 10, 2019 (with permission).

Showing simple steps that users can take to maintain cybersecurity is also essential, as it leads to greater self-efficacy (confidence on one's ability) of action [42]. This is shown in Figure 4.5 (Source University of Notre Dame[6]) which shows university advice on how to be more secure by following a series of simple do's and don'ts. This advertisement mirrors research which suggests that novice users while being aware of cyberthreats, but not really the likely impacts, need also to have the technical knowledge of how to deal with them [54].

Industry research also explains why there is a low level of preparedness amongst computer users in advanced economies, such as the United States, the United Kingdom, France, Germany, and Australia (World Backup Day Survey

[6]https://ltlatnd.wordpress.com/2014/01/16/are-passwords-obsolete/ *Accessed:* 10 Sep 2018.

Do	Have two factor authentication where possible	Save incorrect or unusual answers to security questions	Delete your presence online by removing history when you logout	Use a unique email (not your work email) for password recoveries
Don't	Use the same password for multiple accounts	Use a dictionary word as a password	Use standard number substitutions like "P455W0rd"	Use a short password, no matter how bizarre it is

Figure 4.5: Promoting greater self-efficacy of users to avoid cyberthreats.

2017[7] which can be explained by previously discussed studies (Table 4.1)). Despite just over a third of users experiencing a loss of data in 2017, around 27% of the public did not back up any files. While there were concerns over the loss of personal information and documents (35%) and videos, music, and pictures (32.2%), the prices people would pay someone responsible for a ransomware attack is low (71% would only pay up to $50). This collectively means that the threat (loss of data) is perceived as low, since the amount people would pay to recover their data is low, and therefore protective actions to avoid harm (data backups) are not common.

4.5 The Technology Acceptance Model (TAM) and the Adoption of New Technologies in Cybersecurity

The TAM [37] is a useful model, or framework, for predicting users' intentions to accept new technology and hence by implication safe computing practices and related technology. Though initially applied to predict the acceptance of information technology within an industrial context (e.g., user acceptance of new information technology interventions adopted within organizations), the model has been shown to be relatively robust across a variety of situations and contexts [83,119]. Increasingly, the TAM has been applied to a variety of consumer contexts of both behavior change and acceptance of new technology. For example, the TAM has been used to predict consumers' acceptance of personal computers [143], handheld internet devices [23], online transactions [103], internet

[7] www.acronis.com/en-us/blog/posts/acronis-world-backup-day-survey-results *Accessed:* 6 Feb 2018.

Table 4.1 Backup and Security Behavior of Computer Users in the United Kingdom, United States, France, Germany, and Australia

Question	*Indicative Responses*	*Percent(%)*
Have you or a family member ever lost data on a computer/mobile device?	Yes	34.3
Do you currently back up your files?	Yes, to a local external drive	33.3
	Don't backup anything	26.9
What do you fear losing the most?	Personal information and documents	35.5
	Pictures, videos, and music	32.2
How much money would you be willing to pay to get your files back from ransomware or data loss?	< $50	71.0
	$50–$100	16.8

Source: www.acronis.com/en-us/blog/posts/acronis-world-backup-day-survey-results Accessed: 6 Feb 2018.

banking [79], online auctions [134], sensory enabling technologies [77], e-service systems [87], and a plethora of other consumer products and services. The TAM's appeal and widespread usage seem to be based around its intuitiveness, simplicity, empirical validation, and robustness across a variety of technology contexts.

TAM predicts that the use of a technology depends on two key factors: Perceived Usefulness (Perceived Usefulness (PU)) of the technology and Perceived Ease of Use (PEU). PU is the user's evaluation of how useful a particular technology is. PEU relates to the user's evaluation of how easy it is to apply the technology to a specific task. PEU is closely associated with PU. Regarding the adoption of technology and practices, both components of the TAM model, PU and PEU, are important factors for the manager to consider.

Piccolotto et al. [105], on the use and acceptance of biometrics (Section 7.6), found that while they were seen as more useful, they suffered regarding ease of use by computer users. Conversely, security by passwords provides greater PU, but users were worried about the PEU of passwords, as they were worried that important passwords could be forgotten. Advocates for greater security in cloud devices note that, while PU of greater security protocols and authentication may provide greater user confidence, this may at the same time reduce the PEU [39]. As a related issue, both PEU and PU of computer networks have been shown along with web security to influence the intention to use online services, particularly financial services [29]. The risk here is that if PEU of PU of online services becomes too complicated, due to increased cybersecurity measures, customers may go elsewhere. This means the following needs to be considered by cybersecurity professionals and managers:

PEU and PU of protocols and new technology by users have an important impact on their acceptance.

Cyber Nugget 24: *The Perceived Usefulness of some approaches may not lead to adoption because of low Perceived Ease of Use.*

Cyber Nugget 25: *Very high levels of security authentication and protocols may inhibit online purchase behavior or trigger consumers to switch providers through low Perceived Usefulness and Perceived Ease of Use.*

4.6 Social and Situational Factors in Cybersecurity

While it is understood that there are some factors that may predispose consumers of technology to act in a particular manner regarding cybersecurity, it is essential to understand that situational factors, events, and the background in which the use of information technology occurs also have an important effect on behavior.

4.6.1 *Trust and Risk in the Online Environment*

There is a rich history in marketing, examining the role of perceived risk and trust, in facilitating e-commerce [33,67,82,132]. Generally consumers will look to reduce risks by staying with well-known providers who have good security and privacy practices [33,82], though this is by no means a complete safer computer practice as shown by the high incidence of clickjacking (Section 7.11)[8] on many websites, with some 86% of Indian websites not protected from this attack [40]. Other issues are that user logins from safe and accepted providers such as LinkedIn [53] have been compromised and in the case of Uber are for sale as little as $1 each in the dark web [58]. Research also shows that users underestimate their degree of risk from cyberattacks and see other people as more likely to be vulnerable [25]. In other words the source of security problems is not them, and is something that happens to others and can be managed by providers. A paradox here is that greater trust in providers does not seem to engender greater security concern or vigilance.

[8]clickjacking is a security attack grabbing Keystrokes.

4.6.2 Cybersecurity as Predicted by Personality

While the TRA provides a useful framework for understanding some social phenomena, recent research suggests that personality rather than attitude towards behavior predicts better cybersecurity behaviors [31,127]. Research has found, for example, that the personality traits of conscientiousness and agreeableness moderate the effect of attitudes on the intention to use security software [127].

4.6.3 Stress and Time Pressures on Users

Research on decision-making shows that when under stress and time pressures, people will make suboptimal decisions [16,43,59,63,102]. Stress by itself causes people to engage in emotive, rather than reasoned decision-making [128]. Although some researchers contend that this emotional learning from the outcomes of the miscalculation of risks, rather than a reasoned approach [63,128]. The implications for cybersecurity is that users when faced with stress and time pressures do not understand risk, will base their decisions on fewer pieces or cues of information [57] will use generalizations based on past experiences to understand the choices presented to them (for example, to click or not click on a link in a suspicious email [66]. That is, they do not anticipate the likely results of their actions in a reasoned manner.

What is worrying is that, when faced under time pressure, humans are more likely to repeat tried and true patterns of behavior, even if such behavior still caused errors of judgment [16,24]. This provides considerable challenges to improve behavior in cybersecurity, as users are likely to revert to bad habits when faced with stress and time pressures (clicking on a suspicious link in an email on a Friday afternoon while rushing to meet a deadline). Eye-tracking research suggests that users may engage in random search activity of information presented to them, when under time pressures, and will stop their search when a focal region (a subject heading or logo) is reached [111].

This means for cybercriminals that spoofing emails with well-designed logos, fonts, and subject headings are more likely to be opened when people are under time pressure. It is vital for cybersecurity managers to understand that human behavior in cyber can change at various times of the day and week when people are under higher pressure, and that the tendency will be for less diligence and the use of shortcuts to evaluate material and to be less concerned about known risks.

Cyber Nugget 26: *Greater diligence by system administrators should happen in the days of the week when stress levels or time pressures are higher.*

4.6.4 Information Overload

Greater quantities of information have also been shown to reduce the effectiveness of decision-making [71,74,75]. Consumers, when faced with too much information, are likely to not notice warning labels [88]. Therefore it is possible that they are also less likely to see disbelieving emails or communication. The mood of consumers also influences how they deal with information overload. Consumers in a positive mood are more able to deal with information overload and notice inconsistent information [22]. This last point suggests that while avoiding information overload may not always be possible in many organizations, providing a more positive and happy work environment which assists in positive moods of workers may help them with cybersecurity.

4.7 Improving the Security Behavior of Users

There is an emerging field of research that suggests that to improve the cybersecurity practices of users, Nobel Laureate Richard Thaler's nudge theory [139], that is, providing timely feedback and incentives on behavior, is useful [8,54,142,152]. Furnell et al. [54] showed that providing users with feedback of how strong their passwords were regarding rank and time to crack, along with suggestions for improving passwords, meant that users adopted much stronger and longer passwords.

Some possible cybersecurity nudges might be

- The WiFi daemon does not show unsecured or WEP (deprecated, insecure protocol) networks, and requires a specific checkbox to reveal them.
- If only unsecured networks are available, the daemon could prompt the user to hotspot her phone or switch to using a VPN.
- Some security question prompts (mother's maiden name is a hopeless joke). A better prompt might be *the smelliest boy in your third year class*, with the caveat that he has not been mentioned on social media.

A similar approach has also been found effective in a field experiment [142], whereby interactive menus of password strength and the likelihood of these being cracked were found to produce stronger passwords. Figure 4.6 (Source [142]) shows the interactive experimental treatment that was successful in encouraging stronger passwords.

Nudges can be used in industry. Balebako et al. [8] provide the example of *Flickr.com*, an image and video sharing website, which includes information on each posting along with the privacy settings and who can see it. It could also be argued that many industry sites could adopt similar practices that would significantly increase cybersecurity. Some have argued that this better design and

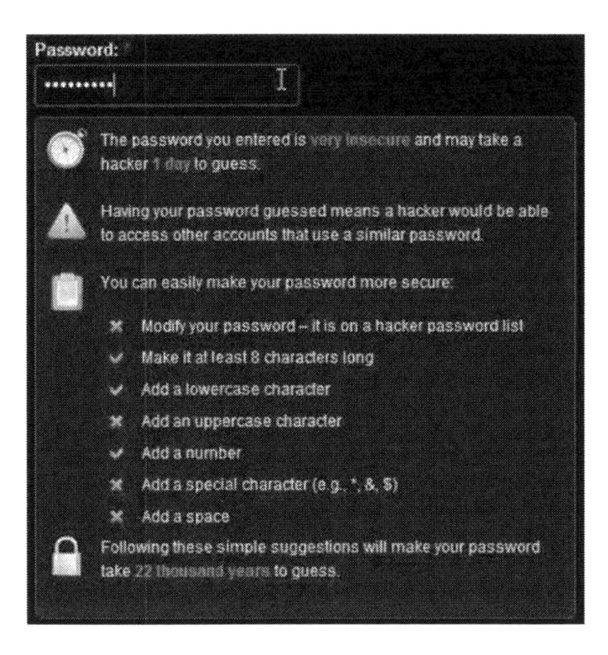

Figure 4.6: Interactive fear appeal treatment for stronger passwords. Source: Vance [141], p. 2993 (with permission).

interactivity in passwords and security settings may be more important than training [120].

4.7.1 A Need for a Systematic Approach to Cybersecurity

It is clear that cybersecurity is an area of existential importance for business, government, and society, yet there is not yet a concerted research effort from social science scholars to address this issue. The adoption of safer computer practices, such as backups of data, keeping up-to-date patches on operating systems (Cyber Nugget 4) and all applications, may well prevent many low-level attacks such as the recent Wannacry ransomware. As can be seen herein, users are not always logical or follow protocols, but their behavior can be understood. This chapter illustrates how this can be achieved.

Technology and cybersafe policies must be accepted by users, be they employees or customers. It is clear from this review that parts of the population (men and people of various age groups) are more vulnerable, or perceive a risk from a cyberattack than less experienced users, those who have not experienced an adverse event. Even if users wish to change their behavior in cybersecurity, there must still be a motivation for them to do so. The theory of MTAH suggests that they must believe they can make the necessary changes (self-efficacy) at a reasonable cost. A high level of perceived threat will conversely mean that a user's self- efficacy cannot cope and that the cost is seen as too high. The solution therefore not only provides accessible solutions at a lower cost but also does not alarm users too high a level. Lastly, organizations may wish to consider the types of people they employ, in very crucial parts of cybersecurity as it seems that people who are more agreeable and conscientious are more likely to adopt safer practices.

Next, managers and security professionals need to consider what is the PU and PEU, not just the technological and systemic improvements proposed. More secure authentication technologies may not be accepted or adopted because of a low level of Perceived Ease of Use. Likewise, harder to use authentication approaches, such as long random passwords, which have a low PEU may suffer from a high PU in the future, caused perhaps by not having to remember important passwords, through the use of password managers/safes. It is also important that if the bar of security is raised too high, the consumers and users may not engage in the use of online services or may change providers. In short the human dimension of cybersecurity is all about understanding and trade-offs (see case study on MyHealth (Section 2.4)).

Chapter 5

Risk Perspectives in Cybersecurity

At present, and maybe long into the future, it is impossible to be totally cybersecure, other than by going off the grid entirely. This chapter looks at the risks and how to address them, posed by cybersecurity threats to business and individuals. Cybersecurity is one risk to balance against others, requiring us to have some estimate of the costs of attacks. Section 5.2 looks at the cost of recent breaches. Threats come in many forms and attack different network levels (Section 7.7.1). Section 5.3 develops a taxonomy of the types of attack.

5.1 Introduction

Risk management is an essential part of any corporate entity. However, the recent spate of attacks, from ransomware to Distributed Denial of Service (DDoS) show that corporations (and possibly insurance companies) do not have a good way of assessing risk. Partly this is because major cyber breaches are black-swan [136] -like events, where the vulnerability was not obvious before the attack. Similarly the cost of such attacks is hard to predict beforehand, since the consequences can range from a small number of computers being comprised to the destruction of an entire corporate database. We discuss the currently available strategies for cyber risk assessment and consider new policies, such as the Australian Government's introduction of mandatory reporting of cyber breaches.

5.2 Costs and Occurrences of Cyberattacks as of 2018

In order to understand the risk of cyberattacks and crime and how individuals, organizations, and nation states can deal with this risk, it is first necessary to quantify and understand the prevalence of the risk. The next step is to examine what frameworks and governance approaches exist to manage this risk. Lastly, there is a need to consider what potential improvements in governance and policy can be made, which can further reduce the risk. This chapter follows this approach. It is important to recognize though that the nature of risk (types and motivations of cyberattacks) is changing as technology and the business models of criminals change, as does the motivations of hostile states.

It is difficult to estimate accurately the extent of cost that can be incurred by an organization or individual from cyberthreats. Estimates of the cost to business and government globally are according to Lloyd's Insurance around US $400 billion a year [135]. A recent survey worldwide survey of security professionals suggests that around 53% of attacks cost an organization US $500000 or more. The internet appears also to becoming an increasingly dangerous place to do business, with security firm Symantec found in evaluating 1 billion web requests in 2017 and that 1 in 13 contained malware, up 3% from 2017.[1] The company also noted a steady increase in "mega breaches" of more than 10 million records as 11 in 2014, 13 in 2015, and 15 in 2016.[2]

The individual costs of data breaches also vary according to country and industry,[3] which makes insurance coverage in this area quite difficult [135][4] Data breaches can involve hundreds of thousands of records or more [106,108], meaning a rise in the individual cost of data breach is significant. In industries the highest cost of a data breach was in healthcare US $380, financial services US $245, media US $119, research US $101, and the public sector US $71 per record.[3] Importantly, the cost of data breach is not just due to legal action but to customer churn, whereby consumers can change providers or stop using an online service. Countries and regions with higher data breach costs per record include the United States (average loss being US $7.35 million per company), Middle East (US $4.94 per million per company), Denmark (US $4.58 million per Company, and Canada (US $4.56 million per company).

The reasons for these differences are complex, but include the fact that North America is a prime target for cybercrime and attacks, the Middle East has a higher churn rate of customers as a result of breach, and Denmark may have a higher reporting rate of data breaches than other European countries. While data breaches are of concern, these are not necessarily the biggest issues for many companies. A worldwide report by Australian telecommunication provider Telstra found that

[1] `Internetsecuritythreatreport.Symantec2018` *Accessed:* 31 Dec 2018.

[2] `Telstrasecurityreport.Australian(2018)` *Accessed:* 31 Dec 2018.

[3] `Costofdatabreachstudy(2018),PoenmonInstituteLLCandIBMSecurity` *Accessed:* 31 Dec 2018.

[4] Swiss Re. (2016). Cyber and beyond *Accessed:* 31 Dec 2018.

the loss of productivity and corrupted business data were the biggest issues faced by 1,252 companies across 15 industries in 13 countries they surveyed.[2] Loss of productivity was an issue for 41% of respondents in Europe and 43% in the Asia Pacific, while corrupted business data was more of a concern for companies in the Asia Pacific (44%) than in Europe (31%). As the report notes, a loss of productivity is important as it can lead to increased costs when operations are disrupted and the potential loss of revenue when, for example, buyers cannot complete purchases.[2] Loss of reputation was the third biggest concern amongst the respondents in the Telstra survey, with 35% of respondents noting this when compared with 33% in Europe. Reputational loss due to a cyberattack can do considerable damage to a brand or a company, and it may take considerable time and resources to rebuild that reputation. A landmark study of identified financial rather than reported costs of cybercrime and attacks from the United States also suggests that data breaches are not necessarily the largest costs faced by organizations [114]. This is shown in Table 5.1. Privacy violations leading to lawsuits and compromised systems have higher median costs than just data breaches per say.

It is important to note that this research shows wide variations in the median and maximum costs that were incurred by US organizations. Data breaches, which for 2002–2016 were the most common reported event, did not cause as high a median cost (US $170 000) and maximum cost (US $572 million) than did privacy violations (median cost US $1.34 million, max US $750 million dollars) and illicit access (a lower median cost US $150 000, but a much higher maximum cost US $710 million dollars). In terms of how common cyberattacks are, the answer seems to be common and increasing in number. According to security firm Symantec's[1] annual report of the worldwide issues in cybersecurity in 2017, there was

1. 92% increase in malware downloader variants.
2. 8,500% increase in coin mining detections.
3. 600% increase on attacks on Internet of Things (IoT) devices.
4. 1,242 ransomware detections in 2017.

Table 5.1 Actual Reported Costs of Cyberattacks and Crime in the United States (2002–2016)

Event Type	*No. of Events*	*Mean Cost*	*Median Cost*	*Maximum Cost*
Data breach	602	5.87	0.17	572
Compromised systems	36	9.17	0.33	100
Privacy violation	234	10.14	1.34	750
Illicit access	49	19.99	0.15	710
Total	**921**	**7.84**	**0.25**	**710**

Source: Romanosky [113], p. 129
Note: Figures are in US $million.

As reported by Zack Whittaker on TechCrunch on information from Symantec,[5] a new coin mining called Beapy led to an upsurge in coin mining

> spread like wildfire across corporate networks to enslave computers into running mining code to generate cryptocurrency. Beapy was first spotted in January but rocketed to more than 12,000 unique infections across 732 organizations since March... In a single month, file-based mining can generate up to $750,000, Symantec researchers estimate...

The Telstra report, alluded to above, noted that business interruptions to cyberattacks occurred with 68% of respondents globally: 70% in Europe and 66% in the Asia Pacific.[2]

To conclude, it appears that cybercrime and attacks are common worldwide, have a range of effects, and that costs are considerable and deserve the attention of organizations and countries across the globe. The wide variation in the types of costs incurred across the globe and industries and the nature of those costs make it difficult for insurance to cover and for there needs to be a coordinated response. While the costs and types of damages from cyberthreats have been discussed, it is also important to understand the actual types of threats and the motivations behind such malicious acts.

5.3 Types of Threats and Their Associated Risks

We now look at different types of attack.

5.3.1 Threats by Source of Attack

It is extremely difficult to determine in many cases the source of the attack and therefore the motivations of the attacker. Nevertheless from a risk perspective, it is important to note that not all attacks are motivated by crime, though it is thought that around half (47%) of all attacks are based on ransom demanded or frauds committed.[2] Table 5.2 shows the various types of attackers, their resources, and motivations. Hacktivists of all groups are likely to disclose their motivation for the attack early, whilst state-sponsored attacks are the least likely to disclose their identity and thus motivation. As a generalization, as we move from left to right in the table the sophistication and depth of the attack increases.

Understanding the potential motivations of attackers is also important, as it gives the nature of the target and the possible type of attack that will be favored. Types of attacks will be discussed shortly, but it is important to understand that

[5] https://techcrunch.com/2019/04/25/cryptojacking-nsa-malware/ *Accessed:* 27 Apr 2019.

Table 5.2 Motivations of Attackers, Their Resources, and Motivations

	Amateurs	*Hacktivists*	*Organized Crime*	*State-Sponsored*
Resources	Limited technical resources	Vast networks Strong emotional commitment	Significant technical resources	Constrained only by government budget
Motivations	Fame and notoriety	Makes as statement, cause, or embarrassment	Economic gain	Boost to innovation; leverage in negotiations
Sophistication	Not professional; uses known exploits	Sometime low-sophistication, Relentless, and targeted.	Professional established syndicates	Highly sophisticated, patient, creative, and persistent
Type of typical attack	Distributed Denial of Service (DDoS), Malware	DDoS Malware	Ransomware social engineering	DDoS Advanced Persistent Threat (APT), Trojans, social engineering

Source: Swales A. (2017, April/May). A race against crime. *Insurance News*, p. 62.

four different types of attackers may not be independent and that there is evidence of cooperation and information flows across all groups. A social network analysis of Russian Hackers [62] found that in terms of risk, very few hackers and malware writers can be considered as dangerous, though they are often centrally located in the network of hackers. This is shown in Figure 5.1. The network density around high-threat hackers (those that develop and disseminate attack tools) is also not large, meaning there are many low-threat hackers (possibly amateurs) who are not centrally connected, though high-threat hackers are all within two degrees of separation of each other (Section 3.3.1), that is, they each know someone who knows someone that has dangerous skills. Importantly, this analysis also shows that most members of the hacker network were young males, with little education and sophistication in hacking, but who may nevertheless become more knowledgeable over time [62, p. 900]. Other research also suggests that a relatively few people in a hacker network (<10) are responsible for the majority of the posts and information flows [118], suggesting that their fame and notoriety are principle motivations for such activity.

While social network analysis tells us something about the nature of threats from armatures and hackers, the type of threat from organized crime is best

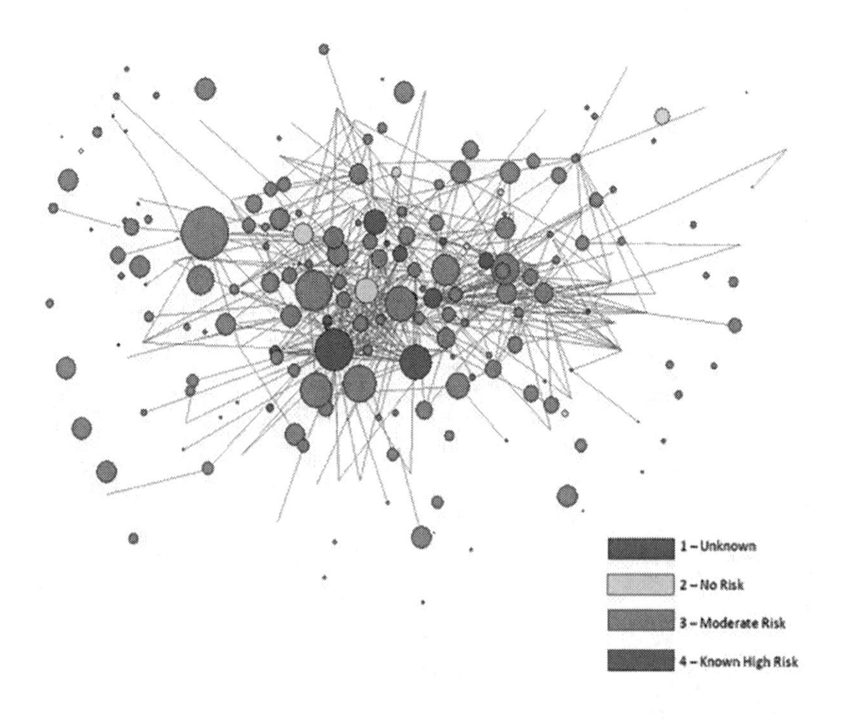

Figure 5.1: Popularity of Russian hacker's network by different groups. (Source: [61], p. 901).

examined by the marketplace conditions in which buyers and sellers engage in this area [85].

5.3.2 Threats by Type of Attack

Identifying the attacker is clearly difficult, but not so the type of attack. It is because of this that most of what we know in cybersecurity is focused on the technological means and not the intentions of attacker. We can categorize five types of attacks:

1. Ransomware/malware attacks (Case Study in Section 2.2.2).
2. Distributed Denial of Service (DDoS) attacks (Case Study in Section 2.1).
3. Middleware attacks (Case Study in Section 2.9).
4. Social engineering (Case Study in Section 2.3).
5. Advanced Persistent Threat (APT) (Case Study in Section 2.10).

Attackers may use a combination of these approaches depending on their motivations, target, and degree of resources and sophistication (see Table 5.2).

Figure 5.2 shows the top ten file extensions that contained malware in 2017.

Cyber Nugget 27: *The risk from malware/ransomware and social engineering attacks can be reduced by simple strategies.*

Such strategies include

1. Having up-to-date operating systems and application versions, with all available patches (Cyber Nugget 4). There needs to be constant vigilance and user training that this is done.
2. Backing up sensitive data on removable hard drives disconnected to the computer or in larger organizations on an off-site server.
3. Being wary of phishing and spam campaigns, the approaches used that get user to click on suspicious links or open files in emails.
4. Having up to date threat intelligence on emerging types of attacks in this area.

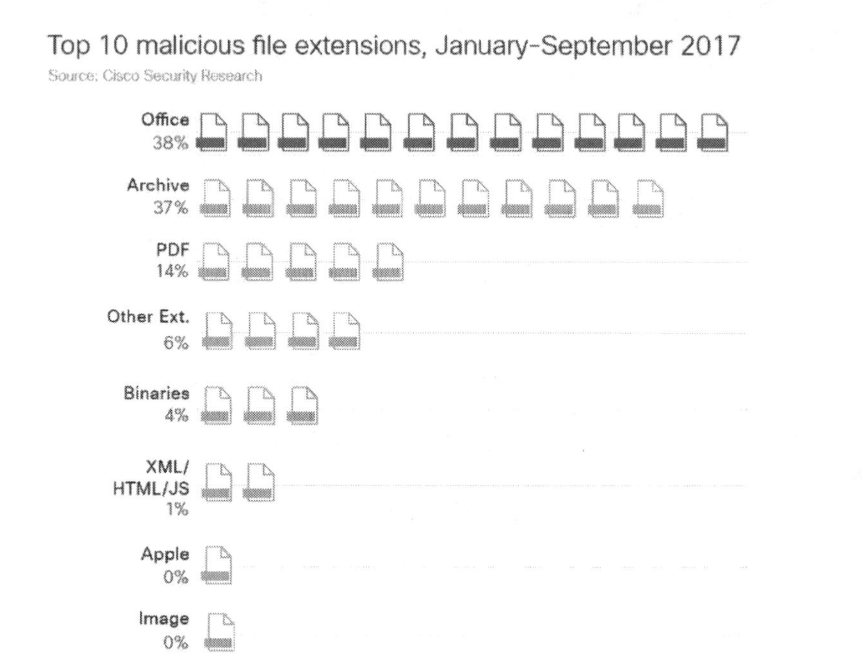

Figure 5.2: Top ten file extensions, which contained malware in 2017. (Source: CISCO 2018, p. 16 (with permission).)

5.3.2.1 DDoS Attacks

The next major category of type of attacks is DDoS (Section 2.1). Attackers may also use third parties in DDoS attacks, that is to amplify attack, they may use hijacked computer systems with larger bandwidth than the target to flood their system. Therefore another risk is that your organization could be used as part of a criminal attack on another without your knowledge. Something that could cause reputational damage and leave an organization open to a claim of negligence on an insurance claim. Figure 5.3 shows the use of a third party in a DDoS attack.

There are several strategies to help reduce DDoS risk, which are not very costly to implement. They include

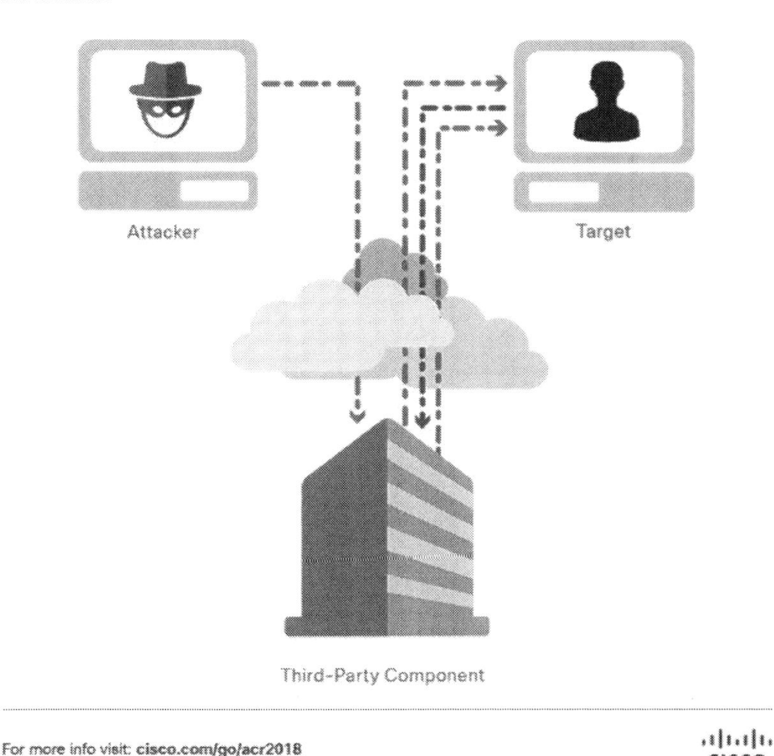

Figure 5.3: DDoS using third party.

- Make sure Internet of Things (IoT) devices and web-connected devices do not provide leak paths, including cloud that does not allow traffic to be forwarded to a location on the internet, such as a malicious website.
- Longer 12-character passwords, containing upper and lowercase letters, and wild characters. As these are harder to crack.
- Make sure all IoT devices and networks are regularly patched and updated.
- Keeping an inventory of all IoT and bring your own devices.
- Educating users to patch and update their own devices used to access organizational information.

5.3.2.2 Middleware Attacks

Middleware attacks, while being less frequent than malware/ransomware and DDoS attacks, are still a concern, given that they are much harder to detect. A middleware attack or a man in the middle (MITM) is an attack where the assailant secretly relays and possibly alters the communication between two parties who believe they are in direct contact. See also Section 2.9.

> **Cyber Nugget 28:** *The risk of middleware attacks can also be reduced by the use of a Virtual Private Network on mobile computing devices.*

Section 7.16.2 considers the advantage of quantum computing for averting Man in the Middle Attack (MITM) attacks.

5.3.2.3 Spoofing Attacks

An emerging variant form of MITM is a spoofing attack. A spoofing attack is when a malicious party impersonates another device or user on a network to launch attacks against network hosts, steal data, spread malware, or bypass access controls. There are several different types of spoofing attacks that malicious parties can use to accomplish this. Some of the most common methods include IP address spoofing attacks, Address Resolution Protocol (ARP), a protocol that is used to resolve IP addresses to Medium Access Control (MAC) addresses for transmitting data spoofing attacks and Domain Name Server (DNS) (Section 7.7.3).

Spoofing attacks are used to access business emails by fooling senders to send invoices to fake bank accounts, from websites and addresses that appear to be genuine. Figure 5.4 shows the structure of a typical spoofing/man in the middle attack.

It is challenging to detect and stop a spoofing attack for most users. The sharing of intelligence on scams may assist this process somewhat. Not allowing access to personal data or identification, usually gained by carelessness or mail theft may help.

> **Cyber Nugget 29:** *The risk of spoofing attacks for individuals and businesses can be reduced by locked letterboxes and mailboxes.*

Usually, victims of this type of crime report a mail theft some time before the fraud occurs. Having a clean desk policy, where password and sensitive information is not written down helps, as does a lockdown of computers when they are not in use.

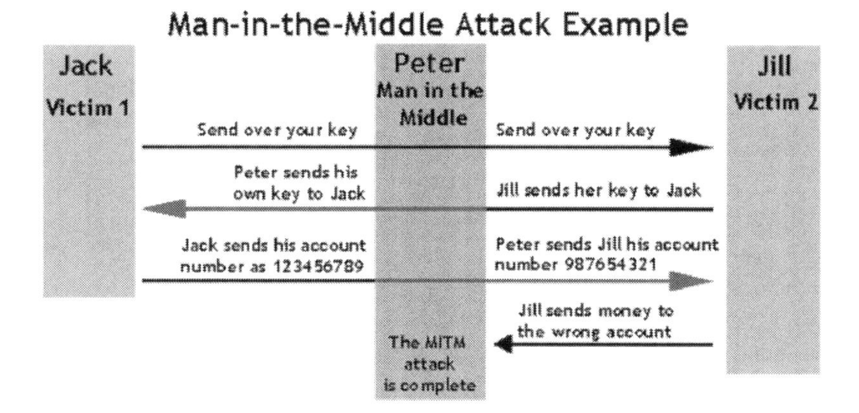

Figure 5.4: Man in the Middle Attack. Source: http://www.asanengineer.com/top-cyber-security-job-interview-questions-and-answers (with permission).

5.3.2.4 Social Engineering Attacks

The next set of attacks are not based on technology, but to use insights into human behavior as a means of accessing a secure network or system. The collective name for this approach is social engineering. Social engineering aims to exploit the one weakness that is found in every organization: human psychology. Using a variety of media, including phone calls and social media, these attackers trick people into offering them access to sensitive information. Some common approaches are

- phishing
- Pretexting
- Baiting
- quid pro quo
- tailgating

Phishing is the attempt to obtain sensitive information such as usernames, passwords, and credit card details (and money), often for malicious reasons, by disguising as a trustworthy entity in electronic communication. This is often the most common way to spread Trojan horses and malware/ransomware. Pretexting is a type of social engineering attack where attackers focus on creating a suitable pretext, or a fabricated scenario, that they can use to try and steal their victims' personal information. For example, a caller claims to be from taxation office and asks for personal information to clear up a claim, or from the police, following up on a traffic violation. In both cases, personal information is sought so that the user's identity can be stolen at a later date.

Baiting is in many ways similar to phishing. However, what distinguishes it from other types of social engineering is the promise of an item or good that hackers use to entice victims. Baiters may offer users free music or movie downloads if they surrender their login credentials to a particular site. Infected USBs have been successfully used in baiting attacks, as most users, being curious, plug them into their computers.

Quid pro quo attacks promise a benefit in exchange for information. This benefit usually assumes the form of a service, whereas baiting frequently takes the form of a good. One of the most common types of quid pro quo attacks involve fraudsters who impersonate IT service people and who spam call as many direct numbers that belong to a company as they can find. These attackers offer IT assistance to every one of their victims. The fraudsters will promise a quick fix in exchange for the employee disabling their antivirus program and for installing malware on their computers that assumes the guise of software updates. Fake updates have been a major scam in the last couple of years. They have invaded content sites, such as Wordpress and Squarespace, and appear as a pop-up window, saying that your browser or other app is out of date.[6] These are realistic looking windows, and it can be tempting to click the update link in order to get on with the job in hand. This would, of course, be a very bad move. Thus Cyber Nugget 32 emphasizes the need for regular system and software updates, but it has to be tempered with an important corollary.

Cyber Nugget 30: *Beware fake updates. Always update from the manufacturer's site (taking due care to avoid spoof sites).*

This approach can also be used to build botnets and use coin mining from a victim's computer.

Another social engineering attack type is known as **tailgating** or **piggybacking**. These types of attacks involve someone who lacks the proper authentication by following an employee into a restricted area. In a common type of tailgating attack, a person impersonates a delivery driver and waits outside a building. When an employee gains security's approval and opens their door, the attacker asks that the employee hold the door, thereby gaining access off of someone who is authorized to enter the company.

Tailgating does not work in all corporate settings, such as in larger companies where all persons entering a building are required to swipe a card. However, in midsize enterprises, attackers can strike up conversations with employees and use this show of familiarity to successfully get past the front desk. It is important to

[6]https://blog.malwarebytes.com/threat-analysis/2018/04/fakeupdates-campaign-leverages-multiple-website-platforms/ *Accessed:* 12 Mar 2019.

note that social engineering attacks evolve as much as the new forms of malware do to compromise systems. Social engineering is also used in combination with the major types of attacks discussed in this chapter. The risk of social engineering attacks can be reduced by

- User training monitoring on cybersecurity practices.
- Avoiding the use of USBs that are provided by third parties.
- Not allowing access to your computer to third parties wishing to assist you, except company IT staff.
- Not providing personal information, if pressured, to cold callers if you are unsure of their identity.
- Reporting such scams to authorities.
- Secure office locks and swipe cards and having a clean desk policy.

The risks of social engineering attacks are significant, since some numbers or identifiers are very valuable and need to be kept secret. One such number is that on a driver's license. Depending upon country and state, this is most likely to be a lifelong number. It is also one of the primary identity checks used by financial institutions.

There may be little choice in giving away your driver's license number to get a credit card or a bank loan. But each time this information is given away, the risk that it will be lost through some cyberattack increases. Sometimes, however, it will be asked for unnecessarily, and one should forcefully decline. For example, stores may require some form of an ID to return or exchange goods. Never ever give them your driver's licence number. Apart from having no idea how secure their computer systems are, they may onsell the data they collect from you, further worsening the security risk.

This can have devastating consequences now that we tie up so much information and do so much with our smartphones. From online banking to SMS security codes, losing our phone is a nontrivial problem. However, you may not need to lose the phone. Sim swapping may achieve exactly the same ends.[7] In this attack the hacker takes a crucial piece of identity information, such as a driver's license number, and uses it to get the telecom company to issue a new sim. Bingo, your phone, has become her phone.

Thus, any form of photo ID that is changeable or ephemeral is better. Tax file numbers are another very valuable number. Usually a tax file number is for life, like a fingerprint or an eyeball. Guard it as you would your eyes.

[7] https://theconversation.com/receiving-a-login-code-via-sms-and-email-isnt-secure-heres-what-to-use-instead-112767 *Accessed:* 6 Mar 2019.

Cyber Nugget 31: *Avoid giving away numbers, such as a driver's license or tax file number, which are hard to change.*

5.3.2.5 Advanced Persistent Threat (APT)

The last type of known attack is an APT. This is an attack in which an unauthorized user gains access to a system or network and remains there for an extended period without being detected. Advanced persistent threats are particularly dangerous for enterprises, as hackers have ongoing access to sensitive company data. Advanced persistent threats generally do not cause damage to company networks or local machines. Instead, the goal of advanced persistent threats is most often data theft. Usually, the goal of an APT attack is not to be detected. APT attacks are more likely to occur in organizations with valuable IP and who are of interest to state espionage. This can include small and medium enterprises working on sensitive government projects.

The risk of an APT attack can be reduced by

- Adopting a policy of least privilege, which is restricting data access to strengthen protection. No organization should have a policy where one person can access all the company data.
- Using multifactor identification.
- Understanding what data is being held, ensuring the protection of that data, and knowing where it is stored.
- Managing regular updates and system patches, a recurrent theme in the book.
- Reviewing existing security measures.
- Undertaking staff training so that employees understand the risk being faced and that that data remains secure at all times.
- Ensure that senior management and boards see cybersecurity as a critical risk to be managed.

Cyber Nugget 32: *Careful human access control with regular review and system updates helps in avoiding Advanced Persistent Threat attacks.*

However, we can't quite let this imperative to update go unquestioned. As we discussed right at the beginning of the book (Section 1.2.1), a system upgrade might break other software. If you're a small business really on some retail software, Albert's Abacus, say, to manage inventory, sales, etc., then downtime is expensive. Upgrading outside of shop hours doesn't necessarily solve the problem. The operating system upgrade might have been released before Albert's Abacus has been tested on the new system. It might be weeks before the two are brought into line.

It is clear that given the complexity and dynamic nature of cyber risks and the costs associated with such risks, it is necessary for organizations and individuals to adopt better governance mechanisms to reduce such risks. These are discussed next and vary from region to country and type of frameworks that aim to mitigate harm from cyberattacks. In this chapter, we examine in detail the use of organizational frameworks, as government policies and structures are dealt with in Chapter 6.

Chapter 6

Government Policy and Statecraft in Cybersecurity

The behavior of nation states, entities, and individuals in cyberspace is guided by peacetime norms—whether legal, policy, ethical, habit, or other. In order for cybersecurity measures to be practical and justifiable, they must respect and engage with existing norms of behavior and those being developed specifically for cyberspace. At the same time, however, the terrains offered by cyberspace force us to reflect on and evaluate those norms with respect to government policy and statecraft. This chapter covers a range of descriptive and proscriptive points of investigation to gain a deeper and broader understanding of just what norms of behavior exist in cyberspace, to ask what norms should exist and to test what impacts the ever-evolving terrain of cyberspace has on those norms.

A fundamentally important set of behaviors in cyberspace, and therefore active cybersecurity, concern how we anticipate and respond to cyberthreats, of which Section 5.3 provided a categorization. This temporal element includes predicting specific or known threats, as well as preparing for generalized and unpredictable challenges. Anticipation also refers to qualitative aspects of preparation and response, in addition to quantitative analytical tools. The aim here is to actively recognize and make sense of the human and seemingly chaotic nature of cyberspace and consider cyberthreats as potential "black swan" [136] and "black elephant" events—black elephants being threats passed off as black swans because they are too politically challenging to acknowledge and/or too unrealistic to be plausible, but on reflection were known and could have been anticipated.

Apart from legal standards and compliance discussed previously, the following certification of governance structures are voluntary and vary in the sort of auditing and scope of their implementation. For schemes such as ISO 2700 (Section 6.2), this is a paid service of ensuring that cyber-risk is being managed effectively. CBEST (Section 6.2.1) developed by the UK Bank of England for the Financial sector, also has an external audit and penetration test of security. The last two National Institute of Standards and Technology (NIST) (Section 6.2.2), developed in the USA and the Australian Signals Directorate (ASD) (Section 6.2.3) essential eight in Australia, are frameworks of recommended practice. All these approaches have strengths and weaknesses, and there is yet a lack of consensuses as to which framework is the best to follow for cybersecurity. Although elements of good practice can be gleamed from each approach, Section 6.1 considers legal frameworks and how they can reduce risk. Closely coupled to legal frameworks are accreditation mechanisms, considered in Section 6.2. Other mechanisms are considered in Section 6.3.

6.1 Legal Frameworks and Their Effects on Reducing Risk

One possible means of reducing risk in the area of cybersecurity is through mandatory reporting of breaches and legislated frameworks of practice. This is cybergovernance influenced by compliance. Another as will be discussed later has assurance mechanisms based on best practice, or some audited standard, which it could be argued is cybergovernance based on reputation or possibly accreditation. Legal or government policies in this area are a broad brush approach to reducing cyber-risks, as they are limited by the sovereign powers of states or economic unions. Nevertheless, they are essential for many firms wishing to do business in different parts of the world to consider how well their business comply with such mandatory requirements. This is also the case if cloud-based services from a domiciled entity are on the server in another country. Table 6.1 presents a summary of legislative approach across selected countries in this area.

As can be seen in Table 6.1, most legislative requirements are focused on the protection of privacy rights and address the issues of notifications of data breaches. Mandatory public notification of data breaches is required in the European Economic Union, the United Kingdom, and Australia. Notification to the government of data breaches is mandatory for severe incidents in China and India, while in New Zealand and Canada, complaints can be made to the Privacy Commissioners in each country, with a failure to notify the public about a data breach being taken into account by authorities in New Zealand. The legislative

Table 6.1 Legislative Approaches to Cybersecurity in Selected Countries

Country	*Legislation Related to Cybersecurity*	*Legal Requirements*	*Possible Penalties*
Australia	Privacy Amendment (Notifiable Data Breaches) Act 2017	Notify the public within 30 days of a data breach likely to result in serious harm.	Compensation orders, civil penalties up to $360,000 AUS for individuals and $1.8 million AUS for corporations.
United States	Varies across states and sectors. Federal Trade Commission has powers in deceptive practices in privacy and security policies.	Other important legislation is: Financial Services Modernization Act, Health Insurance Portability and Accountability Act.	Varies across states and sectors. Uncertain and depends on state jurisdiction. Litigation has only been used in 4% of data breach cases [34, p4]
European Economic Union	General Data Protection Regulation (GDPR)	Right to data portability, the principle of data protection by design and by default. All data breaches must be notified to the public within 72 h of occurrence.	Fines can be up to 2–4% of global turnover (sales). Alternatively, if higher 20–40 million EUR
European Economic Union	Network and Information Systems Directive (NIS)	Essential services and digital services must notify without undue delay breaches or incidents to authorities or response teams. States have powers to require information of an organizations network and information security	With individual member states. The Directive does, however, state that penalties must be effective, proportionate, and dissuasive.

(*Continued*)

Table 6.1 (*Continued*) Legislative Approaches to Cybersecurity in Selected Countries

Country	*Legislation Related to Cybersecurity*	*Legal Requirements*	*Possible Penalties*
The United Kingdom	Data Protection Act 2018	Enacts and extends the GPDR to when the UK leaves the EU. A breach must be reported to affected parties as soon as possible. Data must be correct; there is a right of access and erasure or restriction of processing	Same as the General Data Protection Regulation(GDPR). Directors or members of the organization can be prosecuted if the offence occurred with their consent, connivance or neglect.
New Zealand	Privacy Act 1993 with various amendments.	There is no requirement to notify a data breach to users. However, a failure to notify will be taken into account by the Privacy Commissioner when the complaint is received.	Can seek damages resulting from the breach. The system though is based on dispute resolution. Individuals can appeal to the Human Rights Commission for damages up to $200,000 NZ
Canada	Federal Personal Information Protection and Electronic Documents Act.	There is no requirement to notify a data breach to users. Complaints are made to the Office of the Privacy Commissioner (OPC). OPC does have investigative powers.	Penalties vary according to provincial jurisdictions for individuals from $10,000 to $100,000 CAN.

(*Continued*)

Table 6.1 (*Continued*) Legislative Approaches to Cybersecurity in Selected Countries

Country	*Legislation Related to Cybersecurity*	*Legal Requirements*	*Possible Penalties*
China	Cybersecurity Law	Provides a framework for other laws People's Republic of China (PRC) such as the illegal provision and access to data and data privacy. Security of networks is mandated. Data breaches must be reported to the government.	The graded approach of warnings and requirements to comply. Fines of up to 1 million Chinese Yuan. Corrections orders may be ten times the illegal gains from a data breach. Illegal sale of personal data is subject to the criminal code.
India	No legislation or privacy laws	There are rules of India IT ministry regarding privacy. Every organization must appoint a grievance officer related to privacy. Serious cyber incidents must be reported to the government.	Civil penalties for failure to protect individual data of up to 694,450. There are criminal penalties of 3 years and a fine of up to 6,950 or both for unlawful disclosure of information.

Source: Based on www.diapiper.com Accessed: 3 Sep 2019.

approach in the United States is piecemeal, with data breach legislation varying across states. Many states though follow the example of California, where data breach notifications must be made public past a threshold of harm (a reasonable likelihood or material harm [34, p. 483]). Three important US federal acts also impact on cybersecurity. They are legislation dealing with the Federal Trade Commission (FTC), Financial Services Modernization Act (FSMA), and the Health Insurance Portability and Accountability Act (HIPAA).

The FTC can take action if a company provides misleading claims about the extent of their data security. Since 2002, the FTC has pursued some 60 cases in this area [34]. The FSMA provides that when the financial information of customers is leaked, then there should be public and regulator notification as soon as possible. Lastly, HIPAA seeks to mandate public notifications of data breaches in health insurance and related areas based on a risk assessment. This risk assessment includes the nature and extent of the information leaked, the unauthorized person who used this information, whether the information was acquired or viewed, and whether and to what extent the risk of the data breach was mitigated.

These legislative approaches to reducing cyber-risk may provide an incentive for organizations to tighten processes and controls to avoid legal costs or damages to reputation from public notifications. As can be seen in Table 6.1, this would primarily be so for companies operating in the EU and the United Kingdom, and to a lesser extent, in Australia. The risk of data breaches in China may be more based on the sovereign risk that draws the ire of regulators, than in public exposure. One can also argue that legislative approaches in India, Canada, and New Zealand do not at this stage provide strong incentives in themselves for companies to manage cyber-risk in response to legal compliance. Some scholars also question the efficacy of data protection laws in mandating better cybersecurity, since such laws try "to balance two conflicting concepts, namely the provision of effective consumer protection and the prioritization of corporate cost mitigation [26, p. 302]. The law, in essence, is a blunt instrument in promoting cybersecurity. Another approach though is for the development of self-regulation through the adoption of accreditation and/or national frameworks of good practice in cybersecurity which is discussed next.

6.2 Accreditation and National Frameworks to Reduce Cyber-Risks

ISO 2700 Accreditation in cybersecurity is based on the ISO 2700:2018[1]). This set of audited standards are based on a review of the Information Security Management Systems (ISMS) of an organization. The ISMS is broad and includes policies, procedures, guidelines, and associated resources and activities. The ISMS is made up of the following essential principles:

[1] www.iso.org/standard/73906.html *Accessed:* 18 Jul 2018.

- Awareness of the need for information security.
- Assignment of responsibility for information security.
- Incorporating management commitment and the interest of stakeholders.
- Enhancing societal values.
- Risk assessments determining appropriate controls to reach an acceptable level of risk.
- Active prevention and detection of information security incidents.
- Ensuring a comprehensive approach to information security management.
- Continual reassessment of information security and the making of modifications as appropriate (ISO2700:2018(E)/IEC p. 12[2]).

The standard is based on a review of the process which includes

1. The management system
2. Identification of information assets and their security requirements
3. Assessing security risks
4. Monitoring and maintaining the effectiveness of controls associated with the organization's information assets (ISO/IEC, 2018, p. 14).

Of interest to this chapter are bullet points (3) how security risks are assessed and (4) monitoring and maintaining controls. Regarding risk assessment, this can be thought of regarding impact and likelihood.[3] This is shown in Figure 6.1.

The results of a risk assessment in cybersecurity may mean that for each identified risk there are the following approaches:

1. Tolerate the risk (bottom second dark gray third of the diagram of Figure 6.1).
2. Treat the risk by applying controls (lightest gray and white areas in Figure 6.1).
3. Terminate the risk by avoiding it (darkest gray section in the top right area in Figure 6.1).
4. Transfer the risk through insurance or agreement with other parties (also the darkest gray section, upper right hand corner area in Figure 6.1).

[2]Information technology-Security techniques-Information security management systems-Overview and vocabulary www.iso.org/standard/73906.html *Accessed:* 18 Jul 2018.

[3]IT governance. (2017). Implementing an ISMS: The nine step approach. In IT governance (Ed.), June 2017 ed. www.itgovernance.co.uk/resources/green-papers/implementing-an-isms *Accessed:* 31 Dec 2018.

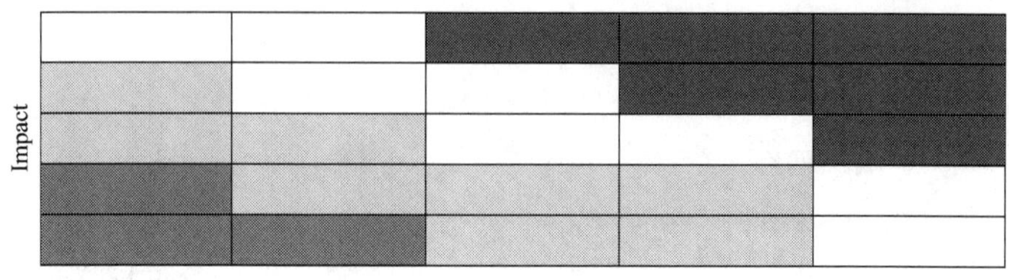

Figure 6.1: Risk Assessment Matrix: bottom second dark gray third of the diagram—tolerate the risk; Lighest gray and white areas—treat the risk by applying controls; darkest gray section in the top right—terminate the risk by avoiding it or transfer it through insurance or agreement with other parties. Gillies [55], p. 233 (with permission).

The organization also needs to have a level of risk tolerance, which may be influenced by legislation in that particular country or trading bloc. Of course, having a proper risk assessment requires three things: knowledge of the risks; the likelihood of occurrence; and the potential impact of the risks. While we discussed this in some detail in Chapter 5, it should be recognized that risks and threats in cyber are always evolving. Therefore, any attempt at accreditation should have an ongoing process of improvement and adaption to the threat landscape.

Controls are acknowledged as best practices to control risks. These include the design of systems, project requirements, and design stage. These can include awareness and training, avoiding risks to specific cyberattacks as discussed in this chapter and beyond. Monitoring and measuring of behaviors of people and systems and recording this are a crucial means of showing that the organization can be audited for an ISO standard. Gillies [56] suggests that a maturity or incremental approach can be used to start the implementation of ISO 2700. This is shown in Table 6.2.

The commitment stage is mostly a planning stage, which when completed leads to the development of systematic processes, which are then monitored. The data from this is then used in the improving stage, and finally, these processes and procedures can be embedded. Throughout all of these components, the risk is assessed and controlled as discussed previously.

There are as expected with such lengthy process barriers to implementation. One is the cost of consultants of around AUS $40,000 on average in 2011 [56]. The other is that certification is more a market signal than an improvement in the process to reduce risk [56]. For example, buyer/seller demands in outsourcing and offshoring have led to increased demands for certification in countries such as Taiwan, Singapore, and India [56]. The process is also much lengthier than other certification regimes and requires significant cultural change within an organization to be accepted [56]. To help overcome these barriers, it is suggested

Table 6.2 Two-Dimensional Matrix to Define Incremental Process of Obtaining ISO 2700 Certification

	F	U	C	K	E	D	!	
	OI	AM	HR	AC	IS	DS	IM	CO
Commitment								
Systematic								
Monitored								
Improving								
Embedded								

Source: Gillies A. (2011). Improving the quality of information security management systems with ISO27000. *The TQM Journal*, 23(4), 363.

Note: AC, access control; AM, asset management; CO, compliance; DS, development and maintenance; HR, human resources security; IM, information security Incident management; IS, information systems acquisition; OI, organizing information security; SP, security policy.

that organizations should motivate staff on the achievement of milestones as shown in Table 6.2. Business benefits (cost savings, efficiencies, reduction of risk) at each stage of the process should also be clearly demonstrated. ISO certification is not for every organization, there are some national frameworks that aim to reduce cyber-risk have been developed which can be implemented at a much reduced cost. These are outlined next.

6.2.1 CBEST

CBEST (not an acronym) is the framework of cybersecurity assurance for the United Kingdom financial system, which is supervised by the Bank of England.[4] Adoption of the framework is voluntary, and the approach of CBEST can also be applied to other sectors of the economy. The framework is intelligence led, that is the risk assessment is based on emerging threats and the threat entity's goals and orientations.[4] These threats are then modeled and intended to be used as a template for conducting a threat assessment by a penetration tester to develop threat-informed test scenarios.[4] There are thus four stages of the CBEST process:

1. Initiation
2. Threat Intelligence (TI) Phase
3. Penetration Testing (PT) Phase
4. Closure Phase

[4]CBEST Intelligence-Led testing (Bank of England, 2016). www.bankofengland.co.uk/financial-stability/financial-sector-continuity *Accessed:* 8 Feb 2019.

The initiation stage consists of outlining the CBEST process to relevant parties, outlining stakeholder roles and responsibilities, a discussion of security protocols, contractual considerations for all outside parties involved in the process, and the project schedule. This process is estimated to take 4–6 weeks.[4]

The TI stage is managed by an outside IT provider. This organization would include expertise in technology and TI. TI is intelligence about relevant threat actors and probable threat scenarios in cybersecurity. While the threat scenarios in this report are fictional, they are based on real-life cyberattacks, including the motivation of the attackers, their objectives, and the methods they employ to meet them.

The objective is to create a credible picture of the cyberthreat landscape based on evidence-backed TI, that is specifically tailored to the firm.[4] The TI prepares the threat report, which is reviewed by the regulator and the PT provider. A workshop is next conducted by the firm and the PT provider to obtain feedback. The TI provider then produces a second draft for management. The TI phase is expected to take around 10 weeks.

The PT phase involves a variety of manual and automated technologies to simulate an attack on the organization's security arrangements. The penetration test is based on tailored scenarios, threat actor goals from the threat report, and the business case to consider these. As a result of the penetration test, a review is compiled of test performance, identified vulnerabilities, any mitigating factors and how such attacks can be mitigated. This process also is expected to be around 10 weeks in duration.

The closure phase concludes this process with the production of an Intelligence, Detection, and Response report, which is reviewed by the regulator. Any issues not met in the CBEST process so far can be included in a further remediation plan. All the TI and PT parties along with the firm then undertake a final debrief that consists of

- Which activities/deliverables progressed well
- Which activities/deliverables could have been improved
- Which aspects of the CBEST process worked well
- Which aspects of the CBEST process could be improved
- Any other feedback.

Overall, this part of the process takes 10 weeks. Following the debrief there are another 6–12 months of supervision of the remediation plan. As with any approach to reducing cyber-risk, there are problems with the CBEST approach. One is a reluctance by organizations to have penetration tests on production systems for fear that the test might accidently cause the real-life system to fail [110]. Also, the accountability to the consumer of this process is also lacking [110].

It is also a lengthy process, taking over a year to complete. Nevertheless, CBEST provides a realistic examination of cyber-risks, tests these risks with a simulated attack, and provides a response and remediation plan as the result of this process. Principles of the CBEST approach may also apply to many large organizations other than financial institutions in the United Kingdom.

Cyber Nugget 33: *All organizations can benefit from the principles in CBEST, especially in being alert to the threat environment and mitigating controls of this to prevent business risks.*

6.2.2 Framework for Improving Critical Infrastructure Cybersecurity or the National Institute of Standards and Technology (NIST) Framework

Often called the NIST framework after the eponymous department which produced these guidelines, NIST, the Framework for Improving Critical Infrastructure Cybersecurity, is a set of procedures to minimize cyber-risk. The NIST framework was developed by executive order in the United States.[5] Like CBEST it is a voluntary governance structure, aimed at managing cyber-risk in critical infrastructure. Unlike CBEST the NIST framework is not audited by regulators or involves PT. The NIST framework is based on the following approaches to manage cyber-risk:

1. **A Framework core**, in which a set of desired cyberactivities, desired outcomes, and relevant references are common across the critical infrastructure sectors. In essence, these are functions described as identify, protect, detect, respond, and recover. When taken together, these functions represent the management of cyber-risk.

2. **Framework Implementation Tiers** provide context on how an organization views and manages cybersecurity risk and the processes designed to manage that risk. The tiers represent a progression of sophistication in dealing with cybersecurity from Partial (Tier 1) to Adaptive (Tier 4). As such, this represents what is called the maturity model of managing cybersecurity.

3. **A Framework profile** This represents the outcomes based on business needs that an organization has selected from the Framework Categories and Subcategories. To develop a Framework profile, a business mission and risk assessment is undertaken for all categories and subcategories.

[5] US Gov doi.org/10.6028/NIST.CSWP.04162018 www.nist.gov/publications/framework-improving-critical-infrastructure-cybersecurity-version-11 *Accessed:* 24 Dec 2018.

> This can be seen as a process as embedding risk assessment with the nature of the business, and therefore, cybersecurity becomes an essential driver of management and governance.[5]

Like the ISO 2700 standard and CBEST, the management of risk is the heart of this framework. This is encapsulated in the framework core, Figure 6.2.

As shown therein, categories represent essential business processes such as asset management and identity management and control. Subcategories are specific technical or management activities that help to support each category. These can include, for example, Data at rest is protected and Notifications from detection systems are investigated. Informative references are standards, guidelines, and practices common across infrastructure sectors, and so provide the benchmarks for categories and subcategories. The five framework core functions can be summarized as follows:

1. **Identify.** Where an organizational understanding is developed to manage cybersecurity risks across systems, people, assets, and capabilities. Examples of this function include asset management, business environment, governance, risk assessment, and risk management strategy.

2. **Protect.** Which involves developing and implementing appropriate safeguards to ensure the delivery of critical services. This may include identity management and control, access control, awareness and training, data security, information management protection processes and procedures, maintenance, and protective technology.

3. **Detect.** This focuses on the activities to identify an occurrence of a cybersecurity event. Example outcomes are anomalies and events, security continuous monitoring, and detection processes.

4. **Respond.** Which focuses on activities to take action regarding a detected cybersecurity incident. This includes response planning, communication analysis, mitigation, and improvements.

5. **Recover.** Which considers the activities to provide timely recovery to normal operations to reduce the impact of a cybersecurity incident. Such activities include recovery planning, improvements, and communications. Across these critical functions for each of the business categories is the maturity level of understanding of risk and participation. These are described in Table 6.3. As can be seen, there is assessment here of how formalized and accepted cybersecurity is in the organization from partial to an adaptive (future-orientated approach). Interestingly, unlike ISO 2700 and CBEST, there is a broader examination of the role of the organization in a supply chain or ecosystem with respect to cyber-risk (see external participation).

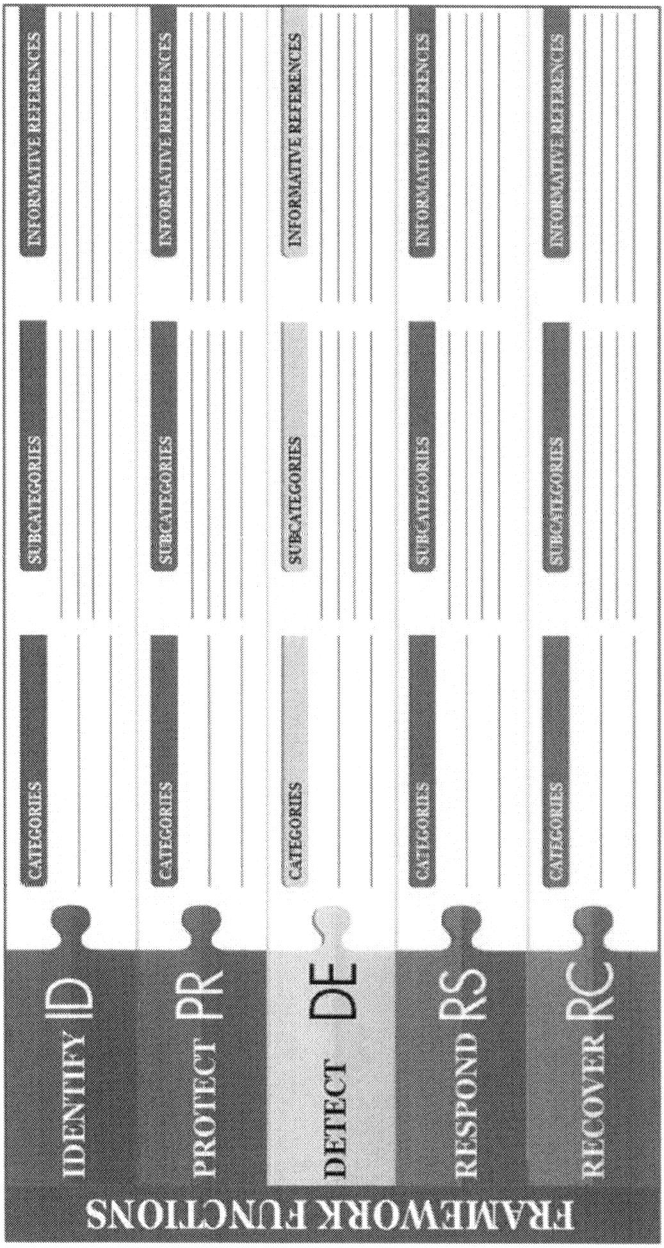

Figure 6.2: NIST Framework core structure. (Source: NIST [9])

Table 6.3 Tiers in the NIST Framework

	Tier 1: Partial	*Tier 2: Risk Informed*	*Tier 3: Repeatable*	*Tier 4: Adaptive*
Risk management process	Risk management is not formalized and is dealt with in an ad-hoc manner	Risk management is approved by management but not established as an extensive organizational policy.	Risk management practices are formally approved and expressed as policy. These are updated concerning the threat landscape.	The organization adapts its cybersecurity practices based on lessons learnt and predictive indicators
Integrated risk management program	Limited awareness of cyber-risk. Risk management is on a case-by-case basis	There is an awareness of cybersecurity risk at the organizational level. However, a broad organizational approach to management of this has not been developed. No processes to share cybersecurity information	There is an organization-wide approach to managing cyber-risk. Risk management policies and procedures are implemented and reviewed. Senior executives ensure consideration of cybersecurity throughout the organization. There is monitoring of cyber-risks on all assets.	The organization-wide approach to managing cyber-risk considers potential events. A clear relationship between organizational and cybersecurity objectives. Budgets based on an understanding of risk. Cyber-risk is part of the organizational culture

(*Continued*)

Table 6.3 (*Continued*) Tiers in the NIST Framework

	Tier 1: Partial	*Tier 2: Risk Informed*	*Tier 3: Repeatable*	*Tier 4: Adaptive*
External participation	The organization does not understand its role in a broader ecosystem concerning cyber. Does not share information or receive information from other entities	The organization understands its role in the ecosystem, concerning either its dependencies or dependents but not both.	The organization understands its role, dependencies, and dependents in the ecosystem. Moreover, many contribute to the community's broader understanding of risks.	The organization understands its role, dependencies, and dependents in the ecosystem and many contribute to the community's broader understanding of risks. It receives and generates intelligence on the threat landscape and communicates this proactively and formally to the supply chain.

Source: NIST (2018, p. 6).

The advantage of the NIST framework over the ISO 2700 and CBEST approach is that it asks organizations in an ecosystem or supply chain to consider cybersecurity as a collective responsibility. The other advantage is the use of graded approaches as shown in Table 6.3, which allows organizations to self-assess their degree of risk minimization. The disadvantage of the NIST framework is the lack of outside audit or oversight, and the complexity of this framework may be beyond many small businesses. For the sake of simplicity and therefore broad adoption, there also exists some more straightforward frameworks to reduce cyber-risk. One of these is the Australian Signals Directorate (ASD) essential eight, which is discussed next.

6.2.3 The Australian Signals Directorate Essential Eight

The ASD essential eight consists of three groups of procedures designed to reduce cyber-risk. These can be broadly grouped as

1. Mitigation strategies to prevent malware delivery and execution in the first place. Four recommendations on the ideas of *whitelisting*, i.e., only allowing approved applications, and commonly used, but risky software.

2. Mitigation strategies to limit the extent of cybersecurity incidents. Three recommendations on access control and patching.

3. Mitigation strategies to recover data and system availability, based on good backup practices.

One recommendation, Table 6.4, outlines this framework in more detail and justifies the eight approaches to reduce cyber-risk (Australian CyberSecurity Centre, p. 2[6]).

The essential eight is a much easier checklist for many organizations to implement quickly to reduce cyber-risk than the other more detailed frameworks discussed so far. The framework is designed to prevent more common forms of cyberattacks. Research by the ASD, for example, in 2011, suggested that around 85% of attacks could be prevented by adopting this framework (ASD, 2013[7]). The essential eight can also be adopted for low- to high-risk environments by the use of a maturity model, or graduated set of mitigation strategies from a maturity level of zero (not aligned with a mitigation strategy), to the maturity level of four for higher risk environments (Australian Cyber Security Centre, 2018[8]). While the essential eight provides an implementable and straightforward

[6]https://acsc.gov.au/publications/protect/essential-eight-maturity-model.htm *Accessed:* 31 Jul 2018.

[7]The top four strategies to mitigate targeted cyber intrusions are mandatory for Australian Government agencies as of April 2013. www.asd.gov.au/infosec/mitigationstrategies.htm *Accessed:* 31 Jul 2018.

[8]`Essentialeightmaturitymodel.Canberra,Australia: AustralianGovernment` Retrieved from https://acsc.gov.au/publications/protect/essential-eight-maturity-model.htm *Accessed:* 31 Jul 2018.

Table 6.4 Essential Eight Mitigation Strategies

Mitigation Strategies to Prevent Malware Delivery and Execution	
1. Application whitelisting of approved/trusted programs to prevent the execution of unapproved/malicious programs, including .exe, DLL, scripts (e.g. Windows Script Host, Power-Shell and HTA) and installers. **Why:** All nonapproved applications (including malicious code) are prevented from executing.	**2. Patch applications,** e.g. Flash, web browsers, Microsoft Office, Java and PDF viewers. Patch/mitigate computers with extreme risk vulnerabilities within 48 h. Use the latest version of applications. **Why:** Security vulnerabilities in applications can be used to execute malicious code on systems.
3. Configure Microsoft Office macro settings to block macros from the Internet, and only allow vetted macros either in trusted locations with limited write access or digitally signed with a trusted certificate. **Why:** Microsoft Office macros can be used to deliver and execute malicious code on systems.	**4. User application hardening.** Configure web browsers to block Flash (ideally uninstall it), ads, and Java on the Internet. Disable unneeded features in Microsoft Office (e.g., OLE), web browsers, and PDF viewers. **Why:** Flash, ads, and Java are popular ways to deliver and execute malicious code on systems.

(*Continued*)

Table 6.4 (*Continued*) Essential Eight Mitigation Strategies

Mitigation Strategies to Limit the Extent of Cybersecurity Incidents	
5. Restrict administrative privileges to operating systems and applications based on user duties. Regularly revalidate the need for privileges. Don't use privileged accounts for reading email and web browsing. **Why:** Admin accounts are the keys to the kingdom. Adversaries use these accounts to gain full access to information and systems.	**6. Patch operating systems** Patch/mitigate computers (including network devices) with extreme risk vulnerabilities within 48 h. Use the latest operating system version. Don't use unsupported versions. **Why:** Security vulnerabilities in operating systems can be used to further the compromise of systems.
7. Multifactor authentication including for virtual private networks (VPNs), RDP, SSH and other remote access, and for all users when they perform a privileged action or access an important (sensitive/high-availability) data repository. **Why:** Stronger user authentication makes it harder for adversaries to access sensitive information and systems.	
Mitigation Strategies to Recover Data and System Availability	
8. Daily backups of important new/changed data, software, and configuration settings, stored disconnected, retained for at least 3 months. Test restoration initially, annually, and when IT infrastructure changes. **Why:** To ensure information can be reaccessed following a cybersecurity incident (e.g., after a successful ransomware incident).	

means to manage most cyber-risks, the degree of adoption of the framework is not audited or monitored. The framework also deals with known risks; it does not, like CBEST, consider TI and how to respond to this. Unlike the NIST and ISO 2700 frameworks, there is no systematic level examination of risk and how it effects the business mission and operations of the organization. For small and medium enterprises, though the essential eight represents a good start on the path to managing cyber-risk.

6.3 Other Approaches to Corporate Governance to Reduce Cyber-Risk

Not surprisingly, there are some related approaches to managing cyber-risk by using existing governance frameworks. One approach is to use auditing standards for service organizations, such as accounting standards. Examples are International Accounting Standards on the Assurance of Engagements and ISE3402 the Assurance reports on Controls at a Service Organization SSAE16 [30, p. 346]. The SSAE16 requires organizations that meet this standard to have audited information on data controls and privacy. The levels of controls and privacy policies are also judged as to how well the objectives of each policy is met. Unfortunately, there is no requirement to disclose the extent of certification of these standards by professional auditors [30]. Another way of reducing cyber-risks is by a governance approach, whereby cybersecurity forms part of the audit committee of the board, and the board is given responsibility to monitor cyber-risks, just as it should provide financial risks of the firm [21,91].[9] The success of this approach has been shown to depend on how well board members understand the cyber-risks and how to deal with them [12]. Rothrock et al. [115] suggested that good governance practices in cybersecurity should be based on the following factors:

1. **Educated company leadership.** Cybersecurity needs to be seen as a business risk and not an IT issue. Having one board member who is knowledgeable on cybersecurity is seen as a good corporate practice.

2. **Developing a universal language of cybersecurity as a risk.** People who provide advice to boards from a specialist area must be able to communicate this as a business risk. Also, the board needs advice on practices that affect the entire company and the priorities that need to be considered in cybersecurity.

[9] CreditUnionDirectorsNewsletter.(2017).Cybersecurityrequiresa vigilantboard.CreditUnionDirectorsNewsletter,43,4--4. *Accessed:* 31 Dec 2018.

3. **Distinguish between security and resilience.** Resilience here is the services the company needs to provide by allowing others to access its data and interact with their systems. For many organizations, this business model must be balanced with the cyber-risks.

4. **Make security and resilience strategic business issues.** As discussed with the previous frameworks (ISO 2700, CBEST, NIST and Essential Eight), there is a need for the organization to adopt these as part of its business strategy. There should also be a discussion of what risks in cyber to avoid, control, and transfer through insurance. Cyber-risks that need to be managed should also have resources deployed (systems, people, and training) to meet them.

6.4 Cyber Warfare

There are different motivations for cyberattacks, ranging as we have already seen, from direct financial gain through to interference at a state level. The last couple of years have seen huge news coverage of interference in national elections by foreign powers. Apart from the dissemination of fake news, there are also vulnerabilities in the mechanism of voting itself. In fact, paper votes may actually be more secure than electronic voting systems.[10]

Such state actors can be devastatingly effective. According to The Economist, a report by CrowdStrike found Russia ranks first in terms of the *breakout time*.[11] This is the time from getting in to a network to reaching something juicy, say a server with secret information. North Korea came second, with China a distant third.

6.5 Conclusion and Recommendations

Can the risk of the unknown be managed? As can be seen in this chapter, the costs of cybercrime and the risks associated with it are considerable and evolving. No one approach can protect any organization entirely from attack in this area. The risks, however, from what we know can be minimized. It is up to organizations and their senior management to consider the nature of the risk and to what extent they accept or manage the risk from cyberattacks. The increased pressure from legislation, and the fact that many organizations have services in

[10] www.nature.com/articles/d41586-018-06611-x?utm_source=briefing-wk&utm_medium=email&utm_campaign=briefing&utm_content=20180907 *Accessed:* 8 Sep 2018.

[11] www.economist.com/science-and-technology/2019/03/09/in-the-cyber-break-in-stakes-the-champion-is-russia?cid1=cust/ddnew/email/n/n/20190311n/owned/n/n/ddnew/n/n/n/nAP/Daily_Dispatch/email&etear=dailydispatch&utm_source=newsletter&utm_medium=email&utm_campaign=Daily_Dispatch&utm_term=20190311 *Accessed:* 12 Mar 2019.

different jurisdictions, mean that cybersecurity should be seen as a fundamentally important board and senior management issue. What time and expense the organization commits to managing cyber-risks needs to be considered within its overall risk profile and viability. There are some framework and approaches discussed in this chapter, which the senior management can implement to reduce and manage cyber-risk. Whatever is chosen, there is an essential role for internal auditing of cyber-risks, separate from those who report these risks and how they are managed, as there is for an outside certification and auditing.

What is also important is that cybersecurity is a movable feast, risks can only be managed against what is known. Advances in technology, human frailty, and business models of criminals and motives of hostile states, mean that no organization can consider itself secure at all times.

Chapter 7

Technical Perspectives

The aim of this chapter is to provide some technical background for the book. From the vast domain of computer and network technology, we pick out the elements that have had, or may have, cybersecurity implications. The dominant area is the nature of computer networks, their structure, and how they may be compromised. An important component of network security is encryption, where we outline the basic ideas and explain the potential threats from quantum computing, and the desire of governments to have backdoor encryption keys.

Trust and identity are essential to computer security, but we currently exist in two parallel universes. In the one we have major advances in identification and certification, from biometrics (Section 7.6) to blockchain (Section 7.14). In the other we have basic security principles subverted by individual and social factors.

We begin with the fundamental element of security and trust on the web, cryptography, how we exchange private keys, compress and sign messages, and the fundamental idea of public–private key (PPK) crytography (Section 7.1). After introducing some basic technical points (Section 7.2), we consider symmetric encryption (shared password) in Section 7.3, and the way the proliferation of cryptographic keys is managed in Section 7.4. Email is a major source of trouble, and we consider it from a variety of angles in Section 7.13.

Some rough knowledge of network architecture is helpful to understanding cyberattacks (Section 7.7), with layers being discussed in Section 7.7.1, general security in Section 7.8, and the Dark Web in Section 7.10.

The chapter ends with a few areas of emerging importance, blockchains (Section 7.14), quantum computing (Section 7.16), and new regulations on privacy (Section 7.15).

7.1 Public–Private Key (PPK) Cryptography

With the huge rise in e-commerce and administration over the Web, one of the most important algorithms in history must be the PPK framework.

Encryption goes back in history way before silicon computers. But historical computing was mostly *symmetric:* the same password, or key, was used to encrypt and decrypt the message (Section 7.3). One of the best, in fact unbreakable, codes of bygone times was the *one-time pad.* The message is matched letter by letter with the text of a code book, say a novel. The two letters are combined in some way to give a new code letter. To decode the encrypted message, the same code book is used. Since each letter almost always becomes a different letter in the code, the code is effectively uncrackable. Stream cyphers, such as RC4 discussed in Section 7.3.2, effectively use this idea.

Suppose our code message is *Aircraft carrier steaming towards Outer Hebrides destined for Scarpa Flow arriving beginning of next week* and our code book is Tolstoy's Anna Karenin and we have from the code book *Happy families are all alike; every unhappy family is unhappy in its own way*, then we XOR the characters one, at a time, to get the coded message (in hex) *090802130b4100154d0a0d1b171a45135216540 40d01490f0b491f0a4c4117121 6523655010b1a4138151b520f05081a4c1d451a07491b0b0c41161f0b003a0d41 1b041200291b024f0041185c.*

This is a *symmetric* cypher—encrypting and decrypting require the same, shared, password or key. Section 7.3 considers symmetric encryption in more detail. But the big challenge is how to manage encryption when there is no shared key. In other words how do we get by without one, or how do we securely exchange a password using the same channel as that on which we would like to use a symmetric key. Thus we consider asymmetric algorithms first.

7.2 Some Preliminary Concepts

Throughout the technical discussion, a couple of concepts recur frequently: trapdoor or hash functions; and discrete logarithms. A trapdoor function does exactly what it sounds like. It's easy to go one way but not back in the other direction. A hash function is its mathematical realization. Many articles have been written on hash functions, measuring their speed and effectiveness, reversibility, and so on. The idea is simple though. We take a big set of something or other and assign the elements to a much smaller set of bins. So finding which bin to put something in is easy. But finding out where something in a bin came from is hard or impossible.

A simple (not very good hash) for a set of numbers, would be to divide them by, say eight, and put them in bins determined by the remainder. One might imagine a hash function for clothes, which has bins for trousers, shoes, shirts, and so on.

But this would not be a very good one, since similar things are in the same bin. Ideally we want completely different things in each bin. Using the country of manufacture would be a little bit better. Even better, closer to an actual hash function, would be to concatenate some identifiers, such as shirtmale32cottonbluechina, view this as a number,

115104105114116109971081015150991111161161111098108117101991041
0511097L

and take the remainder dividing by our old friend the Jupiter number (for 551 bins). We get 16. Now make a tiny change to size 33, we get 361. Size 34 gives 155.

The discrete logarithm is the cornerstone of modern cryptography. Suppose we have an equation

$$x = M^a \tag{7.1}$$

To find a, we can use logs

$$a = \frac{\log x}{\log M} \tag{7.2}$$

This is fine if we want to get an estimate of a. An old-fashioned calculator will do that. However, if M, x, a are exact integers, this turns out to be a hard problem, an extremely hard problem if they are large integers. The discrete logarithm problem underlies two of the major PPK algorithms, RSA (Section 7.2.3) and Elliptic Curve Cryptography (ECC) (Section 7.2.4).

7.2.1 Asymmetric Cyphers

Public-Private Key Cryptography (PPKC) is asymmetric. This is easy to understand. If we take 7 and multiply by 5 we get 35. If we want to get 7 back, we have to multiply by 0.2. To get the basic idea though, let's use English words as an example. imagine a dual code word, say, *snapdragon,* which splits into two words, *snap* and *dragon*. Although this is obvious here, the key idea is that it takes a huge amount of computer time to split up this dual code. We shall come across this idea of computer time thresholds elsewhere, such as when we discuss cryptocurrencies such as bitcoin (Section 7.14).

From *snap*, we now derive a public key in this example by choosing a related word, say, *photo*. From dragon we derive the private key, say, *fire*. Thus our public key is *photo,* and we give this to everybody. Our private key is *fire.* To encrypt a message and sign it, we use *fire*, and anybody can decrypt the document and check the signature using *photo.* Signatures will be an important topic of discussion later (Section 7.4.2). If somebody wants to send a message to us, which only we can read, they encrypt it with *photo*. At this point we need *fire* to read it. Even the sender cannot decrypt the message, since they have only our public key, *photo*.

There are two vulnerabilities in this scheme: *technical,* in that it can be broken with enough computing power; and human, where the private key is not adequately guarded.

Cyber Nugget 34: *Most commonly used cryptographic algorithms can be broken with sufficient computing power (and hence may only last for a finite time).*

Now security agencies and law enforcement are becoming increasingly worried about illicit use of encryption. Two approaches under discussion or already implemented are backdoor keys (Section 7.4.3) and decryption enforcement (Section 8.2). Suppose Angus has a code word *crabapple, crab* his public key and *apple* his private key. Brenda has chosen *pineapple.* A backdoor key might be a word like *granny-smith,* which would decrypt all apple-based code words.

Cyber Nugget 35: *It is essential to know what the crytographic algorithm in use is in order to know if there are backdoor keys.*

7.2.2 Diffie–Hellman, with Apologies to Mary Poppins

A fundamental idea at the heart of PPK exchange is the gslgdh key exchange. If Christine and Doris want to exchange an encrypted document, then they both need the password to encrypt and decrypt. Obviously, they don't want anybody else to know the password, hence they have to choose something really private, for example, the name of the cute boy they met at the fairground where they went for Christine's 12th birthday. Apart from the risk that one of them has mentioned him on Facebook, can they create a truly random password and exchange it over a public channel?

Cyber Nugget 36: *Make sure that secret items from your past do not get shared on social media if you intend to use them as passwords.*

It turns out that they can, thanks to Diffie and Hellman [41]. Let's illustrate this with a simple example using English words. A real mathematical example is given in Section 7.2.2.1. First Christine and Doris choose a big word. They go for broke with *supercalifragilisticexpialidocious*. Since lots of people know this very big word, it's easy to guess. But that doesn't matter. They then need a fragment from this word and choose *list*. Since there are not many real words you can pick out of this monster word, other people might pick this too. Again it doesn't matter. So the big word and the fragment can be shared over a public channel, such as email.

Now it gets serious. Christine chooses a secret fragment, say *doci* and Doris chooses *frag*. Now both of them pass their secret fragment through a special function, which we call a *trapdoor function*. The idea is simple. It's easy to go one way (fall through the trapdoor, but very difficult to go the other way). (In the example, which follows the trapdoor is called a discrete logarithm) (see Section 7.2). Thus Christine ends up with *blue* and Doris with *bong*. Now it's very hard to go back through the trapdoor and convert *bong* to frag. Thus Christine and Doris can exchange these new words over email, Facebook, or anything else, with a small risk that somebody will work out that the secret words are *doci* and *frag*. Remember, though, that this may still be subject to the caveat of Cyber Nugget 34.

So, Christine gets *bong* from Doris and now applies another related trapdoor function (it could be the same one) and gets *expia*. Meanwhile Doris applies the same trapdoor function to *blue* and again gets *expia*. Thus, the shared secret key is *expia*, everything has gone over a public channel, except of course, the secret key.

7.2.2.1 Numerical Example

Here is a simple example. For the underlying algebra, the interested reader could check any number of online resources, or books such as Stallings', such as [133]. The code word we choose is 19. We need a number smaller than 19 called a *primitive root*, in this case, for 19 it is 10.

Ingrid now picks her secret key, say, 3. She then computes 10^3 and finds the remainder after dividing by 19, which is 12. It's easy to do that with pencil and paper.

Horatio picks his secret key, say 16, and does the same, the remainder this time is also 4. That's a bit harder, and you would probably need a computer to do it.

Ingrid sends 12 to Horatio and he sends 4 to Ingrid. Now Ingrid calculates $4^3 = 64$, which has a remainder after dividing by 19 of 7. Pencil and paper suffices for this too. However, Horatio definitely needs a computer to calculate $12^{16} = 184884258895036416$, which also has a remainder of 7. The shared key is 7. Magic!

7.2.3 The RSA Algorithm

Diffie and Hellman have proposed a way of exchanging a secret key, but the next big step forward was to develop a goo trapdoor function and hence the first PPK system. With over 20,000 citations, the RSA algorithm [112], named after its inventors, Ron Rivest, Adi Shamir, and Leonard Adleman, achieved this.

It uses the same modulo arithmetic as Diffie–Hellman, but it masks the private keys. If you know that the product of two big prime numbers p and q is N, then if you know one, you can find the other, albeit with a bit of work. This is such a beautiful algorithm, that we include it here. The details are not essential to the rest of the book and the reader can happily jump onto the next section. However, it is quite useful to know what public and private keys are all about. Some egregious security flaws, through overuse of private keys or the superlarge primes, are discussed in Section 2.9.

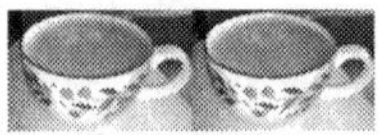

To make life easy, we will work with a smallish product of two primes, we call the Jupiter number. Mozart, like some other composers, was fascinated by numbers[1] and his last symphony, the Jupiter, K551 just happens to factor into the two primes 29 and 19 We now apply some jiggerypokery from 18th century mathematician Euler to get a public key of 41 and. private key of 209 or vice versa. Now a message is just a number (just think of all the bits for each character concatenated to form a very big binary number) So, let's take an arbitrary message, say 304 and raise it to the power of 43 (you need special software for this, but its native to python, for example) We get

58018179210088436959727197583445691443910892153587912023186811
17746
12290743252641752146827919013060662001664L

The L just means a very long integer.

We now take its remainder with respect to 551 and we get 247, which is the encrypted message. Now raise this to the power of 211 (the private key) to get

72286490079395129918244078561406902288041832966123971488063567976
6238
11868046215709265327656893476547521102042235645380013098787834866
8541
15816184714365623025438101603030394604627252707347313795665148255
5208
20290049356146063369515883681011309055647988999470421544271280944
1468
73625850607754689876932104584220233562591810894034479566410152155
1990
71109356553761893812965454749179668529404341768101339681184797411
0618
40445345482476810134452108484117975808339142915174415478006940711
6026
556456767538210867070077752103L

[1]www.theguardian.com/music/2013/apr/05/mozart-bach-music-numbers-codes *Accessed:* 26 Dec 2018.

If we take the remainder of this monster after dividing by the Jupiter number we get 304, the original message (Try it :)

Wikipedia gives the current largest known prime as $2^{82,589,933} - 1$, which has 24,862,048 digits.[2] It would be a bit of an effort to use primes this big. The 2,048 bit encryption, which is about the strongest in current use, uses numbers a little over 600 digits long, still a bit bigger than the Jupiter number.

7.2.3.1 The Really Hairy Part

To get numbers 43 and 211, we need Euler's Totient function [133], which gives the number primes less than some given number. For a product of two primes, p, q, this is simply $(p-1)(q-1)$

$$M^T = M^{(p-1)(q-1)} \mod N = 1 \tag{7.3}$$

where p, q are the two primes (19,29) and $T = (p-1)(q-1)$ is the number of primes less than $N = p * q = 29 * 19 = 551$, in this case $28 * 18 = 504$

Now we pick a number, in this case 43 (there are a few restrictions on what this number can be, but won't elaborate on them here). Then we look for another number, which when we multiply it by 43 and take the remainder with respect to 551 (this is actually called the multiplicative inverse). The number we find is 211, so that $43 * 211 \mod 504 = 1$

So, suppose Fred wants to send a personal message to Fiona. He encrypts the message, say 63 (this would of course be a block of text converted to a number), and raises it to the power of 43 (Fiona's private key). Fiona raises it again to the power of 211 (her private key) and gets the original message back. Here is some python code to do just this

```
#!/usr/bin/python
FredMessage=63**43 # Raise arbitrary number (63) to
   power of 43
print FredMessage  # This is a huge number
             # Fiona's public  key, 43, encrypting the
             message 63
FionaDecode=FredMessage**211 # Fiona her private key,
   211
print FionaDecode # This is an even bigger number
TheMessage=FionaDecode%551 # Take the remainder with
   the Jupiter number
print 'Decoded Message is ', TheMessage # Back to 63,
   Fred's message
```

[2]https://en.wikipedia.org/wiki/Largest_known_prime_number *Accessed:* 26 Dec 2018.

Cyber Nugget 37: *It is possible to create a shared, secret password, using only public channels, thanks to Diffie–Hellman.*

7.2.4 Elliptic Curve Cryptography (ECC)

There is not just one algorithm now: apart from the original prime number-based algorithms, newer methods such as elliptic curve are in common use. They still implicitly rely on the difficulty of the discrete logarithm problem. Also in major use now is ECC. Just like the prime number algorithm, this relies on something that is dead easy using a calculator to get an approximation, but is extremely difficult when pure integers are involved. If we draw an arbitrary curve, $y(x)$, in this case an elliptic curve, which has the cube as its highest power of x, then a few of the points on this curve will have integer x or y values. Finding certain relationships between pairs of points on the curve, which have exact integer values is an extremely hard problem, and hence a candidate for a PPK system. ECC is faster for a given level of breakability (how much computer power would be needed to crack it). So, a 256 bit ECC key is equivalent to a 3,072 bit RSA key. Outside the cryptography world, these numbers don't mean much. But there is an important point to note:

Cyber Nugget 38: *Choose the highest key size for any given method, but don't try to compare key sizes across methods.*

A popular such elliptic curve is Curve25519, which uses integer solutions of the elliptic curve equation [14]

$$y^2 = x^3 + 486662x^2 + x \tag{7.4}$$

which draws numbers from the range up to 2^{255-19}, about 10^{76}. WhatsApp,[3] for example, makes extensive use of Curve25519 for the secret password exchange at the bottom of Figure 7.1. ECC has the advantage that no precomputation (Section 7.5.3.3) attack has so far been found [19]. In May 2019, WhatsApp revealed a serious security breach allowing spyware onto the phone. This was not a problem with the cryptography, but with other aspects of how the app integrates with the phone.

[3]www.whatsapp.com/security/ *Accessed:* 24 Dec 2018.

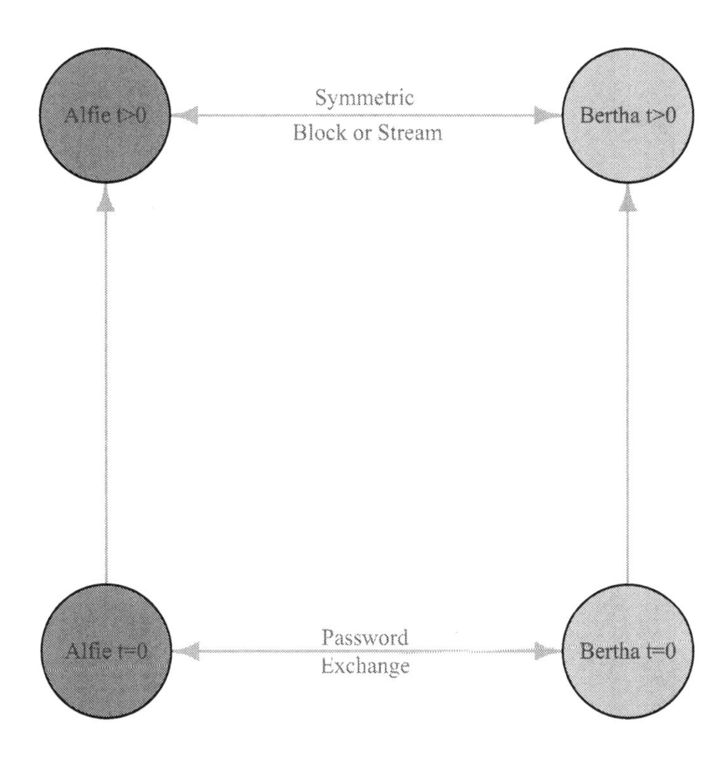

Figure 7.1: The basic principle behind end-to-end encryption for communication. Alfie and Bertha first established a shared password at time zero. They then encrypt all traffic from then on using a symmetric cypher, in this case AES-256, much faster and just as secure.

7.3 Symmetric Encryption

PPK is the gold standard for sending a message to people or machines, where there is no shared key. However, it is considerably slower than *symmetric* encryption, where both parties have a shared password. We saw in Section 7.2.2 that Diffie–Hellman provides a way of establishing a secret, shared key, as does PPK cryptography. This shared key can now be used in faster symmetric encryption.

There are different types of symmetric encryption:

- Block cyphers (Section 7.3.1), where the message, be it text, images, video, or some mixture, is broken up into block, and each block is encrypted with the same password.
- Stream cyphers (Section 7.3.2), where each byte is encrypted individually using a key stream.

7.3.1 Advanced Encryption Standard (AES)

Advanced Encryption Standard (AES), also known by its original name Rijndael, is a specification for the encryption of electronic data established by National Institute of Standards and Technology (NIST) 2001, following an open competition won by Joan Daemen and Vincent Rijmen, hence the portmanteau name. It comes in various strengths. At the time of writing some applications still use 128 bit, but AES-256, 256 bit, is much stronger and to be preferred.

The algorithm is complicated and the details are not needed here. However, the ever important point is to keep the software up to date with the latest standards because

- algorithms continue to improve;
- security flaws may be discovered;
- and computers keep getting faster, meaning that key lengths need to increase.

7.3.2 Stream Cyphers

Before computers, the best encryption used by spies everywhere was the one-time pad, which we saw at the beginning of Section 7.1. Each letter in the message was combined (nowadays using an XOR operation) with a letter from a code book. Such a code book could be anything, a novel even, from which letters were taken one by one and never reused.

The one-time pad is uncrackable without the code book. Online though, this presents a challenge, since the code book would have to be stored somewhere. Thus schemes, which generate a unique, pseudo-random stream of characters are needed. One of the most prominent of these was Ron Rivest's RC4.[4]

RC4 was a clever way of using a string of 256 bytes as the code book, in such a way that it changed every time a byte in the string was used, such that the same letter would repeatedly map to different values in the encrypted output. The algorithm, however, has vulnerabilities, which have been addressed in later versions. Its simplicity, however, makes it very fast and thus useful for encoding long messages.

7.4 Keys Galore

Even a small computer, today, such as a smartphone, has dozens of keys (passwords), which serve a variety of functions, from encrypting the hard disk to communication protocols, such as HyperText Transfer Protocol (HTTP)

[4]http://people.csail.mit.edu/rivest/faq.html#Ron *Accessed:* 24 Dec 2018.

(Section 7.7.1.5). If the hard disk is large, the encrypting might take some considerable time. Thus, every time you change the password, you don't want to re-encrypt it.

Moreover, there might be several users with access to the hard disk, each with a different user password. The way around both problems is to have two keys: the Data Encrypting Key (DEK) is used to encrypt the data, say the hard disk; the Key-Encrypting Key (KEK) encrypts this key, and maybe a lot of other keys besides. On a mac, this is referred to as a key chain. Sometimes access to the KEKs is via the user password, but changing this does not require changing all the keys within it.

Now consider having a giant, encrypted database. Re-encrypting this would be a serious amount of work, yet it may have many users, who come and go frequently. Every time a user leaves an organization, resecuring the database would be a huge effort. A key manager then comes to the rescue.

Access to the database goes via an intermediate authorization agent. It checks to see whether a user can legitimately access the part of the database to which she has requested access. Satisfied that the request is valid, this agent then establishes a secure channel to a key manager. After it has itself validated the requesting agent, it provides the database key. The agent then extracts the data and passes it back to the user. Thus the user never needs to know the database keys. The key manager may look after keys, say to other databases.

7.4.1 Communication Keys

We glibly referred to establishing a secure channel. There are many ways of doing this, with lots of bells and whistles. Using PPK cryptography is computationally expensive, and thus symmetric encryption is preferred. AES-256 is the strongest and most widely used (Section 7.3.1). Figure 7.1 shows what happens. Jeff Moser gives a good description of how this works for setting up and HyperText Transfer Protocol Secure (HTTPS) connection.[5]

This is very much a bird's eye view. Common end-to-end encryption apps, such as (in 2018), *WhatsApp, Facetime, Signal, Telegram, Zoom,* have different optimizations and different implementations. Many make their software or algorithms available for cryptographic analysis, to make sure that they are sound. Others, such as Telegram, use their own proprietary methods, and the absolute level of security is uncertain at the time of writing.

We saw in Section 7.2.2 that Diffie–Hellman provides a way of establishing a shared, secret key. However, raw Diffie–Hellman is vulnerable to an Man in the Middle Attack (MITM) attack (Section 5.3.2.2). It is safer to use an asymmetric, PPK pair. Thus Alfie generates a random password, puts it into a message to

[5] www.moserware.com/2009/06/first-few-milliseconds-of-https.html *Accessed:* 23 Dec 2018.

Bertha and encrypts it with her public key. Only Bertha can decrypt this. See Section 7.5.3.3 for issues related to Diffie–Hellman security.

This is much safer, but Alfie has to be sure that he has Bertha's public key, and not a key from somebody purporting to be Bertha. Thus he needs to get her public key by some secure means, orally, snail mail, stone tablet, Ouija board...

7.4.2 Good and (Very) Bad Signatures

People will often have a cursive signature attached to their email, but this is little more than decoration. Much worse, though, is the use of a photo of the signature pasted into the document. This is dreadfully insecure. Anybody can copy the image and reuse it.

Yet people have been forging signatures for centuries. A proper digital signature is much more secure than any handwritten signature, and it guarantees that the document has not been tampered with. There are many specifications and documents surrounding digital signatures, but for this book the basic principle is enough. There are two elements:

1. Creating a *message digest*;

2. Signing the digest with a private key.

The message digest is yet another hash function, which compresses a document of any size down to a short bit string. One of the early, commonly used digest developed by Ron Rivest, was called MD5,[6] but this has now been superseded by more secure variants, such as SHA. This family of digests comes from NIST, beginning with SHA-1 and now up to SHA-3 (up to 512 bits)[7] Reducing a large document to a string of a hundred or so bits might seem to be a challenge. But even 128 bits could code for 10^{38} documents, which is enough to be going on with.

To sign the digest, it is enough to encrypt it with a private key. Anybody in position of the public key can now extract the digest and compare it with the digest recalculated from the document. Thus the document is validated by the owner of the private key. A change of just one character will lead to a completely different digest value. As discussed in Section 7.4.1 it is essential to know that the public key does indeed belong to whom it claims.

Finally signatures usually have a timestamp. Now computers have a clock and can provide a timestamp. But the clock on a computer can be easily reset. Thus there are numerous *timestamp servers*, which provide an authorized, third-party

---

[6] `butthishasnowbeensupersededbymoresecurevariants, suchas` *Accessed:* 22 Dec 2018.

[7] www.nist.gov/news-events/news/2015/08/nist-releases-sha-3-cryptographic-hash-standard *Accessed:* 23 Dec 2018.

stamp. The basic principle is that the message digest is sent to the server, which returns it signed with its own private key and a timestamp. Some document software already includes options to select a timestamp server when signing documents. The protocols for such servers are defined in RFC3161[8] and are part of X.509 (Section 7.12).

Cyber Nugget 39: *Beware facsimile digital signatures. They are useless unless accompanied by a cryptographic signature and preferably an authorized timestamp.*

7.4.3 Antiencryption Legislation

At present there is a substantial tug-of-war between privacy and state security. Law enforcement, spy agencies, and their ilk want access to encrypted communication. Used to phone tapping in the plain old telephone system, they have lost this option with encrypted systems such as *WhatsApp*—. There are two different issues here:

- Compelling the decryption of documents, messages, or other data. Some jurisdictions already have this. For example, in the United Kingdom, police can with an appropriate warrant, request a document to be decrypted. Regardless of whether or not there is anything illegal in the document, the penalty for simply refusing to decrypt is up to 2 years jail.
- Surreptitious surveillance is surveillance without the communicators' knowledge. This is much harder and has serious implications for the level of security of communication in legitimate domains. We have a look as the current situation in the last chapter Section 8.2.

Cyber Nugget 40: *Some jurisdictions can enforce the revealing of cryptographic keys to law enforcement.*

7.5 Passwords

Passwords are still the bedrock of authentication and, despite endless exhortations to choose good, unique passwords, are still one of the great cybervulnerabilities. The vulnerability is increased by the endless need to create new passwords: bank accounts; commercial websites; government systems; email; work

[8] www.ietf.org/rfc/rfc3161.txt *Accessed:* 25 Feb 2019.

and hobby websites; and so on. To understand password security a little better, we shall have a look at how passwords work (Section 7.5.1) and then what makes a strong password (Section 7.5.2).

But first a little tip. Many people have not heard of password safes/managers, yet there are lots of them. They are a simple way of getting round the ever-growing pile of passwords we have to remember. PCMag picks Dashlane for its top paid password manager in 2018, with LastPass its top free choice.[9]

Cyber Nugget 41: *Get a password safe and ensure it has a local backup option and can export in a nonproprietary format.*

See Section 7.5.3 for considerations in choosing a password safe.

7.5.1 The Password File

At the beginning of the computing era, passwords were stored unencrypted in a password file. If this file got stolen, then it gave immediate access to all accounts on the machine, hence this was not entirely satisfactory. The next stage of development was to encrypt each password and store only the encrypted passwords.

Now, if you think about it, once the password has been encrypted, there is no need to ever decrypt it! When the user types in their password, it is encrypted and compared with the stored encrypted password. So, we don't need a reversible encryption, which would itself need an encryption password. All that is needed is a cryptographic hash trapdoor function (Section 7.2) (with a long drop underneath). There are two minor consequences of this: first, the password can never be retrieved for a user, or the system just has to generate a new one; the system can detect if the new password is the same as the old one (same hash), but it can't easily check for minor variations on the old one. (It's a bad sign if your system can give you your old password instead of just sending you a link to create a new one. It could mean that the password is either stored unencrypted or the encryption key is somewhere on the website).

The message that one should not use the same password for different accounts is all pervasive, although perhaps not universally received. However, it's less clear that just tweaking a password to get a new one is a bad idea, i.e., bison1, bison2, bison3... Users of recruitment website PageUp found this out to their cost. Here is what they say on their website[10]:

> A small number of PageUp error logs from before 2007 may have contained incorrect failed passwords in clear text. Because failed

[9] http://au.pcmag.com/password-managers-products/4524/guide/the-best-password-managers-of-2018 *Accessed:* 07 Jul 2018.

[10] www.pageuppeople.com/unauthorised-activity-on-it-system/ *Accessed:* 8 Jul 2018.

> passwords can be similar to correct passwords, if employees have not changed their password information since 2007, it would be prudent to do this now and anywhere where they may have used the same password.

So, although the password is never stored unencrypted, a mistyped password might end up unencrypted in the error logs. Hence if the log has leppard1, try leopard1.

Cyber Nugget 42: *Don't tweak an old password to use somewhere else.*

7.5.2 Good Passwords

Many systems still have atavistic limitations left over from the early days of computing, such as a restriction to numbers and letters, or a small number of characters. To make a password stronger, we can have a larger number of choices for each character, or just have more characters. The latter usually wins by a huge margin.

To take a simple example, suppose your system allows you an eight-character password, where each character can be a letter, number, or special character. In principle there are 256 such characters, but some of them are not useable in practice. So, our maximum number of possible passwords is $256^8 = 2^{64} \approx 10^{19}$. Not too bad if you can remember `$aq&^f*CK.e`

Password cracking software is a lot cleverer than to just try every possibility. One of the basic tricks is to use dictionaries. The full dictionary would use all the words in the language,[11] in other words about 10^5 for English. So if the password is a word, the number of possibilities to check is a lot less. At the technical side, the password checker can go even faster by checking the most common words first.

Now suppose instead your more advanced system allows you a long string of characters, and your password becomes `chargrilledhippopotamus`. Even if we allow only lowercase letters and numbers, this is about 10^{36} possibilities, which is huge, just like a hippopotamus. Even if we allow for this being made up of words, we could get a rough estimate of the number of possible passwords as, say, testing combinations of four words, but this would still be 10^{20} possibilities, larger than our crude eight-character password (it's tricky to give a precise estimate, because the length of the password is not fixed).

Now a friend, who knows that you weigh 150 kg due to an excessive consumption of giant steaks and a predilection for bush meat, might be able to guess

[11] https://en.oxforddictionaries.com/explore/how-many-words-are-there-in-the-english-language/ *Accessed:* 8 Jul 2018.

this, a computer wouldn't do so well—as yet. However, with more and more of our personal lives online in social media, a future password cracker could trawl your online data and use machine learning to narrow the search for possible passwords.

Despite much publicity about silly passwords and the risks they pose, there are still many egregious examples. Dashlane[12] published a list of the ten worst offenders in 2018. Would you believe it included Google and some very high-level government agencies? Our favorite though was Nutella

> Nutella came under fire for giving some of the nuttiest password advice of the year as the beloved hazelnut-and-chocolate spread company encouraged its Twitter followers to use "Nutella" as their password.

7.5.3 Password Managers/Safes

This book is not generally concerned with recommending specific Products, and it would not be that wise to do so given the enormous churn in the cybersecurity world. As an illustration, Google found a serious bug, now fixed, in LastPass, one of the better password managers, which was a trifle unnerving.[13] One might think that nothing stays safe for very long in the cyberworld. TeamSilk, part of the prestigious Fraunhofer Institute, recently published a report on popular password managers for Android. The results were frightening.[14] They say (our italics)

> In order to answer these questions, we performed a security analysis on the most popular Android password manager applications from the Google Play Store based on download count. The overall results were extremely worrying and revealed that password manager applications, despite their claims, *do not provide enough protection mechanisms for the stored passwords* and credentials. Instead, they *abuse the users' confidence and expose them to high risks.*

These reports date from 2016. They note on their website that *Update 2017-03-01: All reported vulnerabilities are fixed by the vendors*, but this further emphasizes the need to keep security software up-to-date, subject to issues of legacy software discussed in Section 1.2.1.

[12] https://blog.dashlane.com/password-offenders-2018/?utm_source=email&utm_medium=appboy&utm_campaign=19774335-05fd-4bb8-bb48-9e2d05587b38&utm_content=1&utm_term=en&utm_type=news *Accessed:* 20 Dec 2018.

[13] www.theguardian.com/technology/2017/mar/30/lastpass-warns-users-to-exercise-caution-while-it-fixes-major-vulnerability *Accessed:* 24 Sep 2018.

[14] https://team-sik.org/trent_portfolio/password-manager-apps/ *Accessed:* 27 Dec 2018.

There are several different categories of password managers: browser based; cloud based; and local.

7.5.3.1 Using the Browser

When we are using a laptop or desktop computer, a lot of our passwords are entered through a web browser. Often the browser will ask to save passwords, which, in the simplest case, it does locally. Not all browsers tell you how this is done. Firefox being open source reveals its secrets.

But you don't need to look under the hood, to see Firefox has issues. If you look at the saved passwords, you will see an option to show passwords as in Figure 7.2. From our earlier discussion, this should set alarm bells ringing. If Firefox can show the password either it has stored unencrypted or the encryption password is stored somewhere. Either way it is bad news. However, with Firefox version 61.01, the information is stored encrypted in a support file on the mac called *logins.json.*

There is one, nasty, little twist. Firefox will not pressure you into setting a master password, and this might seem to be a hassle one can avoid. Not so! Without a password, anybody with access to the stored Firefox profile can see your passwords. Painful though it may be, unfortunately you have to read the fine print to discover this.

Cyber Nugget 43: *Check the details of how passwords are stored on your browser.*

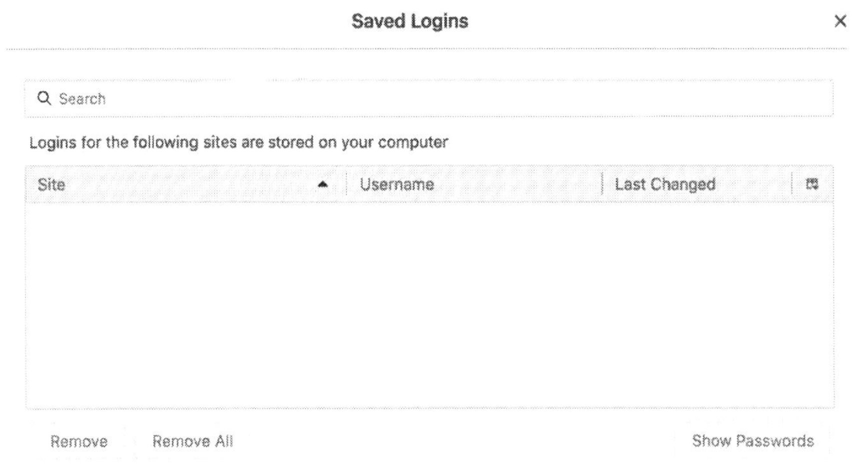

Figure 7.2: Firefox window showing sites for which passwords have been saved.

Even with a master password, the stored passwords are not very safe. The argument now gets somewhat technical[15] and we will avoid the details, since they may have changed by the time this book is read anyway. First, at the time of writing, Firefox was using the weaker SHA-1 as opposed to the current state of the art SHA-256. Second it uses only one salt+hash iteration, as compared, say, to LastPass which defaults to 5,000.

7.5.3.2 Rainbow Tables

Rainbow tables, invented by Philippe Oechslin [101], would take us a bit deeper than most readers would like, but the term occurs so often in security blogs that it might be worth a simplistic description. Cracking a password in principle means trudging through lots of random attempts one at a time. But one of the cheapest ways of getting computing power is to use a GPU, a class of parallel processing chip designed for fast computer graphics.

A very simple way to think about this is to imagine many strings of characters laid out as towns on a map. Each town is connected to another town via the forward encryption algorithm. The brute force approach just trundles methodically through all the towns, trying to find the route backwards from encrypted password to password, which is, of course, very hard. The rainbow table approach now does two things: first it takes the encrypted password and follows the road through a lot more towns, the password route; and it starts at a random town and generates the route out from that town and does this for lots of random starting towns, which it can do in parallel (such as on a GPU).

Since storing every town in every route would take a vast amount of space, we store only the towns at the beginning and end. Now if the password route hits one of the end towns, we've found the route that contains the password. We now start at the beginning of this route and run forward until we hit the encrypted, back up one, and we have the password.

This doesn't work perfectly, of course, since a hash value is a many–one map: there are lots of strings for every hash, thus false alarms are possible (but rare) (see Figure 7.3).

The speed gain comes from precomputing the routes, the left and right of Figure 7.3 and storing just the end values (in order to be able to precompute a very large number of them). This is where salt comes in. Adding a random string at the beginning of the password, the salt, makes it very much more difficult to precompute the rainbow table. The salt does not have to be secret: it can be stored alongside the encrypted password. It has to be different for every password, though.

[15]https://nakedsecurity.sophos.com/2018/03/20/nine-years-on-firefoxs-master-password-is-still-insecure/ *Accessed:* 24 Sep 2018.

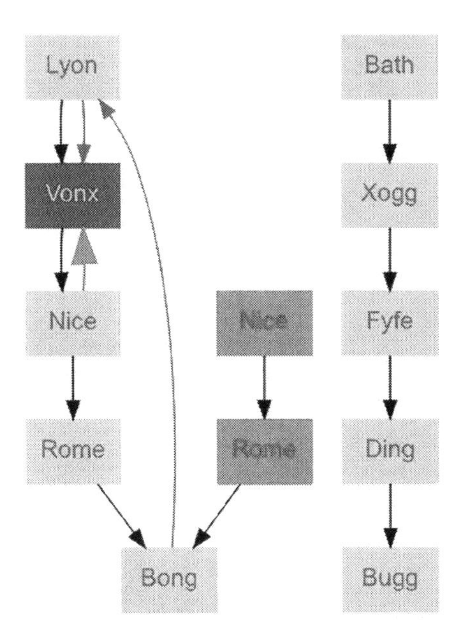

Figure 7.3: Illustration of a rainbow table. The password is Vonx, and its encrypted form is Nice. Running forward in the password route on the right we end up with Bong, which is an endpoint. Going back to the start of the route, Lyon, run forward to Nice and backup one to the password. The route on the right is not used since its endpoint is Bugg, which does not appear in the password route.

7.5.3.3 Key Exchange Precomputation

A similar form of precomputation attack operates on Transport Layer Security (TLS), secure internet packet (IPSec) (Section 7.8.1), key HTTPS (Section 7.4.1) and elsewhere, specifically the Diffie–Hellman exchange (Section 7.2.2). The issue is partly technical and partly human. Since long prime numbers are hard to generate, lots of software tends to use primes picked from quite a small set of 1,024 bit primes, and the same primes get used repeatedly [5,19]. This is fairly secure. However, 512 bit is definitely not.

It's a problem because export restrictions in place at one time restricted full-strength TLS and weak 512 bit primes were used for a modified version of TLS Export This issue has now been remedied in TLS 1.2, but an attack called *logjam* forces TLS1.2 back to the weak export version. TLS 1.3 uses ECC (Section 7.2.4), for which no precomputation attack has so far been discovered.

Cyber Nugget 44: *Ensure that servers and clients use the latest Transport Layer Security.*

7.5.3.4 Storing Passwords Locally

The simplest password-safe is a file with all the passwords stored in it, which is encrypted at all times it is not in use. There are very strong, easy-to-use encryption programs around, such as *bcrypt* and *GnuPG*. Software such as *Adobe Acrobat* and Mac *Preview* offer document encryption options, but the strength of these is often not clearly specified and changes with time. At the time of writing, Preview on the Mac was only 128 bit. For encrypting your own passwords, a sound strategy is to use just one state of the art tool and frequently check news groups and forums for any security issues.

> **Cyber Nugget 45:** *Use a single, high-powered encryption tool, keep it up-to-date and monitor it online for problems.*

Keeping passwords in a file has downsides: it's a bit of a hassle to use, requiring decrypting the file every time you want to use a password; you lose everything in one go if your computer becomes compromised or your file password gets stolen; it has been known for people to lose a master password... If the file is needed on more than one computer, then it has to be moved around (in its encrypted form, of course) and all copies have to be kept in synch.

7.5.3.5 Online Password Safes

In this scenario, the passwords are stored in the cloud somewhere. However, the encryption keys may be stored locally only *LastPass*, one of the popular safe states.[16]

> We've implemented AES-256 bit encryption with PBKDF2 SHA-256 and salted hashes to ensure complete security in the cloud. You'll create an account with an email address and a strong master password to locally-generate a unique encryption key.
>
> Your data is encrypted and decrypted at the device level. Data stored in your vault is kept secret, even from LastPass. Your master password, and the keys used to encrypt and decrypt data, are never sent to LastPass' servers, and are never accessible by LastPass.

At the time of writing, this is about as good as it gets. The advantage of an online system is that it's available whenever and wherever one is online. Unusual circumstances could arise where this is a problem. You might have an important legal document on your laptop, encrypted in case your laptop gets snatched on the train, but when you arrive at the lawyer's office, you find their internet is down.

[16] www.lastpass.com/how-lastpass-works *Accessed:* 26 Sep 2018.

More broadly, though, most of these systems make the implicit assumption that they are around for a long term. *LastPass* has already survived for 10 years. But long term for the IT industry is not archaeological. *LastPass* confronts this head-on with export options and local backup. So far, so good. But the local copy might still be read, and only be readable by the software's app or desktop client. In 10 years, or maybe a lot less, that app might cease to work with newer operating system variants (Cyber Nugget 19).

The best (although not often available) is to have the source code, meaning that the software can be rebuilt way into the future, with one very important caveat. It might use a library random number generator, which of course would change over time. The source would have to include all algorithmically relevant code.

7.5.4 Two-Factor Identification

Some secure websites or devices are now asking for two-factor identification. The simplest example is a pin number in addition to a password. In terms of the number of possibilities, this is no better than having a password longer by the number of digits in the pin. In fact, it's a lot lower, since these extra characters are drawn just from the set of digits. The principle though is sound, in that the intention is that the pin code and password would never be stored together. It is no defense against the common practice of writing things down or using obvious numbers, like your birthday. It is also no defense against key loggers Section 7.11, clipboard sniffing Section 7.11, TLS hijacking Section 2.9 or any of the social engineering traps we saw in Chapter 5.

There are good and bad PINS. All zeroes, nines, whatever, is obviously pretty woeful, but this, it used to be a common default setting, which people did not bother to change. Physics Nobel Laureate Richard Feynman recounted in his memoir, *Sorry you must be joking Mr Feynman* [51] how an army general has this gigantic safe installed in his office. Sometime after its installation, Feynman snuck into the office and tried to open the safe. The password was just that, still the factory setting!!

A more secure technique, now used by some credit card companies, for example, is the sending of a one-time code to a mobile phone. However, this can fail if the mobile phone number can be faked. Suppose a credit-card website is compromised, which will usually have just a password access, or maybe a two-factor system similar to the last paragraph. Now, this website may well have the mobile number (or email address, whatever) stored. Thus the hacker can change this information on the site and get the code sent to some other address.

7.6 Biometrics

We have not said very much about biometrics, mainly because they are outside the main theme of the book, on the psychological and social dimensions of cybersecurity. It is also a rapidly developing field. Many smartphones now use fingerprint recognition, the new iPhone uses face recognition, iris recognition is used elsewhere, and all sorts of experiments are underway looking for distinctive human signatures.

There are a couple of caveats we would raise against biometrics:

1. Their level of security is often not clear cut, in the way that we can calculate the number of possible passwords. Fingerprints may be unique at high resolution, but there are cases where people have difficulty with a fingerprint reader, through skin wear and tear.

2. Crime movies and novels about with examples of people's fingers being chopped off, or their eyeballs extracted, to subvert biometric security. However, fingerprints, iris scans or any other biometrics are just data, which can be stolen just like text. The technology for using this data to fool, say, a fingerprint scanner will undoubtedly get better with time.

3. And here is the rub. Most of us are stuck with our biometrics. Facial plastic surgery is expensive, maybe new fingerprints can be grafted on in some way, but so far eyeball replacement is not an option. Passwords can be changed easily, but biometrics far less easily if at all.

For some time, there have been interests in other biometrics such as gait. Identifying people as they walked through a public space, but too far away for face recognition, could be advantageous to law enforcement as well as for the general Zeitgeist of vacuuming of data about people. This sort of work has led to what one might call hidden biometrics. Smartphones usually contain accelerometers as well as GPS. Thus, they can be used for characterizing gait and other physical activity and for determining daily activity patterns.

Such hidden metrics are already a commercial reality.[17] Whether this will be, as it were, a step too far, remains to be seen.

We now move on to look at some of the basic ideas of computer networks, with a view to how they impact on cybersecurity.

7.7 Basic Ideas of Computer Networks

Computer networks are pretty obviously a huge field of knowledge and research. For this book, which has a strong human/social theme, we can get by with a few basic concepts. The first of these, discussed in Section 7.7.1, is the idea of network layers. We need this because cyberattacks may operate at different layers and different defenses are needed for each. By layers, we mean a hierarchy

[17] www.economist.com/science-and-technology/2019/05/22/online-identification-is-getting-more-and-more-intrusive?cid1=cust/dailypicks/n/bl/n/20190522n/owned/n/n/dailypicks/n/n/AP/243927/n *Accessed:* 23 May 2019.

of mechanisms by which a message gets from one computer to another. In the earliest days of networking, this would simply be a wire connecting two computers together. The lowest level is still the layer of electrical signals between machines. But when we send a message from a computer in Sydney, Australia to the one in Sydney, Canada, we do it via an Internet Protocol (IP) address, the message hopping between many machines *en route*. Section 7.7.2 discusses internet addressing, a fundamental feature of many cyberattacks.

7.7.1 Network Layers

In the early days of computing, the idea of the Open Systems Interconnection emerged, a seven-layer network architecture. Although it is still widely used as a conceptual model and is taught in many courses, it's practical adoption was thwarted through, as Tanenbaum [138] asserts, bad timing, bad technology, bad implementation, and bad politics. The Transport Control Protocol/Internet Protocol (TCP/IP) model, though not so useful theoretically, did get widespread adoption. There are three key ideas to a network architecture: interfaces; services; and protocols. We can imagine the network as a stack, with the level of abstraction (Section 7.7.1.2) increasing at each level. A message actually travels only at the lowest levels, the wires, or electromagnetic waves. At each level of the stack the message is chopped up into chunks (called packets for the internet and frames for ethernet) and repackaged until it gets to the lowest level where it is transmitted. At each level, one machine may communicate with another, but it does so by sending a message down the stack. Thus we have communications vertically, which ultimately become the physical message, and horizontally, which are usually virtual.

Having an idea about these different layers is useful. Cyberattacks often occur at levels below the surface. In the case study of TLS proxies (Section 2.9), we saw an example of this. At the level we work with on the web, HTTPS is supposedly end-to-end encrypted and secure. But things as simple as ad-blockers or ad-insertion agents can interfere with, and reduce the security of, this high, user level.

7.7.1.1 Protocol Stacks. A Simple Analogy

Modern computer software and communication systems are multilayered, one unit encapsulated within another, like a Matryoshka (Russian) doll. To get an idea of how a network protocol stack works, from web page down through HTTP, internet, ethernet, and pulses along wires, imagine transferring furniture between tower blocks. It's a future scenario, where fuel is short and everything is carried by bicycle.

At the top level of Tower A, we have a furniture showroom on Level 4. Fred and Felicity, who live in Tower D, want a dining suite. There is no path between

A and D, thus everything goes via either Tower B or C. They choose their suite, pay for it, and await its delivery. First it is separated into its component table and chairs on Level 3. Each piece has to be labeled with the customer order number and the destination in Tower D. The components then descend to Level 2, where they are disassembled into flat pack pieces, legs, cushions, fasteners, etc. Each of these pieces now needs to be labeled as part of, say, the table, and Fred and Felicity's order.

Finally the pieces arrive at Level 1. Unlike an IKEA flatpack, the disassembly does not stop here. Since there are no trucks, each entity is further disassembled, like LEGO, into bike-deliverable sized blocks, each with a new label, wrapping the former labels. There are now hundreds of pieces setting off for Tower D. They may go via either B or C, depending upon how busy the paths are and are reassembled in Tower D.

The pieces may not have arrived in the correct order and sometimes a piece is missing. Mutant Australian magpies swoop and injure cyclists, while bowerbirds and beavers steal the pieces for their bowers and dams. Thus as each piece arrives an acknowledgement is sent back to Tower A. If A has not received an acknowledgement after a period of time, it assumes it is lost, and just sends another one. At Tower D, a unit, say the table top, does not get send up to Level 2, until all its pieces have arrived and been sorted (to make assembly easy). Eventually Fred and Felicity receive their dining suite on Level 4 of Tower D.

The furniture showroom on level 4 in Tower A has sent the furniture suite to Fred and Felicity on level 4 in Tower D, as if there was a *horizontal* connection between the towers. But this is a virtual connection. There is no physical bridge above ground between level 4 of each tower.

7.7.1.2 Abstraction

One of the important principles across the whole of computer science is that of abstraction. Each level provides a service to the level above and an interface through which this service can be accessed. How the interface is implemented doesn't matter and can change with time as hardware and software technologies change. Many noncomputing systems effectively implement this. When we send a parcel overseas, it gets picked up by a courier and taken to a depot. It then gets aggregated with other parcels to an overseas shipping venue, along with other parcels going, say, to France. It then gets packaged with other stuff going to France and sets off on a ship or a plane, possibly passing through other ports or airports along the way. When it arrives in France a reverse chain on unpacking occurs until it reaches its final destination.

At a horizontal level, the key element is the protocol describing the message structure at this level. The IP defines the protocol for addressing nodes on the internet and hence for getting a large message from one node to another. Such a message is broken up into smaller *packets*, which are sent independently and asynchronously to the destination. They won't all arrive at the same time, they may travel by different routes, and they might not arrive in the right order. TCP sorts all of this out.

7.7.1.3 TCP: The Transport Control Protocol

TCP sets up a virtual connection between two hosts, even though the packets might arrive in the wrong order and by different paths. Since TCP sits on top of IP, a TCP unit has to be put inside an IP packet, which has a maximum size of 64 kB, including the header. Thus the TCP message has to be broken up if it is too big to fit and sent as a number of packets, which do not have to arrive in the right order or follow the same path.

7.7.1.4 UDP: The User Datagram Protocol

The other important protocol at this level is UDP, which is connectionless. A packet sent by UDP may or may not arrive, like a message in a bottle. If there is no response, another packet would be sent.

7.7.1.5 The Application Layer

If we go one level above the transport layer, TCP and UDP, we get the *Application Layer* protocols, such as HTTP used by the World Wide Web, Simple Mail Transfer Protocol (SMTP) used for email, and a host of protocols for multimedia. Malware may target any of these levels or protocols.

7.7.2 Addresses of All Sorts

Without the space to delve into the intricacies of network structure, we shall use a simplistic separation into Local Area Network (LAN) and Wide Area Network (WAN). Basically a LAN is an internal network, say a house or a company, and a WAN is the internet at large (although there are many flavors of WAN). A LAN is connected to the internet through a Point of Presence (PoP), say a modem.

It's a lot more complicated than this, but the two LANs of most significance to this book are ethernet (Section 7.7.2.2) and WiFi (Section 7.7.2.3).

7.7.2.1 IP Addresses for the Internet

Internet addresses exist as IPv4, and the new version with a lot more addresses, IPv6. An IPv4 address is a collection of four hexadecimal number pairs, although these are usually written in decimals.

IP packets contain header information giving source and destination address, protocol information, and other information to reconstitute a longer message.

7.7.2.2 Ethernet

Addresses for the internet are frequently expressed in factors of 16, equal to two bytes, each byte being eight bits. Numbers to base 16 (our everyday numbers are base 10) are called. hexadecimal. 256 is $2^8 = 16^2$ features prominently too as two hexadecimal digits. Hexadecimal numbers are written using the letters A-F for the numbers 10–15. Thus A3 is 163 (decimal).

Every ethernet address on the planet is unique, comprising 12 hexadecimal digits (48 bits). Fortunately, that's quite a lot of addresses (nearly 300 trillion). Ethernet was one of the earliest forms of network and is still widely used within buildings and local areas, capable of speeds much greater than WiFi.

7.7.2.3 WiFi

WiFi uses radio waves in the 100 MHz and 2.4, 3.6, 5, and 60 GHz frequency bands according to IEEE 802.11. A WiFi network is given a name, known as a Service Set Identifier (SSID). WiFi may be unsecured, encrypted with an early standard, WEP, or later, more secure standards, such as Wired Equivalent Privacy (WEP), WiFi Protected Access (WPA), and WPA2.

Creating a home network or mobile phone WiFi hotspot involves inventing an SSID. When a computer or phone scans for networks, these are the names it displays. Now, although the network maybe (should be) protected by WPA, it is still advisable to choose a distinctive (and maybe obscure to outsiders) name for a hotspot, in case attackers are specifically targeting you. This might be an issue, for example, for whaling attacks.

Note that in personal/home WiFi, everybody shares the same password, although enterprise WPA2 can give everybody personal logins and passwords. This can raise security issues, to which we return in Section 7.9.1.

Many nasties have lurked within public WiFi networks, but the use of WPA2 helps get rid of a lot of them. But for organizations, there are technologies for detecting illicit users or potential cyberattackers: Wireless Intrusion Detection System (WIDS); and Wireless Intrusion Protection System (WIPS).

7.7.3 Domain Name Server (DNS)

Those of us without Rain Man's memory do not find Internet addresses, such as 137.166.4.30, easy to remember. This address is actually the website www.csu.edu.au, which is a lot easier to remember. This is called a *domain name* and the conversion between the name, which people use, and the numerical address, which computers use, is done by a Domain Name Server (DNS). There are many DNS throughout the internet. Each contains a list of Resource Record (RR)s, which describe numerous aspects of the domain, which are not especially relevant to us here.

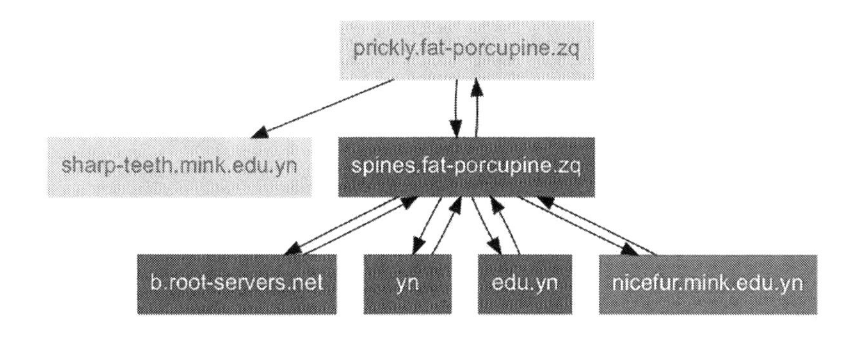

Figure 7.4: Prickly wants to get the IP address of *sharp-teeth.mink.edu.yn.*

The vast number of internet sites is vast, almost 2 billion with the 1 billion mark supposedly passed in September 2014.[18] Thus one name server could not possibly handled domain resolution requests for all internet traffic. Thus computer scientists have resorted to one of their standard tricks: a tree structure.

At the top level are the root servers. Below this are the Top-Level Domain (TLD) servers (such as the country codes) and descending the tree eventually brings us to the leaves, which are the *authoritative servers*, which contain the most accurate information. To speed traffic, flow information is cached along the way and there may be many copies of information, some more up to date than others. Internet protocols often have date of creation and lifetime stamps, to help make sure that information is accurate.

The resolution of an address comprises both *iterative* and *recursive* activities. First within a domain, a host prods the DNS for the IP address of some hostname, and gets back exactly that, an iterative query. The DNS does not get life so easy. It starts at the top, i.e., the right-hand side of the address, such as the country code. It gets back an address of say the country server. It recursively then prods the country server and trundles down the tree until it reaches the authoritative server, from which it gets the IP address.

Thus if *prickly.fat-porcupine.zq* wants to look up *sharp-teeth.mink.edu.yn* (Figure 7.4) it asks its DNS, *spines.fat-porcupine.com*, which then begins the recursive resolution of the address. First, it queries the root server to find the address of the top-level server for country code *zq*. There are 13 root servers, *a.root-servers.net* through *m.root-servers.net*, of which there are numerous copies. The country code then sends back the IP address of the server for the *com* domain, *edu.zq* and so it goes until the authoritative server, *mink.com.zq* is found, which can provide the address for the host *sharp-teeth.mink.com*. Besides, as one might imagine, these servers are all very busy. Thus the queries use UDP, which is connectionless, rather than TCP (Section 7.7.1.4).

[18]http://www.internetlivestats.com/total-number-of-websites/ *Accessed:* 28 Aug 2018.

Table 7.1 Country and Generic Top-Level Domains

Country	*Code*	*Content*	*Code*
UK	.uk	business	.biz
France	.fr	education	.edu
Switzerland	.ch	museums	.museum
South Africa	.za	pornography	.xxx
Germany	de		

It should be pretty obvious that the DNSs are crucial to the functioning of the web and could thus be prime targets of disruptive attacks. Indeed, Section 2.1 discusses one of the biggest such attacks, the DYN attack, which affected giants such as Amazon, PayPal, and Netflix.

TLDs are managed by Internet Corporation for Assigned Names and Numbers (ICANN) and fall into two categories: country and generic. The generic names, such as *edu* for universities and higher education, *.biz* for business and so on (Table 7.1) Andy Tanenbaum [138] points out that sometimes getting names registered may be controversial, such as *.xxx* for pornography.

On the one hand, one might not want to acknowledge that the web is a source of pornography. On the other by concentrating pornography in its own TLD makes it easy to create filters to protect children.

7.8 Increasing Internet Security

We carefully avoided saying making the internet secure, since we don't have now, and won't have in the foreseeable future, defense against all threats. In fact a special term zero day attack has been coined to refer expressly to threats that have not been seen before.

The fine details of what is and is not secure are very technical. But for the readers of this book some intuitive guidelines will be useful. As an illustration, to know why and how much stronger the long keys are than the short ones requires some understanding of number theory and cryptographic mathematics. But it is useful to know that not only are long keys more secure, they are much more secure than might seem. Thus a 256 bit key is *much* stronger than a 128 bit key.[19] At the time of writing, it is essentially uncrackable for a virtual private network (VPN) (Section 7.9) use.[20]

To achieve security over a public channel, we can think of how we might send a secure letter. If we put it in an ordinary envelope and put it in the post, we don't expect it to be very secure. It could easily get damaged and might be left outside in the rain upon delivery. We can reduce the damage risk by putting it in a tough steel box.

[19] in fact it has $2^{128} \approx 10^{38}$, a trillion trillion.

[20] https://www.expressvpn.com/what-is-vpn/vpn-encryption *Accessed:* 2 Sep 2018.

But somebody could still look inside the box and tamper with or replace the letter. Thus we need to put a lock on the box. If we use a combination lock and send the combination by txt from a mobile phone, which the recipient knows the number, we are doing a lot better. Obviously the box has to be strong enough, the combination has to be long enough in a good lock and the txt message serves to identify and validate the sender.

There is yet another variant we can consider here. The above assumes that the sender puts the envelope in the box and locks it. Thus the box has on the label the addresses of the sender and the receiver. This is similar to transport mode below. Alternatively we could let a courier pick up the letter and put it in a box, which would be unpacked at the courier destination depot. Now the box just has the courier addresses on the box, hence there is no information floating around as to who sent or received the package during the transit phase between the courier depots. This is analogous to tunnelling mode.

This is basically how secure internet packets, IPSec work. The strength of the box lies in the cryptographic algorithms and the length of the keys. There are two different modes by which the packet can be put in a secure wrapper: transport mode in which the TCP packet is encrypted and signed, but the original IP header remains the same; and tunnelling mode, in which the entire packet is encrypted and signed and put inside a new packet with a new IP header.

Transport mode can be used end-to-end, from your laptop to your friend's computer a thousand miles away, but it has the disadvantage that the IP header is the original one and provides information about the traffic if not the content.

Tunnelling mode, on the other hand, conceals the traffic, but often is implemented just between the gateways. This is an important distinction. It would mean that, say, the WiFi connection from your laptop to the hotel server would *not* be encrypted, although everything from there on was.

Cyber Nugget 46: *Be sure to know which mode your VPN or secure internet is using.*

7.8.1 IPSec: Going a Bit Deeper

There is a veritable thicket of RFCs surrounding IPSec, and we are going to take no more than a nibble of the content. The three key ideas are

Internet Key Exchange (IKE) (RFC 5996[21]) is used to establish the encryption keys, analogous to sending the lock combination by text, but using some form of Diffie–Hellman (Section 7.2.2)

[21] https://tools.ietf.org/html/rfc5996 *Accessed:* 3 Sep 2018

Authorization Header (AH) (RFC 4302[22]) is a wrapper for the encrypted packed with a digital signature

Encapsulating Security Payload (ESP) (RFC 4835[23]) deals with the encryption and encapsulation of the packet

7.8.2 Ports, Firewalls, and Filters

An IP address gets a message to a server, which may itself be a gateway to a LAN. But at some point, the message gets to an endpoint machine, at which point something else is needed—a port number. Very simplistically, a machine on a network listens to various channels or ports for incoming information. The typical port for the web is 80 or 8080 for HTTP and 443 for HTTPS.

There are numerous other ports, though, and a common security error is to leave these ports open, vulnerable to attack by malware (Section 7.11). To detect open ports see Section 7.8.2.1. Aside from blocking ports, which do not have a legitimate use on any given machine, most machines, home routers, or corporate servers use firewalls. Essentially, these check packets coming in and out and apply filters, allowing some but not others. Hence some internet sites may be blocked.

Organizations may block access for a variety of reasons. They might block social media to prevent employees wasting time. They might block a whole range of other sites for efficiency or confidentiality. Parents might want to restrict what their kids can see.

Firewalls and filters scale up to national level. Within Australia a debate has ranged about national firewalls to block such things as child pornography. But the most egregious example is the so-called *Great Firewall of China*, which blocks Google and many other things (Section 2.6.1). Chapter 6 considers the implications and challenges of filtering at a national level.

7.8.2.1 Detecting Open Ports

A port is not a physical quantity, such as an electrical switch. It refers to a process of some kind, such as a web browser, which is listening to messages for a particular port, usually 443 in the case of HTTPS. There are system commands, which look for processes listening for inputs. Most operating systems have some variants on the *netstat* command. On the mac, to find processes listening for TCP messages, the command is

```
netstat -ap TCP
```

Similar information is often available from GUI (graphical user interface) utilities, such as Activity Monitor on the Mac.

[22]https://tools.ietf.org/html/rfc4302 *Accessed:* 3 Sep 2018.
[23]https://tools.ietf.org/html/rfc4835 *Accessed:* 3 Sep 2018.

7.9 Virtual Private Networks

One of the great facilities and convenience of the 21st century is ubiquitous WiFi. From internet cafes to hotel rooms, internet access is everywhere, but it is often far from secure. Sometimes it may not be password secured at all, sometimes the password is a generic one, such as *coffeebean* used in Fred's Espresso, which hasn't been changed since Fred got WiFi.

Using an HTTPS secure website protects the data going backwards and forwards to the site, but it does not conceal the metadata—the sites being accessed. VPNs solve both security issues. The idea is simple. All traffic is sent encrypted to a special VPN server, which then sends it to its intended destination. Since the server handles traffic from many clients, the destination website has no idea who is accessing it.

VPNs often have additional bells and whistles. They may have multiple servers, switch servers frequently, or bounce messages around multiple servers before sending it to the final target. There are numerous VPN services available, some free, some at costs comparable to cheap internet plans. Some VPNs pride themselves on keeping no logs, meaning that after closing the session, there will be no enduring record thereof. VPNs can slow down access and most providers have multiple servers to help speed up and mask traffic.

It would of course be possible for a fake or deceiptful VPN to log and search all traffic through it. Thus there is some advantage to choosing a well-recognized provider, even if it costs money. Section 3.4.3.7 considers some of the downside of VPNs.

7.9.1 Virtual Private Networks in the Home

VPNs also have an increasingly important role to play within the home. At the time of writing in mid-2018 most low-to-medium priced routers offer some, but rather limited, VPN facilities. A fairly common feature is a guest network, which has a variety of uses. One might want to keep the kids off the adult network, maintain work confidentiality, or other reasons. With more and more people offering AirBnB or its brethren, visitors may want internet access, but sharing the home network might have its downsides.

Another less obvious requirement is the devices that go onto the web—the Internet of Things (IoT). First, there are devices such as TVs, music systems, some white goods, where the security may be lax: the passwords for these devices may be set to obvious defaults and may be quite hard to change, especially if one is not up to setting the clock on the oven. Poor passwords can make these devices vulnerable to hacking and in Section 2.1, we highlight the use of security cameras in botnets. The VPN software, like all computer software, should be regularly updated, since it, too, may have security bugs.[24]

[24]https://www.expressvpn.com/what-is-vpn/vpn-encryption *Accessed:* 2 Sep 2018.

What may be even worse, though, are IoT devices which allow a third-party access for monitoring or maintenance. Solar panels are a good example. This access is something over which the householder has no control and little knowledge of how professional the users are at the other end. Thus all the IoT devices should go on their own VPN, which cannot see the rest of the house network.

7.9.2 Choosing a VPN

An ever-present danger in the cyberworld is deception, something pretending to be something it is not. In principle a VPN could be malicious, harvesting, and exploiting, all your internet traffic. It is not the intention of this book to provide software recommendations. They might easily be outdated by the time it reached the shops anyway. Thus finding a good VPN requires reading a few of the latest blogs and reviews.

There is a couple of important criteria in selecting a VPN, excluding factors such as cost.

- It needs to have a reasonable number of servers to avoid bottlenecks. Sometimes it can seem as if VPN traffic is an attack of some sort. Consider a very popular site, such as Google. If many users are going via the same server, then to Google this looks like a flood of packets from one IP address.
- It should not keep logs. This is not just a paranoid reaction against big brother. VPNs, just like any other server, could potentially be hacked, revealing a great deal about the victims' internet usage.
- It needs to be fast, since all traffic is taking a circuitous route. Both the first two requirements in fact help with speed.

There is a quite a lot of variation in the software strategies used by VPNs, including at least half a dozen protocols for establishing a connection and encryption. These tend to trade-off security with speed and complexity of setup, and VPN providers often offer several of them, user selectable. One of the better protocols is OpenVPN,[25] which has the advantage of being open source (Section 8.1).

7.9.3 Value of a Virtual Private Network

VPNs are really valuable, but are not a panacea for all cyber ills. So

- VPNs give you encryption, subject to the caveats above.
- A website cannot track your URL and determine the location when you use a VPN.
- But cookies, ads, and popup windows still get through.

[25] https://openvpn.net/ *Accessed:* 22 May 2019.

7.9.4 Avoiding the Need for VPNs

Although VPNs offer greatly increased security, they have a potential performance overhead, and are themselves, yet another piece of software, which could get compromised. Google has adopted a different approach, known as BeyondCorp, which obviates the need for a VPN in most cases.[26]

> At Google, we embraced the fact that walls don't work... Rather than have a VPN around all this infrastructure, we decided to get rid of the walls entirely. Neal Mueller, head of infrastructure product marketing at Google.

Figure 7.5 shows the basic framework for the system (reprinted from Ward and Beyer with permission.[27]) It looks complicated, but the principles are fairly simple.

7.10 Onions and the Dark Web

Finally, we turn to an aspcct of the deep web, which is usually thought of as criminal territory, the dark web. It is true that the dark web is used for trading illegal drugs, pornography, and possibly organized crime or terrorist information. It may also serve a social role as a repository for whistle blowers and legal political activists.

7.10.1 The Dark Web and Onion Routing

Like an iceberg, the web we see is just the tip of a much larger set of internet sites and information stores, the *deep web*.[28] Some of these sites have a surface presence, with huge databases underneath. Searching the deep web is a lot more difficult [150].

Because there are so many possible internet addresses, it is quite possible to create private internets within the deep web. These can be open to anybody, providing they have the IP address. However, one particular private network has achieved some notoriety—the Dark Web.

The Dark Web uses exactly the same physical infrastructure as the web we know, but it is not indexed by search engines such as Google. The website names end in .onion, but to find them requires the anonymizing browser, The Onion Router (ToR). There is a search engine, GRAMS, which, according to Rachel Botsman [20] looks very similar to Google. Historically, the Dark Web has been

---

[26] https://thenewstack.io/beyondcorp-google-ditched-virtual-private-networking-internal-applications/ *Accessed:* 19 Jan 2019.

[27] https://ai.google/research/pubs/pub43231 *Accessed:* 15 Jan 2019.

[28] https://quod.lib.umich.edu/j/jep/3336451.0007.104?view=text;rgn=main *Accessed:* 17 Aug 2018.

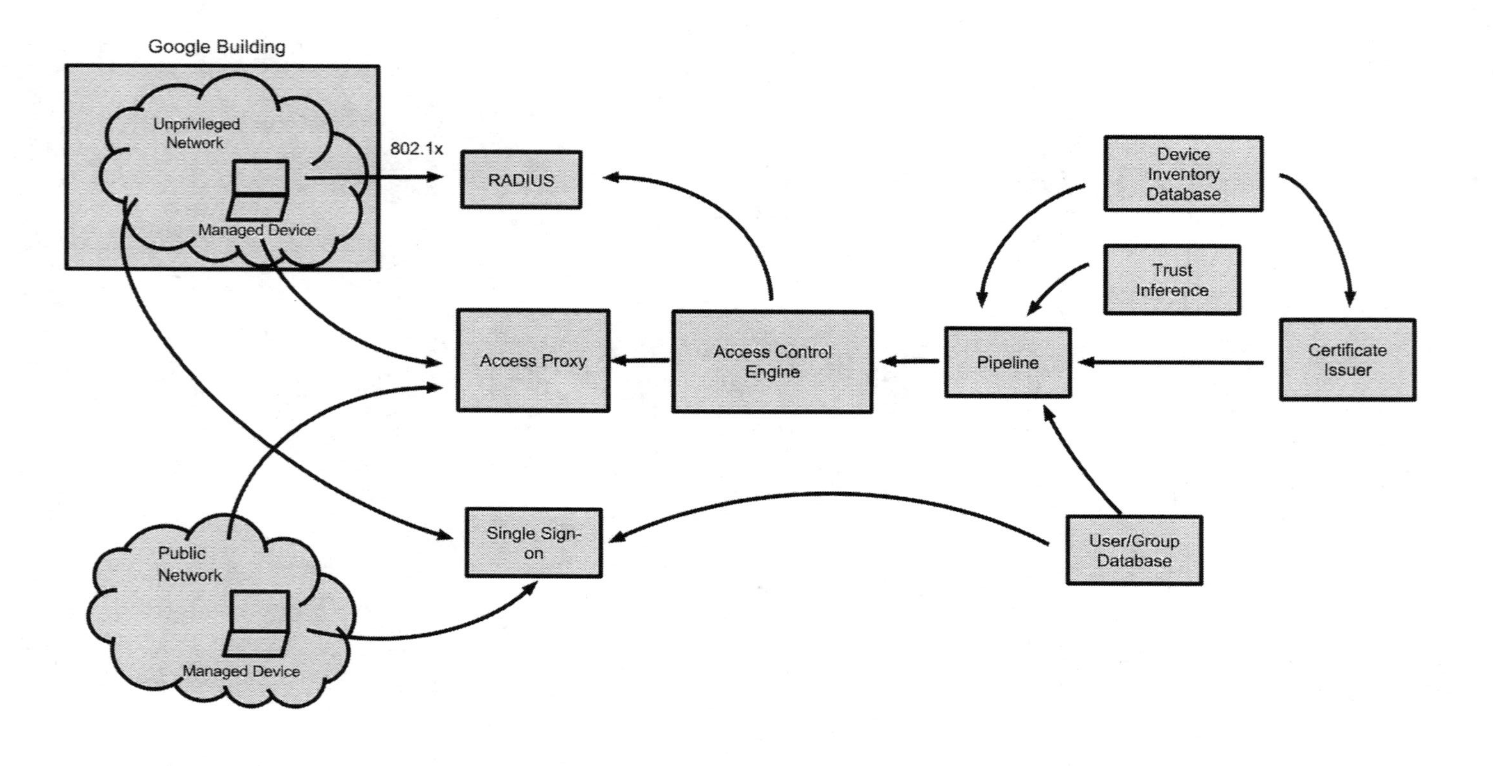

Figure 7.5: BeyondCorp reprinted from Ward and Beyer (see the text).

used for shady or illegal dealings, from arms to drugs. The dark web achieves its anonymity through layers of encryption and access only through specialized browsers such as ToR.

7.11 Local Threats and Malware

The very first computer had one processor and did just one thing at a time. Some time later, a *software* innovation led them to effectively run multiple programs concurrently. This innovation was *timesharing*, where a processor just switched rapidly from one process to another. Since then operating systems have got a whole lot more complicated. Not only do computer chips have multiple processors (cores) on the chip, but they also have the capacity to run lots of program fragments, *threads*, simultaneously. The net result is that a modern computer, even a smartphone is running tens or even hundreds of programs at the same time.

When one of these many programs is not part of the operating system or the user's programs, but has malicious or destructive intent, it is called malware.

A great deal of this book concerns network security, ensuring trust and privacy across networks. This section covers a few nasties, which can take up residence on a computer. They usually arrive as attachments to email, text messages, or other human-level communications, although they may be installed by somebody. The latter situation would be the case for spyware, installed say by a corporation on its computers.

- Ransomware is discussed at length in Section 2.2.
- Coin mining refers to the use of CPU cycles to mine cryptocurrencies, such as bitcoin. When installed illicitly, it steals computer time but nothing else.
- Botnet agents usually do nothing, until called upon to launch a Distributed Denial of Service (DDoS) attack (see Section 2.1).
- Keyloggers are malware, which logs the keys the user types and sends the output to some hacker. This text can be used to look for passwords and other sensitive information. clickjacking is another term for the same process.
- Clipboard sniffers also try to steal information, but they search things like the clipboard. Similar agents scan log files, caches, and other temporary storage.

7.12 Certificates and Trust

In this section we look at the basic network protocols. Email, which can be a major security headache, we consider separately in Section 7.13. Cloud data storage has become ubiquitous. It is almost a prerequisite for using Apple systems, and Amazon hosts a huge amount of data in its cloud services. Generally cloud protocols are secure, but still vulnerable to human error. For example, one of the mainstays of the Amazon cloud is S3. Information is stored in S3 buckets, which can be up to 5 TB in size.[29] In and of themselves they are secure, but vulnerable to human frailty, such as failure to choose correct access privileges, as mentioned in Section 2.5.2.4.

There is one further piece of technology essential to the secure web, the digital certificate. These are hugely important to the secure web. Any website using HTTPS needs to have a certificate signed by a recognized authority, the public key (Section 7.1) of which is readily available.

A certificate is defined according to standard X.509 [138]. It's quite complicated, but the essential elements are

- Who owns it
- Its public key
- Its signature by the authorizing signatory (see the discussion of certificate chains below in Section 7.12.1)
- A signed hash, possibly more than one.

Figure 7.6 shows an example certificate from a Firefox root store.

Verisign (now owned by Symantec) is a major player in the issuing of certificates. Valid certificates for a web page have the following visual clues.[30]

- Padlock to the left of a URL
- The HTTPS URL prefix instead of HTTP
- A trust seal
- A green address bar (when an Extended Validation SSL (EV SSl) certificate is issued)

In Section 2.9 we shall see some examples of malicious software, which perverts the intentions of such certificates, acting as a MITM.

[29] https://aws.amazon.com/blogs/aws/amazon-s3-object-size-limit/ *Accessed:* 15 Aug 2018.

[30] www.verisign.com/en_US/website-presence/website-optimization/ssl-certificates/index.xhtml *Accessed:* 27 Dec 2018.

Issued To	
Common Name (CN)	CloudFlare Inc ECC CA-2
Organization (O)	CloudFlare, Inc.
Organizational Unit (OU)	<Not Part Of Certificate>
Serial Number	0F:F3:E6:16:39:AA:3D:1A:12:65:F4:1F:8B:34:E5:B6
Issued By	
Common Name (CN)	Baltimore CyberTrust Root
Organization (O)	Baltimore
Organizational Unit (OU)	CyberTrust
Period of Validity	
Begins On	14 October 2015
Expires On	9 October 2020
Fingerprints	
SHA-256 Fingerprint	61:72:D7:A1:99:6C:BE:F7:1A:01:82:DD:44:B9:9E:9C: 03:57:42:A9:EB:D0:31:1A:A7:3A:A4:73:33:44:C5:A6
SHA1 Fingerprint	6B:53:C3:B3:58:CE:F3:68:20:1F:87:41:B9:C5:AE:DE:EA:38:61:FA

Figure 7.6: Example certificate from a Firefox root store. It is issued to Cloudflare by Baltimore Root. It provides two different fingerprints, using SHA-1 and SHA-256.

7.12.1 Public Key Infrastructure (PKI)

Managing the huge number of certificate checks which would be needed every second on the web makes a well-designed system essential. Such a system forms the Public Key Infrastructure (PKI). The design enables it to operate with a minimum of web traffic. In brief, it comprises

- The Certificate Authority (CA)s, which provide the *root* certificates. Any certificate signed by a CA can be trusted. There are multiple roots, scattered around the world.

- Even with multiple roots, there is still a potential bottleneck. Thus there are intermediate certificates, forming a chain, each signed by the next one above in the chain, until finally the root is reached.

- Even with chains, there would still be a lot of traffic. This is reduced by a website providing not just its certificate, but all the additional ones in the chain above it, to avoid the client browser having to prod each site in the chain.

- Finally, at the end of the chain, the browser gets to the CA and the root. To avoid further traffic, browsers are usually equipped with a *root store*, which contains a wide range of root certificates preloaded.

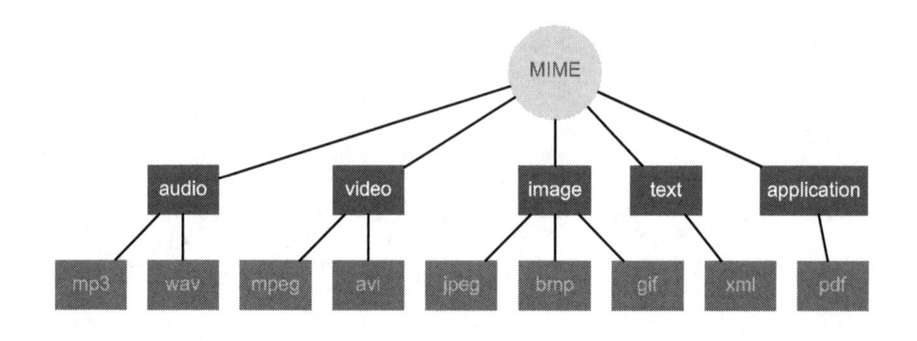

Figure 7.7: MIME types and subtypes. There are seven types and numerous subtypes. Only a sample is presented here.

The *root store* is crucially important and should be modified only with great care. There are legitimate reasons to do so. For example, a large organization might create its own root certificate, which was the ultimate signatory for all its internal certificates. However, other software may have malicious intent, and we study some notorious examples in Section 2.9.

7.13 Email

Email originated before the internet and has since proved extremely popular and useful, even if, at times, a bit overwhelming. The sheer volume of email we often receive these days makes it easy for us to make mistakes through frustration or tiredness (Section 4.6.3), making email a significant cybersecurity risk.

It began so long ago that the first email standard RFC822[31] had all sorts of limitations imposed by the computer limitations of time (1982), such as 7 bit ASCII, some of which continue to hang around today.

RFC822 was a plain text standard, but as computers became more powerful, people wanted to send images and other nontext documents. Hence the next important iteration of the standard, RFC5321[32] introduced Multipurpose Internet Mail Extensions (MIME) to email. There were originally seven MIME types and numerous subtypes proliferated, such as *video/mpeg*.

Most of the MIME details (Figure 7.7) do not concern us here, but there is one very important conceptual issue. Mail servers and clients cannot be expected to handle all of these types and subtypes. Thus nasty things can sneak in and email is a big, very big, source of malware.

[31]www.ietf.org/rfc/rfc0822.txt *Accessed:* 29 Aug 2018.

[32]https://tools.ietf.org/html/rfc5321 *Accessed:* 29 Aug 2018.

A related issue is email privacy. Email fails to adequately protect privacy in two ways:

1. the transmission along the path from mail client, via servers, to mail client at the other end, is frequently unencrypted, and therefore can be read by anybody. Some mail systems (such as Gmail) now utilize client to server encryption.

2. the mail stored on the server is also unencrypted. This is the case for most systems, and, sometimes the email provider will use machine learning, or even human readers, to enhance advertising revenue. Some servers, such as *protonmail*, provide encryption of the user's mailbox.

A consequence of the intrinsic lack of privacy in email is the need to encrypt personal or confidential information. Unfortunately very few people bother (Section 3.4.3.5). Government and law enforcement are quite happy about that. One of the big legal issues under debate at the time of writing is the extent to which encryption should be allowed (Section 8.2).

Cyber Nugget 47: *Private and confidential email should be encrypted and digitally signed.*

Email has now become a major transport vector for all sorts of things, documents large and small. But even if email has been encrypted in transit and remains encrypted on the server, another threat lies beneath the surface. Many email protocols, such as Microsoft Exchange, do not download email permanently from the server. Rather, there is a dynamic relationship between the client and the mail server. Emails withdrawn on the server can be deleted from the client. This could be important if it turns out that an email has some sort of serious legal implications. Another consideration is what happens to an email if a person ceases to have an account on the server, say, when somebody leaves an organization. All of their email may now disappear. Backup is the answer.

Cyber Nugget 48: *Export and backup email at least once a year and important emails immediately.*

The two principal email threats for the unwary: *spoofing*, in which an email is not from whom it purports to be (Section 7.13.1); and *phishing* (Section 5.3.2.4), which is an attempt to get a response to a bogus request of some sort, relying on (false) assumptions the user might make Section 3.2). Both require human error to succeed. Nevertheless, phishing accounts for over 90% of cyberattacks, as noted in the Herjavec 2019 Cybersecurity Ventures report on cybercrime[33]

[33]www.herjavecgroup.com/the-2019-official-annual-cybercrime-report/ *Accessed:* 29 May 2019.

> While the annals of hacking are studded with tales of clever coders finding flaws in systems to achieve malevolent ends, the fact is most cyberattacks begin with a simple email. More than 90% of successful hacks and data breaches stem from phishing.

But spoofing can be reduced with some technical measures as we shall now see.

7.13.1 Spoofing

When email was first set up, it mirrored the sending of a letter by ordinary post, which rapidly got dubbed snail mail. In such a letter, there would be a header, consisting of the addresses of the sender and the recipient and the salutation, Dear Fred, Honorable Sir, whatever. This would be then inserted within an envelope, which would itself be addressed with the recipient and their snail mail address. The envelope could in fact bear no resemblance to the header on the letter, and the wrong letter might end up in an envelope—imagine doing a batch of Christmas cards and getting them mixed up.

An email message, then, comprises a header and body, which are assembled by the mail sending program, which are then put into a virtual envelope, with the recipient address. The email transport system does not look inside the envelope! Hence Odysseus in Section 1.1 could be fooled by the header in the email, which supposedly came from Cutthroat Bank.

From RFC 7208[35]

> The "MAIL FROM" and "HELO" identity authorizations do not provide assurance about the authorization/authenticity of other identities used in the message... Unless the user or the MUA [Mail User Agent] takes care to note that the authorized identity does not match the other more commonly presented identities (such as the From: header field), the user might be lulled into a false sense of security.

7.13.2 Email Security

Email security depends upon three standards: the first two established and given RFCs by the Internet Engineering Task Force (IETF) and the third is quite widely used and awaiting standardization:

For example, eBay and PayPal publish a policy requiring all of their messages to be authenticated in order to appear in someone's inbox. In accordance with their policy, Google rejects all messages from eBay or PayPal that are not authenticated.[34]

[34]https://support.google.com/a/answer/2466580 *Accessed:* 28 Aug 2018.

Sender Policy Framework (SPF) is used to establish the servers, which can send an email on behalf of a domain. Suppose your domain is *fat-porcupine.zq*, the DNS for your server includes an SPF[35] record, which lists the mail servers that can be used for sending mail from *fat-porcupine*.

Domain Keys Identified Mail (DKIM) is an authorization mechanism. The outgoing mail server encrypts the email header information with its private key and adds a digital signature. The receiving server grabs the public key from the sender's DNS to decrypt and check the signature.

Domain-Based Message Authentication, Reporting and Conformance (DMARC) combines both SPF and DKIM and is used, for example, by Gmail[36] The UK government has recommended all departments adopt DMARC, yet a recent report found only 28% of departments outside of central government had done so One successful example is the UK's HM Revenue & Customs, where phishing was a huge problem. However, half a billion emails are blocked by Domain-Based Message Authentication, Reporting and Conformance (DMARC).[37]

> With DMARC, we can now stop almost all of the (500 million phishing emails a year seen in 2014 and 2015) from ever reaching our customers' inboxes," said Edward Tucker, head of HMRC cybersecurity.

Dan Murphy's liquor site has the full works

```
Message ID
 <0.1.2F.447.1D43CC783BD4022.0@omp.email.dansnews.com.au>
Created at: Sun, Aug 26, 2018 at 9:01 AM
 (Delivered after 195 seconds)
From: My | Dan Murphy's <Rewards@email.dansnews.com.au>
To: spikey@fat-porcupine.com
Subject: Hi Spikey  - FREE delivery
SPF: PASS with IP 199.7.206.101
DKIM: 'PASS' with domain email.dansnews.com.au
DMARC: 'PASS'
```

First we begin with the message ID. This is largely free format, but requires the @ symbol: the left-hand side of @ is a unique string; the right-hand side is the server or ADministrative Management Domain (ADMD), which has generated the message ID. This ID is unique to the message for a single passage from

[35]https://tools.ietf.org/html/rfc7208 *Accessed:* 26 Aug 2018.

[36]https://dmarc.org/ *Accessed:* 26 Aug 2018.

[37]www.computerweekly.com/news/450403583/HMRC-blocks-500000-phishing-emails-in-2015 *Accessed:* 21 Mar 2019.

sender to receiver. If the message is forwarded, a new ID is generated. The following fields are self-evident, concluding with the three security fields discussed above.

7.13.2.1 Sender Policy Framework Results

The SPF query to the DNS can return seven results.[35] The most desirable result is PASS, meaning that the server is authorized. NEUTRAL means that the ADMD opts out, not asserting whether the IP address is authorized. FAIL is bad news, an explicit statement that the IP address is *not* authorized by the ADMD.[38]

So here is how it all works; (Figure 7.8) *spikey@fat-porcupine.zq* wants to send an email to *cutebutvicious@mink.edu.yn*. His Mail User Agent composes the email, telling *cutebutvicious* he loves her teeth, and sends it to theMail Transfer Agent (MTA) (the mail server), *spines@fat-porcupine.zq*. The MTA creates the message ID, encrypts, and signs the headers (DKIM), adds an envelope, and prods the DNS to get the IP address of *cutebutvicious@mink.edu.yn*. Once he has the email address, he sends the message on its way.

When *mink.edu.yn* receives the message, it does some security checks. First it gets the public key for *fat-porcupine.zq* and successfully decrypts the message and checks the signature. Then it checks the DNS SPF Resource Record(RR) for and gets back a PASS. It then puts message into *cutebutvicisous* mailbox for her to read at her leisure.

7.14 Blockchains

Blockchains are a new and exciting technology that originated with Satoshi Nakamoto, but, like Banksy, nobody knows who he, or she, is. This is extraordinary, since many computer scientists would regard blockchains as a major breakthrough, worthy of the highest awards. Satoshi invented blockchain as part of his introduction of the first cryptocurrency, bitcoin, although blockchains have now gone way beyond crytocurrency in their application domains. Since they are a hot research area, we shall give here just the basic concepts.

A blockchain is often referred to as a *distributed ledger.* It is a record of transactions, which is not stored centrally but is kept by everybody. Communication is peer-to-peer, with no central authority or database. Cryptographic techniques are used to ensure that the record (blockchain) cannot be tampered with. Pretty much anything can go into the payload of a block. It could be a document listing land rights, some financial information, or maybe personal health data. At an abstract level, there are three components: a consensus mechanism; the creation of a new block for the chain; and the process of adding the new block. The consensus mechanism is used to ensure that the new block is a valid entity to add to the

[38]https://tools.ietf.org/html/rfc5598 *Accessed:* 01 Aug 2019.

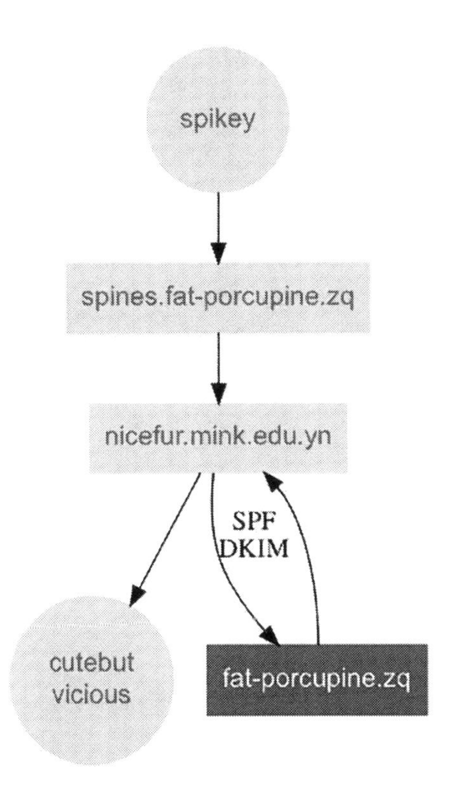

Figure 7.8: Spikey sends email to cutebutvicious. *mink.com* checks with spikey's DNS via SPF and DKIM that the email is really from spikey's authorized domain server (in dark gray).

blockchain. The essential technical feature here is a *trapdoor function,* known as a hash (Section 7.2). Such a hash function is used to in effect sign the block, which will contain the signature of the chain until that point in time. Creating the block is akin to climbing up the wall by one's fingernails to get back through the trapdoor. But for the network to validate the block, it requires only the computational effort to fall through the trapdoor in the first place. PPK crytography, which we discussed above, is used to achieve a very high level of security of individual node failures and to prevent individuals faking messages, to achieve what is technically referred to as Byzantine Fault Tolerance [80].

Although the application of blockchains is growing rapidly, Fedorov et al. [50] caution that quantum computing (Section 7.16) may render them useless within a decade. Thus there is active research [15] to find algorithms that will survive in a postquantum world.

Much hype surrounds the use of blockchains and trust. However, Bruce Schneier[39], inventor of Blowfish points out that there are numerous human factors in blockchain and bitcoin technology. These include issues of determination of blocksize, vendors of hardware, validation of software, and so on[39]:

> People have to trust the software and the operating systems and the computers everything is running on. And we've seen attacks against wallets and exchanges. We've seen Trojans and phishing and password guessing. Criminals have even used flaws in the system that people use to repair their cell phones to steal bitcoin.

7.14.1 The Hard Fork

One of the much touted features of blockchains is their immutability, Some Ethereum (one of the other big blockchains outside of bitcoin) users lost around US $50 million due to a cyberattack on the Decentralized Autonomous Organisation (DAO). At this point, the immutability of the blockchain came under scrutiny.

As Patrick Murch wrote[40]

> But, at the end of the day, too many Ethereum community members, including some of its most prominent leaders, suffered losses, having traded their ether for DAO tokens. They felt that action had to be taken to reverse their losses. The Ethereum leadership was able to coordinate with the network stakeholders to create a so-called "hard fork," a permanent split of the Ethereum blockchain, so that control of the siphoned-off funds would be shifted to a group of trusted leader

Thus human factors came into play in a big way, to agree that the hard fork should happen. But there was a huge principle at stake here. If the blockchain could be changed, would any blockchain *ever* be safe? Murch again[40]

> For some members of the community, the decision to hard fork was a wanton violation of the community's core principles, akin to burning down the house to roast the pig. In protest, they decided to keep running the original Ethereum blockchain unadulterated, and thus there are now two Ethereum networks.

So, what was the hard fork. Essentially it meant winding back all the Ethereum transactions to just before the hack. Backward

[39] www.schneier.com/blog/archives/2019/02/blockchain_and_.html *Accessed:* 16 Feb 2019.
[40] https://hbr.org/2017/04/who-controls-the-blockchain *Accessed:* 16 Feb 2019.

compatibility is lost. At that point the software protocols were changed, and the blockchain carried on along a new fork in the path/chain on 20 July 2016.[41]

However, more benign motivations underlie further hard forks in Ethereum blockchains.

Ethereum hard fork Constantinople is scheduled for 27 Feb. 2019, Following.[42]

> Ethereum has decreased by more than 10× from its all-time high in 2018, and numerous platforms and companies, launched via Ethereum have been facing enforcement pressures from the US Securities and Exchange Commission for the trading of securities and unregistered issuance. The developers have figured out that the difficulty bomb programmed into Ethereum has caused the blocks to become extremely slow after a point, after which no more blocks can be mined. The developers have to hard fork periodically so that ETH keeps on getting updated with the latest technology.

7.15 EU Data Protection Rules

Buried within the terms and conditions for internet services, which not everybody reads, are often all sorts of rights to use or onsell data. Most of the time we don't have any option but to agree if we want access to the service. However, this is such an important issue that the United Nations has adopted resolutions to extend offline privacy to online information.[43] In fact the International Covenant on Civil and Political Rights declares in Article 17[44]:

1. *No one shall be subjected to arbitrary or unlawful interference with his privacy, family, home or correspondence, nor to unlawful attacks on his honour and reputation.*

2. *Everyone has the right to the protection of the law against such interference or attacks.*

In May 2018, the EU General Data Protection Regulation (GDPR) came into force across the EU. It gives comprehensive protection of personal data, what can be collected, and how and when it can be used. Moreover, it extends to issues such as automated use of data for decisions affecting the user: such decisions are now subject to three user rights: the right to know; the right to request a person review the decision; and the right to contest.

[41] https://blog.ethereum.org/2016/07/20/hard-fork-completed/ *Accessed:* 17 Feb 2019.

[42] https://coinswitch.co/news/ethereum-hard-fork-jan-19-know-everything-about-3-upcoming-eth-hard-forks *Accessed:* 17 Feb 2019.

[43] www.ohchr.org/en/issues/digitalage/pages/digitalageindex.aspx *Accessed:* 17 Aug 2018.

[44] www.ohchr.org/en/professionalinterest/pages/ccpr.aspx *Accessed:* 17 Aug 2018.

7.16 Quantum Computing

We end this chapter with a brief look at the Jekyll and Hyde of cybersecurity, quantum computing. As yet it is still in the potential application stage, at least for common commercial use. Quantum theory is unusual in science, in that, since its inception over a century ago, it has passed every experimental test. Yet philosophically it remains bizarre.

One of its more spooky characteristics is *entanglement*, discussed in Section 7.16.2, which is given by Dr Jekyll. Another is *superposition*, which, for this largely nontechnical book, we might loosely call the parallel universe side, the Mr Hyde side.

7.16.1 Mr Hyde: Superposition and Parallel Computation

Edwin Schrödinger, one of the pioneers of quantum theory, came up with a Gedanken (thought) experiment, his eponymous cat. Fortunately it was a thought experiment only and no cats were ever harmed. The central idea is that a quantum system (which is any system in our universe) progresses over a time in many states simultaneously if left to its own devices. When somebody prods it, it selects just one of these states, or in some interpretations, one of the many parallel universes. Philosophers have agonized over what this means and entire books have been written on this aspect of the quantum world alone.

So, going back to Schrödinger's cat, our poor feline is put in a chamber with a radioactive source [121] and a container of poisonous gas. If the source emits a particle it releases the gas. But radioactivity is random, thus at any given time, the cat may be alive or dead. Schrödinger argued that before looking inside the chamber, the cat was in a superposition of live and dead states, and one was only selected at the time of checking.

The reason this is important for cryptography appeared over 60 years later, when Peter Shor [126] demonstrated that quantum computers could solve the integer factorization and hence the discrete logarithm problem (Section 36) is *much* faster than conventional computers, essentially by exploring lots of solutions all at the same time. Thus if quantum computers become readily available, and Shor turns out to be right in practice, the whole edifice of public–private cryptography will come crumbling down. Mr Hyde will triumph.

7.16.2 Dr Jekyll: Entanglement

One of the ever-present risks in cybersecurity is known as the Man in the Middle Attack attack. Alice and Brenda have come up with a clever cryptographic system along the lines we have already discussed. But suppose now that Cornelius has inserted himself in the middle. He now intercepts Alice's messages and forwards them to Brenda, who still thinks they are from Alice. Likewise,

Alice is deceived into thinking her communications are coming directly from Brenda.

Without going into technical detail, the MITM is very hard to detect. Quantum entanglement has the potential to completely protect against it. To get the idea, we need to think of light as a stream of particles, known as photons. There is an interesting historical twist to light as particles. Isaac Newton in the 17th century argued light as a stream of particles, which he referred to as corpuscles. His theory lost out to Christian Huygens' wave theory. Quantum mechanics in the early 20th century provided a compromise: light could behave both as a particle and a wave.

Photons have a property called spin, which may point up or down. When they are created in pairs, the spins are entangled. Each photon does not know its spin until the spin is measured. At that point its twin adopts the other spin, *instantly*. By instantly, we mean exactly that. There is no time for a message to travel from one photon to the other, even at many times the speed of light. The photons may have ended up at opposite ends of the galaxy, but still the same happens. Much discussion has taken place over how one photon knows that its twin, somewhere, has taken a particular spin state. Suffice it to say that there is no way either photon can know what is going to happen. Each remains in a superposition of spin up and spin down until one is measured.

Entanglement is so spooky and counterintuitive that it has been subject to the most stringent tests, involving greater and greater distances. In 2017 the distance was pushed out to an incredible 1,200 km [154].

And now to the punchline, without going into detail, entanglement completely destroys MITM. Any interference with a message between Alice and Bob forces superposition to collapse, and they know that somebody has been snooping. Thus, the MITM attack becomes impossible. Quantum mechanics has potentially a huge role to play in computing and cryptography.

Chapter 8

The Future

In times of peace prepare for war.

Sun Tzu, *The Art of War*

We conclude the book with some guesses as to the immediate future. We consider burgeoning risks, such as security in the internet of things, and the implications they carry for government policy, and the need to consider international actors and nation states. To this end, our recommendations are tailored to specific recommendations for specific types of nation states. We also look at the challenges posed by technologies, such as quantum computing and DNA storage. We also examine the real possibility of a zero day attack and how a coordinated response can prevent or respond to such an event.

8.1 Keeping Nasties Out

We saw earlier in the book that companies, such as Uber (Section 3.4.3.2) and Bose (Section 3.3.3), have been covertly, although not necessarily illegally, vacuuming user data. There is a need for consumers to be sure that an app they download will not be a Trojan horse of this kind.

It is already commonplace for free/open source software to be distributed with certificate keys, enabling the user to determine that the download site is genuine and that the software is what it is supposed to be. However, this does not get around the problem of the software creator adding spyware of some kind.

In the open-source world, it is possible for third parties to read and confirm that software is free of nasties. The mechanisms of distributed trust we discussed will come into play to ensure that these third parties are honest. Thus, although open source might seem to be cheap and flaky, it can offer extra security through being inspected and checked by lots of people.

Cyber Nugget 49: *Open-source software has the advantage that it can be checked by a lot of people for bugs and hidden nasties.*

For proprietary software, new methods are needed. Legal mechanisms are not likely to be effective. The examples above are probably already illegal in some jurisdictions, but globalization makes any sanctions very hard to enforce. Third party validators are needed. Since organizations entrust confidential data to lawyers and accountants, in principle software source code can be entrusted to a suitably accredited body.

It seems feasible that validators, which have emerged to check open-source software, could morph into accredited entities in the way professional bodies monitor accountants, doctors, and so on. Professional computing societies could act as accrediting bodies. To gain accreditation a validator would need to demonstrate

- Adequate professional expertise. This is commonplace for professional accreditation of higher education courses, and is already something the Association for Computing Machinery (ACM) does across numerous computing and engineering domains.
- Adequate protection of data, presumably encrypted. Already one would assume that lawyers, accountants, and doctors would keep data secure. However, Anthem (Section 3.4.3.2) did not manage to keep patient data secure; hence, the security bar needs to be raised.
- Theft by employees. Rogue employees (Section 2.10) are an ever-present threat to data security as we saw with in Section 2.10. Hardware and authentication systems can reduce the risk of data theft. It is much harder to control the theft of intellectual property, since this may not require anything physical being removed.

On balance, the risk of something going adrift should be acceptable for the assurance that the software is not toxic.

Cyber Nugget 50: *Be wary of apps possibly containing nasties, such as spyware.*

8.1.1 Formal Validation

Some software validators have already appeared, with applications in safety critical areas such as medical imaging. Here the focus is not on keeping out malware, but on making sure that the software does what it is supposed to do. With electric cars, fly-by-wire aircraft, and other potentially life-endangering systems proliferating, such testing is of paramount importance.

DeepSpec is a consortium aiming at formal software verification. In other activities, formally correct operating systems, such as CertiKOS [124], are under development.

8.2 Use of Encryption

Encryption enables us, in principle, to communicate with other individuals without others being privy to the exchange. In the days of snail mail, countries often had severe penalties for tampering with mail. However, security agencies, where authorized, could open and read any letter. These same agencies now want decryption of electronic communications. A lot of confusion surrounds these issues, particularly with regard to the algorithms. But as Bruce Schneier (Blowfish, etc.) notes, the issues are not cryptographic, so much as human/social/political.[1]

Australia has a legal framework, which will give authorities increased access to encrypted communication. At this time, it is also not clear how this will work. Corporations may offer encryption services, which they themselves cannot crack. This became a matter of major news coverage when the FBI asked Apple to unlock a phone associated with the San Bernardino shootings.[2] Apple refused on the grounds that whether it wanted to or not (and its public position was that it did not want to interfere with the privacy of its users), it simply could not.

There are signs that this may have a negative effect on Australian business. Microsoft president, Brad Smith, said that his customers had in some cases asked to avoid building data centers in Australia. They saw a risk in weakened encryption as a result of these laws.[3]

The authors concur with the UN position we have already noted (Section 7.15) that the UN regards privacy as a human right and has extended its thinking to the digital age. There is a fine line to tread and it is no time to be apathetic. One is that encryption may become illegal, just as guns are illegal in many countries, except for designated applications. Thus, the encryption of HyperText Transfer Protocol Secure (HTTPS) would be allowed, since it is fundamental to commercial and government activity. But general encryption apps, such as PGP,[4] or bcrypt (an implementation of Blowfish,[5] even homegrown encryption), could

---

[1] www.schneier.com/blog/archives/2018/05/ray_ozzies_encr.html *Accessed:* 31 May 2019.

[2] www.theguardian.com/technology/2016/feb/17/apple-challenges-chilling-demand-decrypt-san-bernadino-iphone *Accessed:* 21 Nov 2018.

[3] www.theguardian.com/technology/2019/mar/27/tech-companies-not-comfortable-storing-data-in-australia-microsoft-warns *Accessed:* 28 Mar 2019.

[4] www.openpgp.org/ *Accessed:* 21 Nov 2018.

[5] www.schneier.com/academic/blowfish/ *Accessed:* 24 May 2019.

become illegal. We are some way away from this privacy storm as yet and, hopefully, it will remain a black cloud in the horizon.

8.3 Encouraging Good Cyber Practice

Mobile phones, tablets, laptops, home computers, WiFi, cellular data, and almost everybody in the developed world have some form of computer access and much of the rest of the world does too. Facebook is now reported to have over 2 billion users,[6] over a quarter of the world's population. Many African financial transactions are carried out over mobile phones.

Given such huge computer usage, it is unrealistic to expect most of these people to be anything more than simple users, rather like the many people who slavishly follow recipes, rather than the chefs who invent them. Computer users are still thought of as nerds, albeit sometimes rather wealthy nerds, and not many people have the slightest inclination to dig into the details of how their computing devices work.

The ever-increasing prevalence of cyberattacks of one form or the other means that ignorance and lack of interest are no longer viable choices. Apart from individual risk, one person's risk and cyber compromise may impact on others, say by letting a hacker into a large system.

8.3.1 The Scourge and Salvation of Email

Email is undoubtedly useful. It also has proliferated. Many people, especially if they use email at work, are inundated with messages. Sometimes, messages languish on the server for days, and sometimes, they never get read or attended to. We've seen numerous examples of cyberthreats through email, from phishing to ransomware. Yet email is also a good source of information about cyberthreats, since it is a push service. It arrives on your computer, whether you asked for it or not.

There are numerous good email services for cybersafety alerts. For Example, the Australian government runs *Stay Smart Online*,[7] a website and regular alert email, such as the December 2018 breach of the Quora forum.[8] Two problems impede the success of such initiatives: getting people to subscribe in the first place; and making sure that the emails are read or at least scanned for relevance.

Making sure that emails get through depends upon another mild knowledge requirement: effective use of an email client. The more popular email clients

[6] www.statista.com/statistics/264810/number-of-monthly-active-facebook-users-worldwide/ *Accessed:* 09 Dec 2018.

[7] www.staysmartonline.gov.au/alert-service *Accessed:* 10 Dec 2018.

[8] www.staysmartonline.gov.au/alert-service/data-breach-public-qa-forum-website-quora *Accessed:* 10 Dec 2018.

offer ways of automatically sorting emails. Security emails need to be prioritized and spruiked until they have been opened.

Organizations, such as banks, frequently send out security emails (and lots of malware often purports to be from a bank), along with other advertising and general information they send to customers. Thus security emails need to be tagged in some way, although any constant tag could be easily exploited. One possibility might be to integrate a weekly code, sent, say by SMS, with the email header or subject line. Another would be to establish a tag within the email security features discussed in Section 7.13.

8.4 Teaching People Safe Practices

There is a lot going on in this area and even more to do. We just give a couple of examples: gamification in Section 8.4.1 and marketing campaigns in Section 8.4.1.1.

8.4.1 Gamification

One of the exciting developments over the last decade or so has been the use of computer games for teaching and learning [55,123]. Where the material to be taught benefits from simulation, role playing or scenario analysis, games are a natural tool. However, there was also a growing interest in making games out of things, which are not intrinsically game-like. Jane McGonigal [90] describes how she turned domestic chores, such as cleaning the bathroom, into a game with her partner. This is called *gamification.*

There is already gamification activity in teaching good cybersecurity practices. Antiphishing Phil is a game that grew out of research at Carnegie Mellon [125]. As you might expect, it teaches people about how to recognize phishing and believe it or not features fish (Figure 8.1).

Gamification is engaging the few times one encounters it, but it can become tedious thereafter. Partly, this is because the so-called games are not actually very good games. However, there is a lot of scope for development here, since hacker stories have become best sellers — think of the Girl with the Dragon Tattoo.[9]

8.4.1.1 Marketing Campaigns for Cybersecurity

Another way of educating people about cybersecurity is to develop social marketing campaigns, which use nudges (Section 4.7). Hayden[10] suggests cybersecurity can be promoted in campaigns which feature

---

[9] the first of Stieg Larsson's monumental trilogy.

[10] Why marketing principles can help a security awareness program succeed (2014). https://searchsecurity.techtarget.com/tip/Why-marketing-principles-can-help-a-security-awareness-program-succeed *Accessed:* 7 Jan 2018.

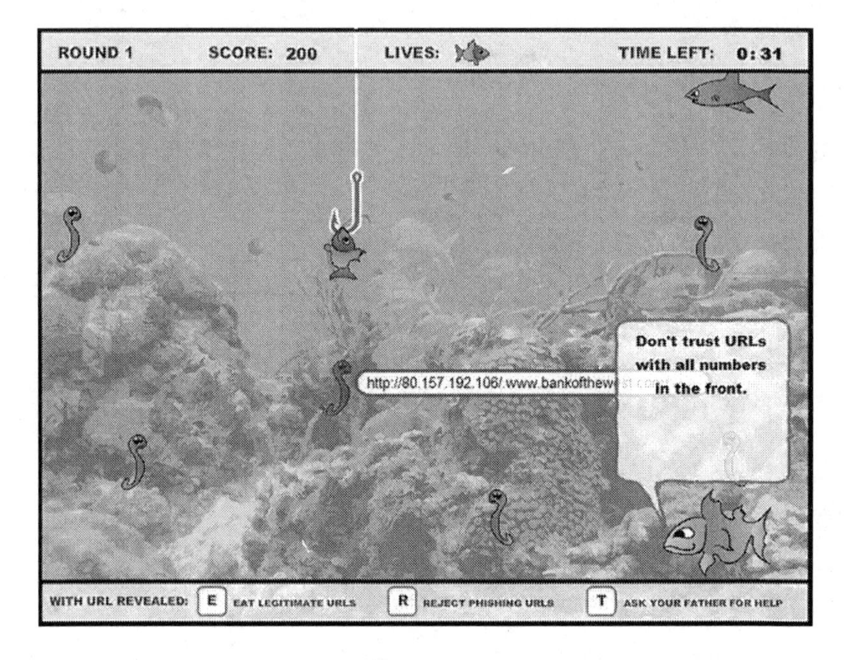

Figure 8.1: Screenshot from Antiphishing Phil.

- Social currency
- Triggers
- Emotion
- Public
- Practical value
- Stories

Social currency means that cybersecurity issues should be explained in a manner that involves the wider public in what and how to protect themselves and how to respond to data breaches. The information should not be presented as talking down to people, but in a language and style that makes individuals empowered and intelligent. Triggers or cues should be designed in any cybersecurity program so that security is at the top of the mind. Nudges, as discussed in Section 4.7, such as feedback on poor passwords and not using poor security questions, may also serve an important part of this program.

Emotion is important, as emotional content may often be shared. Crafting messages in terms of humor or anger, or even sympathy and compassion may help. An example may be to show the effect on an elderly lady. All cybersecurity programs should focus on providing tangible cues and evidence of what good practice looks like. This can include rewards for clean-desk policies, having a no piggybacking policy of visitors to the building. In short it is important that cybersecurity policies become apparent and visible in our workplaces and homes.

People are more likely to take onboard messages that have practical value, such as preventing a cyberattack or reducing cyber insurance premiums. It also suggested that incentives may be used to encourage cybersecurity, such as providing software to encrypt hard drives that may benefit both the user and the company.

Stories are important because lessons or morality about cybersecurity can be shared online. Police-type lessons do not work well, as opposed to a focus on characters and the humor involved in sometimes unpleasant situations of cyber breaches. Simply put content that is fun and engaging is more likely to be shared and discussed at home and in the office. What these hallmarks of good cybersecurity communication show is that it is not the amount of information that is important, but the nature of communication and how this information about cybersecurity is communicated to different groups or niches in society.

8.5 Changing Criminal Models and the Arms Race with the Authorities

It is possible that criminal and hostile states are more organized than those who seek to protect our cybersecurity. As noted in Chapter 5, the threats faced by all of us are constantly evolving both in technology, vector of attack, but more importantly by the business model criminals and hostile states wish to use. Examples are the use of ransomware, business email compromises, threats of denial of service, and the stealing of IP by criminal insiders, and members of hostile states. The use of social engineering also shows that cybercriminals can adapt quickly to the frailty of human behavior to get around security design and technology. A worrying trend is the use of criminal networks such as the Necrus group by hostile states as privateers to steal information and/or disrupt the infrastructure of opposition countries. For many in the population, this means that keeping up to date with the intelligence of threats and how to avoid them is vital.

It should be noted that reactions to cyberattacks and threats are fragmentary and depend on cooperation across different jurisdictions with different legal and regulatory frameworks. Also many technologies and systems used to prevent attacks are not coordinated to provide overall enterprise security. A good example is the use of cloud technology to store critical data. As noted in Chapter 6, this is seen as an out-of-sight out-of-mind solution of contracting out security of vital assets to a third party. On the other hand, those who seek to disrupt, steal, threaten, and even destroy our security are better organized through criminal networks working with hostile states, where intelligence and knowhow on how to conduct cyberattacks is easily shared. As noted also in Chapter 6, the costs and expertise now to engage in cybercrime are minimal, or can be provided on a percentage of return basis. We are therefore likely to see cyberattacks becoming more common with small and medium businesses, and more individuals as barriers reduce entry of criminals, while the competition to provide services increases.

8.5.1 Do People Learn?

Despite media reports of massive breaches, popular fiction of cyberthreats in films like Die-Hard 4.0 or in television series such as Mr Robot, it seems that human behavior in cybersecurity is difficult to change, even for those who work in national security or in technology companies. In a recent report by security company Dashlane, Katz noted in 2018[11]

- The Government Accountability Office (GAO) in the United States government was able to guess Admin passwords in the Pentagon in just 9 seconds, as well as discovering that passwords for multiple weapon's systems were protected by default passwords, that any member of the public could find online.
- The state of Texas left 14 million electoral records exposed on a server that was not password protected.
- There are around 1 million corporate email and password combinations of top UK law firm available in the Dark Web. Most of the credentials stolen were in plain text.
- An Indian engineering student hacked into one of Google's pages to access a TV broadcast satellite. The student logged in using his mobile device on the Google Admin pages with a blank username and password.
- A White house staffer allegedly wrote down his email login and password on White house stationary, which he then left accidently at a DC bus stop.

No technology can really protect us from our carelessness. The examples all show the problem of having only one weak link in security can cause serious breaches. Organizations and individuals need to see cybersecurity as fundamental risk and not just an IT issue. Governance, training, and monitoring of people with access to important information is also the most perplexing but important issue for the 21st-century political economy.

[11] Kanye West Tops Dashlane's List of 2018's "Worst Password Offenders" https://blog.dashlane.com/password-offenders-2018/?utm_source=email&utm_medium=appboy&utm_campaign=19774335-05fd-4bb8-bb48-9e2d05587b38&utm_content=1&utm_term=en&utm_type=news *Accessed:* 20 Dec 2018.

8.5.2 New Legal Agendas

We have seen a number of examples of where vendors have sought to exploit information in a deceptive way. Bose (Section 3.3.3) used their control app for harvesting musical activity. Superfish and PrivDog hijacked HTTPS security (Section 2.9). Such vendors may have already obtained permission to do this when the user agreed to the terms and conditions.

Lengthy legal contracts are a fact of life in the cyberworld, and most users have little option but to agree. Thus, entry to the Apple store *for any app* requires a blanket agreement. The GDPR helps a little with this, but we believe that terms and conditions should be legally required to state in everyday language right at the beginning, an executive summary if you will, a number of important conditions, such as

- Whether the app harvests data to onsell to other vendors. Some companies, we have seen earlier in the book, have been less than perfect in this regard. **It should be clearly stated what information an app harvests and whether it onsells it.**
- Whether the app interferes with security protocols such as HTTPS.
- Whether personal data can (a) be exported in a universal, nonproprietary format and (b) how personal data can be completely expunged, including backups, log files, clipboards, and innards of algorithms.

As this book goes to press, Bloomberg reported that Amazon has huge teams of people listening to Alexa,[12] its home assistant.[13]

> In a response to the story, Amazon confirmed to CNN Business that it hires people to listen to what customers say to Alexa. But Amazon said it takes "security and privacy of our customers' personal information seriously." The company said it only annotates an "extremely small number of interactions from a random set of customers."

The situation is slightly less sinister for Apple, again according to Bloomberg,[14] its home assistant[15]

[12] www.bloomberg.com/news/articles/2019-04-10/is-anyone-listening-to-you-on-alexa-a-global-team-reviews-audio *Accessed:* 13 Apr 2019.

[13] https://edition.cnn.com/2019/04/11/tech/amazon-alexa-listening/index.html *Accessed:* 13 Apr 2019.

[14] www.bloomberg.com/news/articles/2019-04-10/is-anyone-listening-to-you-on-alexa-a-global-team-reviews-audio *Accessed:* 13 Apr 2019.

[15] https://edition.cnn.com/2019/04/11/tech/amazon-alexa-listening/index.html *Accessed:* 13 Apr 2019.

> Apple's Siri also has human helpers, who work to gauge whether the digital assistant's interpretation of requests lines up with what the person said. The recordings they review lack personally identifiable information and are stored for six months tied to a random identifier,

8.6 Hyperstorage and Machine Learning and Privacy

Facebook went under intense scrutiny following the apparently illicit use of over 50 million user's personal data by firm Cambridge Analytica. The information was used to generate personal ad campaigns in the 2016 US presidential election (Section 2.8). The threat, and possible benefit, from machine learning is increased manyfold by the ease of storage of extremely large volumes of data, what we call hyperstorage. Data storage costs energy, thus new storage technologies with much higher information density and lower energy costs could be transformative. One such technology is DNA storage—using the DNA molecule itself as a storage medium (as opposed to it storing a genetic code). It has already been demonstrated, but currently costs around $3K/MB and thus needs to come down in price significantly.

The significance of hyperstorage combined with rapid progress in machine learning means that very little online information will remain secret. For example, telcos could record every single phone call, convert it to text and search it for anything, from advertising opportunities to criminal intent. To see how easy this is, imagine you spend 2 h everyday on the phone at 64 Kbps (a decent MP3 rate), which would amount to about 20 MB. Thus, 10 years of calls would equate to 200 GB. Peanuts. Hence, the need for increase privacy.

8.6.1 Protecting the Vulnerable from Themselves

It could also be argued that the threats of cyberattacks, beyond those of carelessness, are too complex and dynamic for many in society to deal with. Examples may be the elderly, less educated, and small businesses who lack the infrastructure and resources to be able to defend or rebuild after an attack. Designing in security for a society may therefore become an important option. This could include the use routers that monitor individual WiFi hotspots for homes and business that report suspicious behavior, provide greater security and guidance on stronger passwords, have built-in password safes and VPN capabilities. These routers could also have reminders on updates on operating systems. These systems could be produced at low cost and become mandated or distributed by government to vulnerable consumers. Of course technology cannot protect us from our own carelessness and lack of forethought, or new social engineering risks, but it can at least like a burglar alarm make a cybercrime less likely.

8.7 The Mink and the Porcupine

Porcupine defends herself from predators with her sharp spines, difficult to strike or bite. You need kevlar gloves to pick up a porcupine. Mink on the other hand has a beautiful soft coat, but he is a voracious predator with very sharp teeth. You need kevlar gloves to pick up an angry mink too.

Most of the cybersecurity measures discussed in this book are porcupine defenses, making it as difficult as possible to get in. At the state level, cyber warfare is starting to emerge as a national strategy, although Stuxnet was very likely an example of a state attack. Thus, mink-like strategies of hunt and kill are increasingly prevalent at this level, but much less so at a corporate or home level.

We began the book with the story of the first computer virus, Creeper, and Reaper, a cyber mink sent out to destroy it. Perhaps we need legal and accreditation frameworks for more attack software. Why wait for a network of unsecured Internet of Things (IoT) devices to become a botnet for a Distributed Denial of Service (DDoS)? Why not be more proactive and search out and get their owners to secure them in some way. We need more cyber minks.

There are some powerful tools already out there. Marcin Kleczynski found *Malwarebytes* after picking up a nasty virus in 2004. Now a company with over 700 people,[16] it develops tools for hunting and destroying malware, beyond the usual antiviral software.

Another mink comes, Falcon OverWatch, from CrowdStrike[17] that searches out threats of all kinds, known and unknown, in real time.

8.8 Take It Away, Renatus

The message of this book is that good cybersecurity depends on people as much as, or even more than, technology. We have seen how destructive and costly a cyberattack can be, from ransomware to fake news. When computers have been set up and configured, there is a strong urge to leave well alone. This is not irrational. An operating system upgrade can sometimes break existing software, perhaps with very high cost. However, we believe that good cyber hygiene to avoid attacks pays off in the long run. Deception, such as email spoofing, and false assumptions—nobody could possibly know my mother's maiden name—lead us into trouble. Thus, we give the last word to Roman writer Publius Flavius Vegetius Renatus, a millennium and a half ago, often wrongly attributed to Sun Tzu in the *Art of War*

Si vis pacem, para bellum. *If you want peace, prepare for war*

[16]www.malwarebytes.com/company/ *Accessed:* 12 Mar 2019.
[17]www.crowdstrike.com/why-crowdstrike/ *Accessed:* 12 Mar 2019.

References

[1] Harold Abelson, Ross Anderson, Steven M. Bellovin, Josh Benaloh, Matt Blaze, Whitfield Diffie, John Gilmore, Matthew Green, Susan Landau, Peter G. Neumann, Ronald L. Rivest, Jeffrey I. Schiller, Bruce Schneier, Michael A. Specter, and Daniel J. Weitzner. Keys under doormats: Mandating insecurity by requiring government access to all data and communications. *Journal of Cybersecurity*, 1(1):69–79, 2015.

[2] Brigitte Acoca. Online identity theft. *OECD Observer*, 268:12–13, 2008.

[3] Anne Adams and Martina Angela Sasse. Users are not the enemy. *Communications of the ACM*, 42(12):40–46, 1999.

[4] Anne Adams, Martina Angela Sasse, and Peter Lunt. Making passwords secure and usable. In: Thimbleby H., O'Conaill B., Thomas P.J. (eds.) *People and Computers XII*, pages 1–19. Springer, London, 1997.

[5] David Adrian, Karthikeyan Bhargavan, Zakir Durumeric, Pierrick Gaudry, Matthew Green, J. Alex Halderman, Nadia Heninger, Drew Springall, Emmanuel Thomé, Luke Valenta, Benjamin VanderSloot, Eric Wustrow, Santiago Zanella-Béguelin, and Paul Zimmermann. Imperfect forward secrecy: How Diffie-Hellman fails in practice. *Communications of the ACM*, 62(1):106–114, 2018.

[6] Catherine L. Anderson and Ritu Agarwal. Practicing safe computing: A multimethod empirical examination of home computer use security behavioral intentions. *MIS Quarterly*, 34(3):613–643, 2010.

[7] Dmitriy Ayrapetov. Cybersecurity challenges in 2013. *CIO (13284045)*, page 8, 2013.

[8] Rebecca Balebako, Pedro G Leon, Hazim Almuhimedi, Patrick Gage Kelley, Jonathan Mugan, Alessandro Acquisti, Lorrie Faith Cranor, and Norman Sadeh. Nudging users towards privacy on mobile devices. In *Proc. CHI 2011 Workshop on Persuasion, Nudge, Influence and Coercion*, pages 193–201, 2011.

[9] Matthew P. Barrett. *Framework for Improving Critical Infrastructure Cybersecurity Version 1.1.* National Institute of Standards and Technology, Gaithersburg, MD, 2018.

[10] Albert-László Barabási. *Linked: The New Science of Networks.* AAPT, New York, 2003.

[11] Albert-László Barabási and Réka Albert. Emergence of scaling in random networks. *Science*, 286(5439):509–512, 1999.

[12] Solms Basie Von. Towards a cyber governance maturity model for boards of directors. *International Journal of Business and Cyber Security*, 1(1), 2016, also presented at the *1st International Conference on Business and Cyber Security*, 11–12 May 2016, London, UK.

[13] Hannah Beech, Gu Yongqiang, Victor Luckerson, and Sam Frizell. The other side of the great firewall. *Time*, 185(23):48–51, 2015.

[14] Daniel J Bernstein. Curve25519: New Diffie-Hellman speed records. In *International Workshop on Public Key Cryptography*, pages 207–228. Springer, 2006, 24–26 April 2006, New York.

[15] Daniel J. Bernstein and Tanja Lange. Post-quantum cryptography. *Nature*, 549:188–194, 2017.

[16] Tilmann Betsch, Susanne Haberstroh, Beate Molter, and Andreas Glckner. Oops, i did it againrelapse errors in routinized decision making. *Organizational Behavior & Human Decision Processes*, 93(1):62, 2004.

[17] Merim Bilalić, Peter McLeod, and Fernand Gobet. Inflexibility of expertsreality or myth? Quantifying the einstellung effect in chess masters. *Cognitive Psychology*, 56(2):73–102, 2008.

[18] Douglas Bonderud. Leaked mirai malware boosts iot insecurity threat level. https://securityintelligence.com/news/leaked-mirai-malware-boosts-iot-insecurity-threat-level/, Accessed 11 June 2018, 2016.

[19] Dan Boneh. Attacking cryptographic key exchange with precomputation: Technical perspective. *Communications of the ACM*, 62(1):105, 2018.

[20] Rachel Botsman. *Who can You Trust.* Penguin, London, 2017.

[21] Sezer Bozkus Kahyaoglu and Kiymet Caliyurt. Cyber security assurance process from the internal audit perspective. *Managerial Auditing Journal*, 33(4):360–376, 2018.

[22] Kathryn A. Braun-LaTour, Nancy M. Puccinelli, and Fred W. Mast. Mood, information congruency, and overload. *Journal of Business Research*, 60(11):1109–1116, 2007.

[23] C Bruner, Gordon and Anand Kumar. Explaining consumer acceptance of handheld internet devices. *Journal of Business Research*, 58(5):553–558, 2005.

[24] Tad T. Bruny, Matthew D. Wood, Lindsay A. Houck, and Holly A. Taylor. The path more travelled: Time pressure increases reliance on familiar route-based strategies during navigation. *Quarterly Journal of Experimental Psychology*, 70(8):1439–1452, 2017.

[25] Joseph Bullington. Self-other perceptions in user judgments of internet computing risks. In *Proceedings for the Northeast Region Decision Sciences Institute*, pages 484–508, March 2014, Philadelphia, PA.

[26] Mark Burdon, Bill Lane, and Paul von Nessen. Data breach notification law in the eu and australia where to now? *Computer Law & Security Review*, 28(3):296–307, 2012.

[27] Mary A Burke and H Peyton Young. Social norms. *Handbook of Social Economics*, 1:311–338, 2010.

[28] Geoffrey Cain. The cyber-empire strikes back. *Far Eastern Economic Review*, 172(2):50–52, 2009.

[29] Fida Hussain Chandio, Zahir Irani, Akram M. Zeki, Asadullah Shah, and Sayed Chhattan Shah. Online banking information systems acceptance: An empirical examination of system characteristics and web security. *Information Systems Management*, 34(1):50–64, 2017.

[30] Charika Channuntapipat. Assurance for service organisations: Contextualising accountability and trust. *Managerial Auditing Journal*, 33(4):340–359, 2017.

[31] Coye Cheshire, Judd Antin, and Elizabeth Churchill. Behaviors, adverse events, and dispositions: An empirical study of online discretion and information control. *Journal of the American Society for Information Science and Technology*, 61(7):1487–1501, 2010.

[32] Nicholas A Christakis. *Connected: The Amazing Power of Social Networks and How They Shape Our Lives*. HarperCollins, London, 2010.

[33] Steven D'Alessandro, Antonia Girardi, and Leela Tiangsoongnern. Perceived risk and trust as antecedents of online purchasing behavior in the usa gemstone industry. *Asia Pacific Journal of Marketing and Logistics*, 24(3):433–460, 2012.

[34] Angela Daly. The introduction of data breach notification legislation in Australia: A comparative view. *Computer Law & Security Review*, 34(3):477–495, 2018.

[35] Stefan R. Dandelles and Jean Y. Liu. Insurance coverage for social engineering scams under review. *Property & Casualty 360*, 122(3):16–17, 2018.

[36] Duy Dang-Pham and Siddhi Pittayachawan. Comparing intention to avoid malware across contexts in a byod-enabled australian university: A protection motivation theory approach. *Computers and Security*, 48:281–297, 2015.

[37] Fred D Davis. Perceived usefulness, perceived ease of use, and user acceptance of information technology. *MIS Quarterly*, 13(3):319–340, 1989.

[38] Michael R. Davisson and Patricia Michelena Parisi. Imposter fraud: Courts may decide this year on key coverage questions tied to email scams that dupe employees into transferring company funds to fraudsters. *Best's Review*, 119(3):22, 2018.

[39] Saurabh Dey, Srinivas Sampalli, and Y. E. Qiang. Security and privacy issues in mobile cloud computing. *International Journal of Business and Cyber Security*, 1(1):31–43, 2016.

[40] Vijaya Geeta Dharmavaram. Clickjacking: A study on popular websites in India. *Journal of Money Laundering Control*, 18(4):447–456, 2015.

[41] Whitfield Diffie and Martin Hellman. New directions in cryptography. *IEEE Transactions on Information Theory*, 22(6):644–654, 1976.

[42] Matias Dodel and Gustavo Mesch. Cyber-victimization preventive behavior: A health belief model approach. *Computers in Human Behavior*, 68:359–367, 2017.

[43] Itiel E. Dror and Jerome R. Busemeyer. Decision making under time pressure: An independent test of sequential sampling models. *Memory & Cognition*, 27(4):713, 1999.

[44] Geoffrey B. Duggan, Hilary Johnson, and Beate Grawemeyer. Rational security: Modelling everyday password use. *International Journal of Human-Computer Studies*, 70(6):415–431, 2012.

[45] The art of concealment. *The Economist*, 407(8830):8–10, 2013.

[46] Cat and mouse. *The Economist*, 407(8830):5–7, 2013.

[47] Creating a digital totalitarian state. *The Economist*, 421(9020):20–22, 2016.

[48] I Hilmi Elifoglu, Ivan Abel, and Ozlem Tasseven. Minimizing insider threat risk with behavioral monitoring. *Review of Business*, 38(2):61–74, 2018.

[49] Paul Everton. Traveling for work? You're a prime target for hackers. *Harvard Business Review Digital Articles*, pages 2–4, 2016.

[50] Aleksey K Fedorov, Evgeniy O Kiktenko, and Alexander I Lvovsky. Quantum computers put blockchain security at risk. *Nature*, 563(7732):465–467, 2018.

[51] Richard Phillips Feynman and Ralph Leighton. *"Surely You're Joking, Mr. Feynman!": Adventures of a Curious Character*. Random House, New York, 1992.

[52] Nicola Field. Cyber gender gap. *Money (Australia Edition)*, Issue 118:13, 2009.

[53] Thomas Fox-Brewster. Linkedin warns users to reset passwords as 117m logins for sale on dark web. *Forbes.com*, page 1, 2016.

[54] Steven Furnell, Warut Khern-am nuai, Rawan Esmael, Weining Yang, and Ninghui Li. Enhancing security behaviour by supporting the user. *Computers & Security*, 75:1–9, 2018.

[55] James Paul Gee. *What Video Games Have to Teach Us About Learning and Literacy*. Palgrave, New York, 2003.

[56] Alan Gillies. Improving the quality of information security management systems with ISO27000. *The TQM Journal*, 23(4):367–376, 2011.

[57] Sandra Godinho, Marlia Prada, and Margarida Vaz Garrido. Under pressure: An integrative perspective of time pressure impact on consumer decision-making. *Journal of International Consumer Marketing*, 28(4):251–273, 2016.

[58] Robert Hackett. Stolen uber user logins are for sale on the dark web: Only $1 each. *Fortune.com*, 2015.

[59] Minhi Hahn, Robert Lawson, and Young Gyu Lee. The effects of time pressure and information load on decision quality. *Psychology & Marketing*, 9(5):365–378, 1992.

[60] Tejaswini Herath, Rui Chen, Jingguo Wang, Ketan Banjara, Jeff Wilbur, and H. Raghav Rao. Security services as coping mechanisms: An investigation into user intention to adopt an email authentication service. *Information Systems Journal*, 24(1):61–84, 2014.

[61] William R. Hobbs and Margaret E. Roberts. How sudden censorship can increase access to information. *American Political Science Review*, 112(3):621–636, 2018.

[62] Thomas J. Holt, Deborah Strumsky, Olga Smirnova, and Max Kilger. Examining the social networks of malware writers and hackers. *International Journal of Cyber Criminology*, 6(1):891–903, 2012.

[63] Yixin Hu, Dawei Wang, Kaiyuan Pang, Guangxing Xu, and Jinhong Guo. The effect of emotion and time pressure on risk decision-making. *Journal of Risk Research*, 18(5):637–650, 2015.

[64] Yasheng Huang. Can big data tame big brother? *MIT Technology Review*, 121(5):42–43, 2018.

[65] Liang Huigang and Xue Yajiong. Understanding security behaviors in personal computer usage: A threat avoidance perspective. *Journal of the Association for Information Systems*, 11(7):394–413, 2010.

[66] John S. Hulland and Don N. Kleinmuntz. Factors influencing the use of internal summary evaluations versus external information in choice. *Journal of Behavioral Decision Making*, 7(2):79–102, 1994.

[67] Ha Huong and Ken Coghill. Online shoppers in australia: Dealing with problems. *International Journal of Consumer Studies*, 32(1):5–17, 2008.

[68] J. Hyman. Cybersecurity for insider threats. *Workforce*, 97(6):24, 2018.

[69] Rafiqul Islam, Ronghua Tian, Lynn M Batten, and Steve Versteeg. Classification of malware based on integrated static and dynamic features. *Journal of Network and Computer Applications*, 36(2):646–656, 2013.

[70] Rafiqul Islam, Ronghua Tian, Veelasha Moonsamy, and Lynn Batten. A comparison of the classification of disparate malware collected in different time periods. *Journal of Networks*, 7(6):946–955, 2012.

[71] Jacob Jacoby. Perspectives on information overload. *Journal of Consumer Research*, 10(4):432–435, 1984.

[72] J. Jaeger. Mitigating cyber threats from the inside out. *Compliance Week*, 13(146):50–59, 2016.

[73] David M. Katz. The corporation of cyber crime. *CFO*, 33(1):26–31, 2017.

[74] Kevin Lane Keller and Richard Staelin. Effects of quality and quantity of information on decision effectiveness. *Journal of Consumer Research*, 14(2):200–213, 1987.

[75] Kevin Lane Keller and Richard Staelin. Assessing biases in measuring decision effectiveness and information overload. *Journal of Consumer Research*, 15(4):504–508, 1989.

[76] Josh Kessler. Banks are expected to use more behavioral biometrics technology. *ABA Bank Marketing*, 38(2):5, 2006.

[77] Jiyeon Kim and Sandra Forsythe. Sensory enabling technology acceptance model (se-tam): A multiple-group structural model comparison. *Psychology and Marketing*, 25(9):901–922, 2008.

[78] Jonathan J. Koehler and Andrew D. Gershoff. Betrayal aversion: When agents of protection become agents of harm. *Organizational Behavior and Human Decision Processes*, 90(2):244, 2003.

[79] Vincent S Lai and Honglei Li. Technology acceptance model for internet banking: An invariance analysis. *Information and Management*, 42(2):373–386, 2005.

[80] Leslie Lamport, Robert Shostak, and Marshall Pease. The Byzantine generals problem. *ACM Transactions on Programming Languages and Systems (TOPLAS)*, 4(3):382–401, 1982.

[81] Christina Larson. The best and worst internet experience in the world. *MIT Technology Review*, 119(4):108–110, 2016.

[82] Thomas Lauer and Xiaodong Deng. Building online trust through privacy practices. *International Journal of Information Security*, 6(5):323–331, 2007.

[83] Paul Legris, John Ingham, and Pierre Collerette. Why do people use information technology? A critical review of the technology acceptance model. *Information and Management*, 40(3):191–204, 2003.

[84] David E Levari, Daniel T Gilbert, Timothy D Wilson, Beau Sievers, David M Amodio, and Thalia Wheatley. Prevalence-induced concept change in human judgment. *Science*, 360(6396):1465–1467, 2018.

[85] Weifeng Li, Hsinchun Chen, and Jay F. Nunamaker. Identifying and profiling key sellers in cyber carding community: Azsecure text mining system. *Journal of Management Information Systems*, 33(4):1059–1086, 2016.

[86] Thomas A Limoncelli. SQL is no excuse to avoid devops. *Communications of the ACM*, 62(1):46–49, 2018.

[87] Chien-Hsin Lin, Hsin-Yu Shih, and Peter J Sher. Integrating technology readiness into technology acceptance: The tram model. *Psychology and Marketing*, 24(7):641–657, 2007.

[88] Wesley A. Magat, W. Kip Viscusi, and Joel Huber. Consumer processing of hazard warning information. *Journal of Risk & Uncertainty*, 1(2):201–232, 1988.

[89] D. McCauley. Millions to opt out of my health record as backlash builds, 24 July 2018.

[90] Jane McGonigal. *Reality is Broken*. Jonathan Cape, London, 2011.

[91] Susan McLean. Beware the botnets: Cyber security is a board level issue. *Intellectual Property & Technology Law Journal*, 25(12):22–27, 2013.

[92] Stanley Milgram. Six degrees of separation. *Psychology Today*, 2:60–64, 1967.

[93] Ron Milo, Shai S. Shen-Orr, Shalev Itzkovitz, N. Kashtan, Dmitri B Chklovskii, and Uri Alon. Network motifs: Simple building blocks of complex networks. *Science*, 298(5594):824–827, 2002.

[94] Andrew Moloney. Online banking security and consumer confidence. *Credit Control*, 30(4/5):28–29, 2009.

[95] Steve Morgan. 2017 cybercrime report. Report, Cybersecuirty Ventures, sponsored by Harjavec Group, 2017.

[96] David Z. Morris. China will block travel for those with bad social credit. *Fortune.com*, page 1, 2018.

[97] George E. Newman, Ravi Dhar, and Margarita Gorlin. Communicating eco-friendly benefits: Why accidental improvements may be better received by consumers. *GfK-Marketing Intelligence Review*, 8(1):42–45, 2016.

[98] Mark EJ Newman and Michelle Girvan. Finding and evaluating community structure in networks. *Physical Review E*, 69(2):026113, 2004.

[99] Boon-Yuen Ng, Atreyi Kankanhalli, and Yunjie Xu. Studying users' computer security behavior: A health belief perspective. *Decision Support Systems*, 46(4):815–825, 2009.

[100] George Nott. Govt backs 15 trials of tech built around my health records. *CIO*, page 1, 2018.

[101] Philippe Oechslin. Making a faster cryptanalytic time-memory trade-off. In *Annual International Cryptology Conference*, pages 617–630. Springer, 2003, Berlin, Heidelberg.

[102] Hanna Oh, Jeffrey M. Beck, Zhu Pingping, Marc A. Sommer, Silvia Ferrari, and Tobias Egner. Satisficing in split-second decision making is characterized by strategic cue discounting. *Journal of Experimental Psychology. Learning, Memory & Cognition*, 42(12):1937–1956, 2016.

[103] Paul A Pavlou. Consumer acceptance of electronic commerce: Integrating trust and risk with the technology acceptance model. *International Journal of Electronic Commerce*, 7(3):101–134, 2003.

[104] Simon J. Pervan, Liliana L. Bove, and Lester W. Johnson. Reciprocity as a key stabilizing norm of interpersonal marketing relationships: Scale development and validation. *Industrial Marketing Management*, 38(1):60–70, 2009.

[105] Pablo Piccolotto and Patricio Maller. Biometrics from the user point of view; Deriving design principlese from user perceptions and concerns about biometeric systems. *Intel Technology Journal*, 18(4):30–44, 2014.

[106] Joanna Plucinska. 200,000 comcast customers told to reset passwords after data offered for sale. *Time.com*, 2015.

[107] David Poole. Identity and verification in the digital age: Where we are today and what the future could hold. *Journal of Payments Strategy and Systems*, 10(4):383–388, 2017.

[108] Brian Prince. Yahoo confirms 400,000 passwords stolen in hack. *eWeek*, page 7, 2012.

[109] Wayne Rash. Advanced phishing scam targets ceos, cfos for phony cash transfers. *eWeek*, page 1, 2015.

[110] Tom Reeve. What's wrong with CBEST? *www.scmagazine.com*, pages 19–20, July-August 2015.

[111] Elena Reutskaja, Rosemarie Nagel, Colin F. Camerer, and Antonio Rangel. Search dynamics in consumer choice under time pressure: An eye-tracking study. *American Economic Review*, 101(2):900–926, 2011.

[112] Ronald L Rivest, Adi Shamir, and Leonard Adleman. A method for obtaining digital signatures and public-key cryptosystems. *Communications of the ACM*, 21(2):120–126, 1978.

[113] Garry Robins, Pip Pattison, Yuval Kalish, and Dean Lusher. An introduction to exponential random graph (p*) models for social networks. *Social networks*, 29(2):173–191, 2007.

[114] Sasha Romanosky. Examining the costs and causes of cyber incidents. *Journal of Cybersecurity*, 2(2):121–135, 2016.

[115] Ray A. Rothrock, James Kaplan, and Friso Van Der Oord. The board's role in managing cybersecurity risks. *MIT Sloan Management Review*, 59(2):12–15, 2018.

[116] Nader Sohrabi Safa, Mehdi Sookhak, Rossouw Von Solms, Steven Furnell, Norjihan Abdul Ghani, and Tutut Herawan. Information security conscious care behaviour formation in organizations. *Computers and Security*, 53:65–78, 2015.

[117] Mohamad Saleh, E Paul Ratazzi, and Shouhuai Xu. Instructions-based detection of sophisticated obfuscation and packing. In *Military Communications Conference (MILCOM)*, pages 1–6. IEEE, 06–08 October 2014, Washington, DC.

[118] Sagar Samtani, Ryan Chinn, Hsinchun Chen, and Jay F. Nunamaker. Exploring emerging hacker assets and key hackers for proactive cyber threat intelligence. *Journal of Management Information Systems*, 34(4):1023–1053, 2018.

[119] Jeroen Schepers and Martin Wetzels. A meta-analysis of the technology acceptance model: Investigating subjective norm and moderation effects. *Information and Management*, 44(1):90–103, 2007.

[120] B. Schneier. On security awareness training, 2013.

[121] E. Schrödinger. Die gegenwrtige situation in der quantenmechanik (the present situation in quantum mechanics). *Naturwissenschaften*, 23(48):807–812, 1935.

[122] Ted Scott. Green gauges. *Money Marketing*, page 62, 2006.

[123] David Williamson Shaffer. *How Computer Games Help Children Learn*. Palgrave Macmillan, New York, 2006.

[124] Esther Shein. Hacker-proof coding. *Communications of the ACM*, 60(8):12–14, 2017.

[125] Steve Sheng, Bryant Magnien, Ponnurangam Kumaraguru, Alessandro Acquisti, Lorrie Faith Cranor, Jason Hong, and Elizabeth Nunge. Anti-phishing phil: The design and evaluation of a game that teaches people not to fall for phish. In *Proceedings of the 3rd Symposium on Usable Privacy and Security*, pages 88–99. ACM, 2007.

[126] Peter W Shor. Polynomial-time algorithms for prime factorization and discrete logarithms on a quantum computer. *SIAM review*, 41(2):303–332, 1999.

[127] Jordan Shropshire, Merrill Warkentin, and Shwadhin Sharma. Personality, attitudes, and intentions: Predicting initial adoption of information security behavior. *Computers and Security*, 49:177–191, 2015.

[128] Boban Simonovic, Edward J. N. Stupple, Maggie Gale, and David Sheffield. Stress and risky decision making: Cognitive reflection, emotional learning or both. *Journal of Behavioral Decision Making*, 30(2):658–665, 2017.

[129] Allan Snyder. Explaining and inducing savant skills: Privileged access to lower level, less-processed information. *Philosophical Transactions of the Royal Society of London B: Biological Sciences*, 364(1522):1399–1405, 2009.

[130] Allan Snyder, Terry Bossomaier, and D John Mitchell. Concept formation: 'Object' attributes dynamically inhibited from conscious awareness. *Journal of Integrative Neuroscience*, 3(01):31–46, 2004.

[131] Allan W Snyder, Elaine Mulcahy, Janet L Taylor, D John Mitchell, Perminder Sachdev, and Simon C Gandevia. Savant-like skills exposed in normal people by suppressing the left fronto-temporal lobe. *Journal of Integrative Neuroscience*, 2(02):149–158, 2003.

[132] Ray Soumya, Ow Terence, and Sung S. Kim. Security assurance: How online service providers can influence security control perceptions and gain trust. *Decision Sciences*, 42(2):391–412, 2011.

[133] William Stallings and Mohit P Tahiliani. *Cryptography and Network Security: Principles and Practice*, volume 6. Pearson, London, 2014.

[134] B Stern, Barbara, B Royne, Marla, F Stafford, Thomas, and C Bienstock, Carol. Consumer acceptance of online auctions: An extension and revision of the tam. *Psychology and Marketing*, 25(7):619–636, 2008.

[135] Andy Swales. A race against crime. *Insurance News*, pages 62–64, April/May 2017.

[136] Nassim Nicholas Talib. *The Black Swan*. Random House, New York, 2007.

[137] L. Tam, Myron Glassman, and Mark Vandenwauver. The psychology of password management: A tradeoff between security and convenience. *Behaviour and Information Technology*, 29(3):233–244, 2010.

[138] Andrew S. Tanenbaum and David J. Wetherall. *Computer Networks, 5th Ed.* Prentice Hall, Upper Saddle River, NJ, 2011.

[139] Richard H Thaler. From homo economicus to homo sapiens. *Journal of Economic Perspectives*, 14(1):133–141, 2000.

[140] Bob Toxen. The NSA and Snowden: Securing the all-seeing eye. *Communications of the ACM*, 57(5):44–51, 2014.

[141] Ahmad Kabir Usman and Mahmood Hussain Shah. Strengthening e-banking security using keystroke dynamics. *Journal of Internet Banking and Commerce*, 18(3):1–11, 2013.

[142] Anthony Vance, David Eargle, Kirk Ouimet, and Detmar Straub. Enhancing password security through interactive fear appeals: A web-based field experiment. In *2013 46th Hawaii International Conference on System Sciences*, pages 2988–2997, 07–10 January 2013, Washington, DC.

[143] Viswanath Venkatesh and Susan A Brown. A longitudinal investigation of personal computers in homes: Adoption determinants and emerging challenges. *MIS Quarterly*, 25(1):71–102, 2001.

[144] Maya Wang. Chinas chilling social credit blacklist. *Wall Street Journal - Online Edition*, page 1, 2017.

[145] Steven Ward, Kate Bridges, and Bill Chitty. Do incentives matter? An examination of online privacy concerns and willingness to provide personal and financial information. *Journal of Marketing Communications*, 11(1):21–40, 2005.

[146] Duncan J. Watts and Steven H. Strogatz. Collective dynamics of 'small-world' networks. *Nature*, 393(6684):440–442, 1998.

[147] Michael Weinstein. Business email compromise and wire fraud: How to protect your clients and firm in the year ahead. *National Real Estate Investor*, page 14, 2017.

[148] Monica Whitty, James Doodson, Sadie Creese, and Duncan Hodges. Individual differences in cyber security behaviors: An examination of who is sharing passwords. *CyberPsychology, Behavior and Social Networking*, 18(1):3–7, 2015.

[149] Richard Wickliffe. Gone phishing. *Claims*, 64(9):24–26, 2016.

[150] Alex Wright. Searching the deep web. *Communications of the ACM*, 51(10):14–15, 2008.

[151] Yang Xia, Zafar U. Ahmed, Morry Ghingold, Goh Sock Boon, Goh Sock Thain Su Mei, and Hwa Lim Lee. Consumer preferences for commercial web site design: An asia-pacific perspective. *Journal of Consumer Marketing*, 20(1):10–27, 2003.

[152] Aiping Xiong, Robert W. Proctor, Weining Yang, and Ninghui Li. Is domain highlighting actually helpful in identifying phishing web pages? *Human Factors*, 59(4):640–660, 2017.

[153] Jeff Yan, Alan Blackwell, Ross Anderson, and Alasdair Grant. Password memorability and security: Empirical results. *IEEE Security & Privacy*, 2(5):25–31, 2004.

[154] Juan Yin, Yuan Cao, Yu-Huai Li, Sheng-Kai Liao, Liang Zhang, Ji-Gang Ren, Wen-Qi Cai, Wei-Yue Liu, Bo Li, Hui Dai, et al. Satellite-based entanglement distribution over 1200 kilometers. *Science*, 356(6343):1140–1144, 2017.

[155] D. Zahn. Combating insider threat. *Processing*, 29(9):28–30, 2016.

[156] David Zweighaft. Business email compromise and executive impersonation: Are financial institutions exposed? *Journal of Investment Compliance*, 18(1):1–7, 2017.

Index